MACROECONOMIC POLICY

DEMYSTIFYING MONETARY AND FISCAL POLICY

MACROECONOMIC POLICY

DEMYSTIFYING MONETARY AND FISCAL POLICY

FARROKH K. LANGDANA

Rutgers Business School

"Macroeconomic Policy is a lively and informative introduction to the diverse doctrines of macroeconomic theory."
Robert E. Lucas, Jr.,
Recipient of the 1995 Nobel Prize in Economics

Foreword by Dr. W. Michael Cox,
Chief Economist and Senior Vice President of the
Federal Reserve Bank of Dallas,
and co-author of *Myths of Rich and Poor*

KLUWER ACADEMIC PUBLISHERS
Boston / Dordrecht / London

Distributors for North, Central and South America:
Kluwer Academic Publishers
101 Philip Drive
Assinippi Park
Norwell, Massachusetts 02061 USA
Telephone (781) 871-6600
Fax (781) 681-9045
E-Mail: kluwer@wkap.com

Distributors for all other countries:
Kluwer Academic Publishers Group
Post Office Box 322
3300 AH Dordrecht, THE NETHERLANDS
Telephone 31 786 576 000
Fax 31 786 576 474
E-Mail: services@wkap.nl

 Electronic Services < http://www.wkap.nl>

Library of Congress Cataloging-in-Publication Data

A C.I.P. Catalogue record for this book is available
from the Library of Congress.

To my wife,

Mary

CONTENTS

Dr. W. Michael Cox

Macroeconomic policy analysis has been in a state of flux since the early 1970s. Although the casual student of macroeconomics might expect that economists would have come to some agreement in our quest to model the so-called real world, the analysis of macroeconomic policy has perhaps never been so confounding as it is today. Each monetary or fiscal policy event is almost inevitably followed by at least two completely different and conflicting sets of analyses.

Consider, for example, the question of whether government spending affects GDP growth. One can find just about any answer to this question possible—some say it increases GDP, some that it decreases GDP, and some claim no effect. Others go on to claim that the answer depends on whether the economy is a developed one, such as the US, or an emerging one, like China.

Another central source of confusion is the proverbial Phillips Curve, which, as originally conceived, related the unemployment rate to wage inflation. Some researchers have found an inverse relationship between these variables; others have found no link at all. What's more, the economics profession has introduced new and improved variants on Phillips' tradeoff theme—inflation versus unemployment rates, inflation versus GDP growth, inflation versus capacity utilization, and so on. For each of these postulated relationships, virtually any conclusion can be found. And to confound things even more, the conclusions appear able to change over time as the economy changes. The statistical evidence from the much-heralded "New Economy" of the late 1990s seems to suggest that rapid GDP is linked more to *low* than high inflation. Will the real Phillips curve relationship please stand up?

Conceivably, there are as many interpretations of economic phenomenon as there are economists to interpret them. All this may be well and good from the standpoint of the passionate researcher, who makes a living in an endless search for the Holy Grail. But for the typical student, less interested in contrast and more interested in conclusions, the result can be a state of confusion as he or she moves from class to class, from book to book, or from publication to publication. Finding the truth for economics students has become a bit of a mystery.

Enter Farrokh Langdana's book, aptly titled *Macroeconomic Policy: Demystifying Monetary and Fiscal Policy*. Not only does the book shine a bright light through the dense fog surrounding economists' centrist position on macroeconomic thought, it does so with a set of tools virtually all readers can handle. The cumbersome mathematics that most modern economists love but most students loathe are put aside in favor of teaching tools with wider appeal.

Even economists have recognized that as our profession has aged, our language—both verbal and quantitative—has become more convenient and precise for us, but less accessible and attractive to the general audience. So, what should the economics professor do? Economist Francis Edgeworth, writing nearly a century ago about Alfred Marshall, one of economics' original and first-class mathematicians, said that "Marshall, who desired above all things to be useful, *deferred to the prejudices of those that he wished to persuade* (emphasis added)." In other words, we should speak in the language of our audience, not our profession. Increasingly, the economics profession shuns this communication principle in favor of "rigor," all the while knowing that, as economist Robert Heilbroner said, "Mathematics has given economics rigor, but alas, also mortis."

The Bureau of Labor Statistics estimates that there are roughly 135,000 economists in the U.S. out of a population of roughly 287 million. This figures out to be 1 economist for every 2126 people. Must not it be important to speak to the other 2125, not just to the one? Of course, and thus this book is written for you, not for economists.

When Richard Alm and I wrote Myths of Rich and Poor, we set out to debunk a series of widely accepted myths that the U.S. was lagging behind economically, and that its citizens were getting progressively worse off. We accomplished the complete dismantling of such myths by presenting systematic overwhelming evidence that the U.S. has been prospering splendidly in recent decades, and we did so using the only tool possible for such a large audience—common sense. The reaction to our book has been tremendous because we spoke eye to eye with folks, not above their heads.

Macroeconomic Policy: Demystifying Monetary and Fiscal Policy takes on an equally important task—to show the reader that modern macroeconomic analysis is systematic, with logical frameworks within which economies can be successfully analyzed, and to do this without the use of overly fancy techniques. The applied and intuitive approach to the theory centers on diagrammatic derivations, using only the minimal techniques necessary to prove its points. While the book approaches analysis primarily via applications and analysis, the vital theoretical underpinnings have not been sacrificed.

As a long-time professor of economics, a practicing economist and an author, the teaching approach that I find most compelling is the "applications method." Begin with an important issue (such as supply side economics) at least vaguely familiar to just about anybody, set out the central opposing views with the intuition behind each side, then examine the evidence and thrash out the conclusion. That's the best teaching approach because that's the way people think and work.

And thus it is with Professor Langdana's book, we have a text that is first and foremost applications oriented. That's why MBA and Executive MBA students will find this book indispensable, financial analysts may like to have it on hand as an essential reference, and even a general audience can find it useful.

The overview chapter clearly and concisely states the book's position regarding its focus on intuition and applicability. The notion of allowing the reader the freedom of choice between the Keynesian or the Supply-Side paradigm for developed economies is fresh and radically different from most conventional macroeconomics texts. In addition, it is an honest approach, given that both monetary and fiscal policymakers in Washington D.C. still make policy based on assumptions behind each paradigm.

The author states that he has taken care not to influence the reader towards either paradigm and he has faithfully managed to keep the promise throughout the text. The coverage is carefully balanced, with the excellent chapter on the New Economy (Chapter 10) being especially pertinent to the two-model approach. In the chapter on monetary policy (Chapter 11), Farrokh Langdana and Giles Mellon actually discuss the fact that reserve requirements are not binding any more in the United States. This is one of very few texts that has managed to cogently explain how the conventional textbook explanation of open market operations and the "money multiplier" has substantially changed in several major economies.

The simulated "media articles" following each chapter are vital to this text and to truly analyzing macroeconomic policy in general. It rapidly becomes evident through the clarity of exposition why the author has been consistently rated so highly as a teacher.

Dr. W. Michael Cox is Senior Vice President and Chief Economist at the Federal Reserve Bank of Dallas, Professor of Economics at Southern Methodist University, and co-author (with Richard Alm) of the highly acclaimed *Myths of Rich and Poor: Why We're Better Off Than We Think.*

About the Author

Dr. Farrokh Langdana is a professor in the Finance/Economics Department at Rutgers Business School, New Jersey. In addition to this volume, he is the author of three other research-oriented books (two co-authored with Prof. Richard C.K. Burdekin), and several publications pertaining to macroeconomic policy and macro-experimentation.

Dr. Langdana is currently the Director of the Executive MBA program at Rutgers Business School and teaches Macroeconomic Policy as well as International Trade and Global Macroeconomics in the program.

He is the recipient of the Rutgers University Warren I. Susman Award for Excellence in Teaching, the Paul Nadler Award for Teaching Excellence, the Horace dePodwin Research Award, three Executive MBA Teaching Excellence Awards, and over 15 Rutgers MBA teaching awards. In addition to teaching in the US, Prof. Langdana also teaches MBA and Executive MBA students in China, Singapore, and France.

ACKNOWLEDGMENTS

This book would, quite simply, not have been possible without the assistance and encouragement of many people.

I begin by thanking Prof. Robert E. Lucas of the University of Chicago, the recipient of the 1995 Nobel Prize in Economics, for his comments and suggestions pertaining to my experimental testing of his paradigm-busting "islands" model (Chapter 10). Prof. Lucas' work has been a source of encouragement and inspiration to me as well as to generations of macroeconomists over the last three decades.

Dr. Michael Cox, Chief Economist and Senior Vice President of the Federal Reserve Bank of Dallas, and co-author of *Myths of Rich and Poor: Why We Are Better Off Than We Think,* took time off from his busy schedule to write the foreword for this book, and for that I am most grateful. Dr. Cox, who is also Professor of Economics at Southern Methodist University, has drawn upon his experience as economist, professor, and author to eloquently describe the challenges faced in analyzing as well as teaching macroeconomic policy today. In a few short pages he has deftly managed to home-in on the very essence of the book.

I remain extremely grateful to my colleague Professor Giles Mellon at Rutgers Business School with whom I co-authored most recently, "Monetary Policy in a World of Non-Binding Reserve Requirements." I thank Giles for his invaluable assistance with Chapter 11 in which we "blow the whistle" on the fact that, in reality, central bank open market operations in most developed economies have very little in common with conventional textbook discussions on the subject.

I am indebted to my co-author of two books (and a well received paper on Confederate financing in the US Civil War), Prof. Richard C.K. Burdekin of Claremont McKenna College and Claremont Graduate School, for his comments, suggestions, and detailed structural advice related to the draft of the first proposal. Thanks also to Professors Mark Castelino, Leonard Goodman, and Menahem Spiegel for their extremely valuable comments that enabled the proposal to evolve into the first draft.

Thanks to my Dean, Dr. Howard Tuckman, for further developing the highly regarded Rutgers Global Executive MBA programs that contributed so much to the global nature of this book and to numerous macroeconomic insights that could only be obtained by actually interacting with individuals overseas.

Many thanks to Prof. Michael Crew, Director of the Rutgers Center for Research in Regulated Industries and author of numerous books in the area of Utilities Regulation, for his support and strategic advice at all stages of this project and for steering me to a wonderful working relationship with Kluwer Academic Press.

The book would not have been completed on schedule and in its final form without the assistance of Prof. Ivan Brick, the Chairman of the Finance and Economics Department at Rutgers Business School. In addition to allowing me the flexibility to work on this project, Dr. Brick also made possible the editorial assistance of my colleague, Prof. Carter Daniel, wordsmith par excellence, by providing funding from The Whitcomb Center for Research in Financial Services. For all this I am most thankful.

Prof. Daniel and my wife, Mary Langdana, deserve a special note of thanks for patiently and laboriously proofreading the manuscript—not once, but several times, often at very short notice. I deeply appreciate their efforts.

Two of my former students, Wenjeng Lee and Amir Razzaghi, provided me with copies of their excellent notes from my macroeconomics classes at Rutgers Business School. These notes were invaluable in ensuring that the sequence and intensity of my classroom discussions were faithfully captured in this book.

Many of the questions discussed towards the end of each chapter have been asked in class, and I thank all my past students in the MBA and Executive MBA programs in the US, China, Singapore, and France for their contributions. In addition, some of my former students have made extremely valuable comments and suggestions on the early drafts of the chapters, most of which have been incorporated. I owe a special note of thanks to former students Michael Perron for his excellent insight into the Keynesian nature of the yield curve, and Sarah Boltizar for her suggestions pertaining to the figures in Chapter 5.

Over the years, several former students have kindly supplied me with some truly excellent articles from major news publications for which I remain grateful. These articles have allowed me to widen my resource net and include as much relevant and current material as possible. Facts from these articles have been included in several chapters.

Prof. Issac Gottlieb, software specialist extraordinaire, has come to my assistance on numerous occasions—often responding to very nocturnal distress emails pertaining to plots, fonts, formatting, etc., and I owe him a huge debt for his prompt help and assistance. The assistance provided by the Rutgers computer-support staff, Martin O'Reilly, Rob Torres, Ted Durand, and Bernice Fair, is also much appreciated.

My editor, Tom Randall, has been most patient with my queries and I thank him for his excellent advice, particularly in the early formative stages of this book and with the numerous "end-game" questions as this volume neared completion.

My parents in Bombay, Zarrin and Keki, instilled in me a thirst for reading, a quest for knowledge, and a sense of humor from my very early childhood. It was only many years later that I came to truly appreciate the significance of this aspect of upbringing, and I thank them for this.

Many thanks to my stepson, Christopher Jennelle, for his assistance and encouragement over the years.

Above all, I remain most grateful to my wife, Mary. Not only was she one of the two proofreaders for the whole manuscript as mentioned above, but for several years she graciously endured a perpetually distracted husband, his nocturnal working hours on the computer, and the sight of manuscripts stacked obtrusively in almost every part of the house. She endured all this to allow this book to be published. This is partly why *Macroeconomic Policy: Demystifying Monetary and Fiscal Policy* is dedicated to her.

1. INTRODUCTION AND OVERVIEW

In recent times, authors of macroeconomics texts have faced a series of daunting challenges. The primary challenge lies in the very nature of the subject. Monetary and fiscal policies influence wages, employment, inflation, output, interest rates, and exchange rates and affect virtually all individuals in emerging as well as in developed economies. The applicability and pervasiveness of macroeconomics have never been in doubt. In fact, it is these very aspects that pose the major challenges to authors of texts pertaining to the analysis of monetary and fiscal policies.

Texts that cater primarily to current global macroeconomic events, focusing on the real-world implications of macroeconomic policies on employment, inflation, etc., immediately run into one serious challenge. Given the rapid pace of macroeconomic change and the frequency of global macroeconomic crises, such texts often become outdated by the time they appear. In fact, the greater the emphasis on actual current events, the greater the likelihood of the textbook becoming "dated", and hence the shorter its shelf life.

Another challenge is that theoretical models that drive macroeconomic policy are usually complex time-series models involving significant familiarity with mathematical and statistical techniques. Texts that attempt to incorporate large tracts of cutting-edge theory have been received favorably by researchers and students in PhD programs. But, such texts have not done so well with practitioners such as financial analysts and MBA students, where the focus is on learning how to analyze the implications of actual fiscal and monetary policies, rather than the construction and development of theoretical/mathematical models. This mutual exclusivity has thus compartmentalized macroeconomic texts into generally two groups based on either the emphasis on research or on policy analysis.

Finally, perhaps the most daunting challenge faced by authors of macroeconomics texts is that in several developed economies, such as those of the US, Western Europe, and perhaps Japan, two dramatically different macroeconomic models compete for the center-stage of macroeconomic policy. In this book we will describe one of these as "Keynesian/Traditional" and the other as "Supply-Sider/New Classical."

The differences between these two models are anything but academic. In fact, their policy implications are diametrically and fundamentally different. For example, some key issues that produce resoundingly different responses from these two models are:

- Should the government increase spending to promote employment and growth?
- Should the central bank change monetary growth to actively lower/raise interest rates to manage employment and GDP?

- Should tax cuts be based mainly on personal income or geared primarily towards businesses?
- Should the government maintain at least some optimal degree of regulation over business enterprise or is unfettered deregulation and privatization the mantra of growth?

Given these challenges—focusing on either the applied real-world aspects of policy or on the hard-core theory, and resolving two-model issue—the analysis and interpretation of macroeconomic policy has become a largely mystifying process. Individuals grappling with the implications of recent announcements from domestic and foreign policy makers have often been confronted by wildly different analyses, at times in the same publication!

The objective of this book is to demystify macroeconomic policy analysis. Specifically, this book attempts to accomplish this demystification in the following manner:

(1) The primarily emphasis of this book will be on practical real-world aspects of fiscal and monetary policy analysis. The book is, first and foremost, an applications-oriented macroeconomic policy analysis guide, designed to cater to individuals who need to analyze fiscal and monetary policies in the context of their personal or professional lives.

All the theory included in the chapters is "must know" theory that is absolutely essential for interpreting policy announcements and analyzing macroeconomic news. Furthermore, whenever possible, the emphasis is on an intuitive diagram-based approach to the models, with the models themselves gradually increasing in sophistication. For example, the Keynesian multiplier effect is first introduced in Chapter 4, then discussed in detail in the context of the ISLM-ADAS model in Chapter 9, and then again in Chapter 10 in the context of the Keynesian explanation of the New Economy. Similarly, the Classical Model is first introduced in Chapter 4, then in an ISLM-ADAS framework in Chapter 8, and then again in Chapters 10 and 11 while discussing the New Economy and the monetary policy objectives of the European Central Bank.

One key feature that truly anchors this textbook to the real world is the inclusion of the simulated "media articles" at the end of each chapter. These articles, written by the author and designed to mimic actual articles in periodicals such as the Economist, Wall Street Journal (US and Asian Edition), Business Week, and Financial Times, simulate the form and manner in which macroeconomic "news" is presented to managers in the real world.

The reader should be able to relate the relevant underlined parts of these innovative "articles" to the theoretical course context presented in the current and preceding chapters. These exercises at the conclusion of every chapter are specifically designed to train the reader to relate, interpret, and analyze macroeconomic news as encountered in the work-place. Solutions to these exercises are provided at the very end of each chapter. At times, some of the "solutions" are mostly hints designed to enable readers to arrive at the correct solution by themselves—in fact, some of these hints are even in the form of additional leading questions.

In addition, the book and all the "media articles" are designed to be "time-neutral". All the real-world examples and exercises at the end of the chapters are carefully placed in historical context, and a conscious effort has been made not to allow this text to be dated to a particular era, administration, or country. Furthermore, the book balances macroeconomic policy analyses for emerging economies such as China, Central Europe, and South America with developed economies such as the US, Japan, and Western Europe. In short, this book is designed to be applicable for readers in both emerging and developed economies.

(2) While this book includes a significant body of theory vital to monetary and fiscal policy analysis, it relegates some of the more quantitative mathematical derivations to texts that cater primarily to research economists. Our focus remains on <u>macroeconomic policy analysis</u> and not on the derivation of theoretical time-series models *per se*. The mathematical-statistical derivations of the theoretical models necessary for research in macroeconomics and integral to PhD education, lie outside the domain of this book.

(3) This book attempts to resolve the Keynesian-Supply Side challenge by explaining exactly how and why two fundamentally different models can indeed legitimately coexist in some economies. Both models are constructed, described, and analyzed in equal detail. This text is careful not to introduce any bias—readers will be presented with the strengths and weaknesses of each model in equal detail.

We will discover that different economies enact policies in radically different paradigms (models) determined by factors such as the nature and sophistication of their labor markets and the quality of information. For example, emerging and transitional economies will be described as "primarily Keynesian" while many developed economies will be described as displaying "supply-side" tendencies. Interestingly, for some developed economies both models vie the role of "primary policy model." In these cases, the reader will be presented with all the macroeconomic tools necessary to make the choice of the more suitable model. This text will ensure that no editorial bias creeps in to influence the reader to choose one model over the other in economies where the "jury is still out" regarding the operative paradigm.

3

(4) Each chapter includes discussion questions along with solutions. In 15 years of teaching MBA and Executive MBA students in the US, China, Singapore, and France, these are the most commonly asked questions pertaining to the respective topics, and their inclusion should go a long way towards demystifying macroeconomic policy.

In summary, the book is designed for individuals who want an applied, hands-on approach to analyzing the effects of macroeconomic policies. The primary audience is MBA and Executive MBA students who have been in the work force long enough to appreciate the importance of monetary and fiscal policies. Intermediate-level undergraduate students will also find this book to be a good supplemental text. Individual investors, analysts, consultants, and in fact anyone who needs to strip away myths, jargon, and theoretical ambiguity in order to systematically analyze the effects of current and future monetary and fiscal policies will find this text useful.

1.1   CHAPTER OVERVIEW

Chapter 2 begins with an overview of macroeconomic policies and the definitions of key variables such as GDP and inflation. The link between budget and trade deficits, interest rates, exchange rates, and global capital flows is discussed within the context of the National Savings Identity in **Chapter 3**.

The early groundwork for demand-side stabilization begins with **Chapter 4**. The first reference to Keynesian macroeconomics is made here along with the concept of the multiplier effect. In the milestone **Chapter 5**, we discuss key concepts such as the overheating, soft landing, and hard landing of economies. This chapter also discusses the measurement of unemployment and the complexities of that particular statistic. **Chapter 6** essentially extends the content of Chapter 5 to include the effects of expected risk and inflation on long-term interest rates. The yield curve and the Fisher Effect are included in this chapter. The latter part of Chapter 6 describes the ultimate macroeconomic meltdown—hyperinflation.

The first encounter with the core model underlying macroeconomic policy analysis in this book occurs in **Chapter 7**. The ISLM-ADAS model is introduced here along with several policy exercises. In this chapter, we introduce an economy where inflation is artificially held constant in order to allow readers to gradually gain confidence with diagrammatic ISLM-ADAS policy experiments. In **Chapter 8**, we increase the sophistication of the ISLM-ADAS by allowing inflation to change: the Classical paradigm is analyzed here. The Keynesian model follows in the context of ISLM in **Chapter 9**. This chapter also includes a non-traditional analysis of the Great

Depression, along with several exercises pertaining to emerging economy macropolicies.

The supply-sider paradigm is constructed and analyzed in **Chapter 10**, along with a discussion of the technology driven New Economy. This chapter includes elements of rational expectations theory, crucial to the development of the supply-side model. The driving influences in this portion of the chapter will be concepts of imperfect and asymmetric information. This capstone chapter also includes significant discussion of the Identification Problem, whereby it is possible to legitimately allow two fundamentally different models to co-exist simultaneously. The Keynesian explanation for the New Economy is also presented in this chapter along with a detailed summary of the differences between emerging and developed economies and the Keynesian ("traditional") and supply-sider (New Economy) models.

Finally, **Chapter 11** discusses central banks and the role and conduct of monetary policy. The organization and structure of US Federal Reserve System and the European Central Bank are included here. This chapter also includes an update on the current state of reserves in the US banking system and the implication of these reserves on the future conduct of monetary policy. This section on the state of US reserves and the implications thereof incorporates elements of a paper co-authored with Professor Giles Mellon of Rutgers Business School.

Each chapter ends with a section featuring the most common questions asked by students and several simulated "media articles" that will allow readers to relate the theory to real-world macroeconomic news.

Readers may often find serious passages discussing rigorous theory juxtaposed with livelier, and almost whimsical anecdotal discussions of real-world macroeconomic events. This format, which mimics my teaching style in class, ensures that the "tone" of the book changes often and that readers fully appreciate that the demystification of monetary and fiscal policy is not only important and relevant, but exciting as well.

2. NATIONAL INCOME ACCOUNTS

This foundation chapter begins with definitions of key macrovariables and policy instruments essential to macroeconomic policy analysis.

The conventional definition of macroeconomics is the analysis of economy-wide, aggregated variables such as national output, interest rates, employment, wages, inflation, and exchange rates. These are defined as **endogenous** variables, determined by and "within" the macroeconomy. These variables cannot be directly influenced or changed by degree but are a product of the interaction of domestic and global demand and supply pressures.

For example, policy makers cannot simply have a meeting, vote to increase growth from 2% to 3%, and expect national output to conveniently comply. National output is an endogenously determined variable, and the final change is, instead, a result of simultaneous interactions of consumer and investor expectations, domestic and foreign disturbances (shocks), and, of course, macroeconomic policies.

The macroeconomic policies that influence the endogenous variables are deliberately implemented and directly controlled by policy makers. These policies are considered to be **exogenous**, or determined independently "outside" the model.

The three exogenous policy instruments available to implement macroeconomic policy are changes in tax rates (t), changes in government spending (G), and changes in the growth of the money supply (M). The first two policy instruments constitute fiscal policy implemented by the government. Changes in the growth of the money supply and, to some extent, in national interest rates are determined and conducted by the nation's central bank, and constitute monetary policy.[1]

In addition to macroeconomic policies, exogenous variables also include "shocks" that unexpectedly slam into the economy. The endogenous macroeconomic variables such as national output, inflation, and employment are influenced, and at times traumatized, by exogenous shocks such as the oil shocks of 1973 and 1979, which resulted in the Great Stagflation in the US, and, more recently, the events of September 11, 2001.[2]

Table 1 summarizes the exogenous variables, namely, fiscal and monetary policy instruments, and shocks. The interplay between these variables and factors such as consumer and investor confidence and expectations then determines the host of endogenous macroeconomic variables that we encounter on almost a daily basis in the news.

The following endogenous variables will be represented interchangeably: National output = GDP = Y; inflation = P; employment = n; and interest rates = i.

Table 1

Fiscal Policy	Monetary Policy	Shocks
Changes in tax rates (t) Changes in government Spending (G) (Government controlled)	Changes in money supply (M) and in short-term interest rates (Controlled by the nation's central bank)	Wars Weather Oil Shocks, for example

In addition to the conventional discussion and analysis of macrovariables, one major feature of this book will be the explicit incorporation of the role of **expectations** in formulating and analyzing macroeconomic policy. A key feature introduced below and presented in forthcoming chapters is the concept of "paradigm shifts" where an entire macroeconomic model (paradigm) undergoes a fundamental and unexpectedly drastic change in a relatively short time period.[3]

2.1 PARADIGM SHIFTS: AN INTRODUCTION

This concept explains how macroeconomic models that may have performed wonderfully in certain periods may suddenly fail within the space of just a few years. It also illustrates how models that are tremendously successful in one economy may be frustrating disasters in another. This book will make the case that paradigm shifts were largely responsible for several major macroeconomic crises. The US in the Great Depression of the 1930s and the stagflation of the 1970s, and the macroeconomic problems experienced by Japan since the early 1990s, will be among the cases to be discussed in this context in later chapters.

A special feature of this book will be in-depth discussions of the implications and policy prescriptions of each individual paradigm and the linking of these paradigm shifts to the expectations and actions of forward-looking consumers, producers and investors.

Building a Bridge: An Early Intuitive Example

Why is macroeconomic policy-making such an imprecise science? With all this computing power at our disposal and with even more accurate and sophisticated data-gathering systems in place, why can't a conventional engineering optimization problem design optimal fiscal and monetary polices that will ensure continuous recovery?

These questions hit at, perhaps, the core of macroeconomic policy design. Prescribing macropolicy is, unfortunately, not an optimization problem like those encountered in engineering. (Having acquired an engineering undergraduate degree, this author remembers agonizing over similar issues in graduate school in macroeconomics). The answer lies in the aspect of macroeconomics that results in paradigm shifts. The following simple example will provide intuition at this early stage. (A more detailed analysis will be presented while studying the JoAnna Grey/Lucas model in chapter 10.)

A bridge has to be designed to cross a river in Year 1. The design specifications are {A, B, C}, where A is the width and depth of the river, B is the load and cycles/second to be experienced by the bridge, and C is the nature of the bedrock, geology, etc. With these specifications, the engineer produces the optimal design, X, which is the blueprint for the bridge.

Now, in Year 5, if another bridge is to be built in a different part of the country, and if, coincidentally, the specifications {A, B, C} are to remain exactly the same, the civil engineer can indeed dust-off blueprint {X} and submit it again. It will work.

However, this procedure would be practically impossible in the world of macroeconomic policy. If a set of "optimal" fiscal and monetary polices {Z} were designed and implemented to improve an economy laboring under the specifications {J, K, L}, where J is high inflation, K is high unemployment, and L is low output growth, they may indeed work in Year 1. But, say, in Year 5, if the economy is facing the same problem specified by {J, K, L}, it is more than likely that the set of macroeconomic policies {Z} which were successful in Year 1 would fail or even be counterproductive in Year 5.

The reason is that engineering policy {X} is set against a time-invariant backdrop of nature. Isaac Newton's three laws of motion will always be valid in Year 1 as well as in Year 5. Macroeconomic policy, on the other hand, is set against a backdrop of individuals who have expectations which are constantly changing and which are, in turn, functions of the results of past fiscal and monetary policies.

In our example here, individuals remember the effects of macropolicy {Z} in Year 1. They remember what happened to interest rates, employment, exchange rates, etc., soon after {Z} was enacted. So in year 5, when they realize that policies {Z} are about to be implemented again, this time they indulge in hedging behavior. They anticipate the effects of {Z} based on their past experience, and they take action to minimize any and all adverse effects of {Z}. Thus, the cumulative actions of these individuals may end up minimizing or totally negating policy {Z} in Year 5. In this case, a paradigm shift is said to have occurred. Policy {Z} which may have been a huge success in Year 1 may now be rendered totally ineffectual in Year 5.

Some examples of such paradigm shifts are presented in **Table 2**.

Until the early 1930s, the US economy was well-represented by the classical model. Macroeconomic policies dictated by the model and its underlying assumptions of wage and price changes fit the economy well. However, the macroeconomic trauma of the Great Depression of 1929-1933 ushered in a shift to the Keynesian paradigm (named after the British economist, John Maynard Keynes) that reigned supreme from the late 1930s and was generally considered to be a globally effective model. The shift from the classical to the Keynesian model is now labeled Paradigm Shift 1. Macroeconomic policies dictated by the Keynesian model—activist fiscal and monetary policies—enabled economists to fine-tune macrovariables such as inflation and output growth with respectable precision.

This macroeconomic Camelot, however, collapsed in spectacular fashion in the oil-shock decade of the 1970s. The Great Stagflation of the 1970s in the US (characterized by double-digit inflation and unemployment) ushered in yet another paradigm shift to the supply-side model, now described as Paradigm Shift 2.

Table 2

Till Early 1930s	Late 1930s to Late 1970s	Late 1970s to present
Classical Model	Keynesian Model	**Developed Economies** Supply-side (rational expectationist) leading to the New Economy since the mid-1990s **Or** New Keynesian **Emerging Economies** New Keynesian

This paradigm, with its theoretical underpinnings in the "rational expectations" models, has policy implications and assumptions that are fundamentally different from its Keynesian predecessor. Here, the roles of government spending and monetary policy in influencing employment and output are minimal at best. The emphasis is on deregulation, tax cuts, and "less government" in general. Adherents of this model, the supply-siders, have claimed responsibility for the US macroeconomic performance of the 1980s through the early 2000s. In fact, as discussed in Chapter 10, the internet-assisted and technology-driven "new economy" has been linked to the deregulatory backdrop of the 1980s.

We will see, however, that in the US, Paradigm Shift 2 is by no means incontrovertible. As discussed in the preceding chapter, since the early 1980s, both the Keynesian and the supply-sider models have been competing for the center stage of macroeconomic policy dominance. Both models claim distinguished and experienced economists and policy makers as adherents. And both seem to be able to "explain" the behavior of key macroeconomic variables reasonably well.[4] It is this two-model coexistence in the US since the early 1980s that has resulted in the conflicting policy analyses, policies, and interpretations discussed in chapter 1. This duality of models exists only in developed economies such as the US, Western Europe, and Japan. Emerging economies are well described by individual and incontrovertible macromodels to be discussed in detail in later chapters.

Each model will be chronologically discussed in the following chapters, beginning with the classical model, followed by the Keynesian and supply-side models, and finally ending with the New Economy. For the US economy at present, the reader will have to decide which model—New Keynesian or supply-sider—is most applicable, based on the information and analyses presented in the following chapters. Unlike other texts, which may steer readers towards one of the two models for the US, this book will not impose the author's choice of the "true" US macroeconomic model. Since a consensus for a single model is conspicuously absent in the US at present (even the governors of the Federal Reserve are strongly split), it would be pedagogically inappropriate to unequivocally claim one or the other as the dominant macromodel for the US.

2.2 SOME FUNDAMENTAL DEFINITIONS

The total value of a country's output is the gross domestic product, or GDP. In the US, this statistic is measured by the Commerce Department. It is defined as the total market value of all final goods and services produced within a given time period by factors of production located domestically.

This seemingly innocuous definition has several interesting aspects. Only final goods and services are included with their final prices inclusive of all taxes. Intermediate goods are not included to avoid the problem of double-counting. For example, an electronic component that is part of a laptop screen is counted in the price of the final laptop. Including it separately at some earlier stage of the production process would simply double-count the component.

Only goods produced (and services rendered) in the current period are included. Unsold inventory is also included with the emphasis on current production, and not necessarily on market clearance. The sale of a used car, or the resale value of a home, for example, would not be a current GDP statistic as these items have already been included in the year in which they were initially produced.

The goods produced and services rendered must be within the current period, and the output must be produced by factors of production (labor, capital, or land), located within the country, hence, gross "domestic" product. This includes output produced (and profits earned) by foreigners and foreign companies in the domestic country, but does not include output produced by domestic citizens abroad. Profits earned by domestic companies abroad are, similarly, not included.

The less widely used gross national product (GNP) statistic measures the output produced by a country's factors of production (domestic workers), regardless of where the production takes place. The following simple example helps differentiate the GDP and GNP statistics. A Japanese company making light trucks in the US would have all its output included in US GDP. However, only the wages of the American workers employed in the truck factory would be included in US GNP.

In late 1999, the Bureau of Economic Analysis significantly revised the measurement of GDP. (i) Business software purchases were included in a component of GDP (specifically in the Equipment and Software component of nonresidential fixed investment), (ii) government employees' pensions were reclassified as personal savings, and (iii) a new measure of banking output was designed to measure banking productivity gains more accurately. All these revisions may have boosted the annual growth rate of real GDP by as much as 0.4 percent annually in the expansion of the late 1990s.

While GDP is one of the most frequently encountered and tracked statistics, it is far from being a perfect measure. By itself, per capita GDP – total GDP divided by the population—says very little about the overall level of pollution, quality of health care, education, government services, financial and legal institutions, etc.[5] In addition the average per capita GDP ignores the vast asymmetry in income distribution experienced in countries where most of the national wealth is concentrated in only a few individuals. In short, the link from per capita GDP to "quality of life" is often tenuous.

Even if per capita GDP were to increase over time, a large portion of this increase could be due to inflation and not to real increases in output. The next logical step, therefore, is to measure national inflation and to determine the "real" or inflation-adjusted output.

2.2.1 INFLATION

Inflation is defined as the percentage rate of change of a price index. Two important and frequently encountered price indexes that allow us to measure inflation are the GDP deflator and the Consumer Price Index (CPI).

The following examples will best describe these two frequently encountered indexes.

2.2.1 GDP DEFLATOR

The GDP deflator, also known as the **personal consumption expenditure (PCE) deflator**, is a nation-wide generalized price index focusing on the change in prices of goods and services that constitute the GDP. This economy-wide index attempts to determine the percentage change in price for all the goods and services produced in an economy.

GDP Deflator = Nominal GDP / Real GDP

In the following simple example in **Table 3**, the inflation rate is measured from some benchmark or base year in the past (Year 1) to the current time period (Year 5).

In Year 1, country K produced 15 units of X at $0.20 per unit, and 50 of Y at $0.22 per unit. In Year 5, as shown below, it produced more of both goods, but the prices also increased. To calculate the real (physical) increase in the value of national output, our first task is to measure the rate of inflation and then to sift it out to compute the real inflation-adjusted increase in GDP.

Table 3

Base year (Year 1)	Current Year (Year 5)	Real GDP Current year (Year 5)
15 of X at $0.20 = $3.00 50 of Y at $0.22 = $11.00	20 of X at $0.30 = $6.00 60 of Y at $0.25 = $15.00	20 of X at $0.20 = $4.00 60 of Y at $0.22 = $13.20
Total = $14.00 Nominal GDP in Year 1 (in Year 1 Dollars)	Total = $21.00 Nominal GDP in Year 5 (in Year 5 dollars)	Total = $17.20 Real GDP in Year 5 is $17.20 (using Year 1 prices)

The nominal GDP from the formula is computed by simply multiplying both quantities and prices of each individual good for the particular year in question. Hence, nominal GDPs for Year 1 and Year 5 are $14.00 and $21.00, as presented in Table 3. However, computing a growth rate for GDP based on these numbers would certainly overstate the real increase in output. We need to subtract—deflate—the increase in nominal GDP due to inflation.

13

The next task, therefore, is the computation of the real GDP in the current year. As displayed in the third column, real GDP is computed by multiplying the quantities produced in the current period (Year 5) not with the current prices, but by our base year (benchmark) prices from Year 1. Real GDP is therefore a more modest $17.20 in Year 5. This is the "real" increase in goods and services from Year 1 to Year 5.

The rate of growth of real GDP is defined as the **"growth rate"** of an economy. A decline in real GDP over two consecutive quarters constitutes a **recession;** this is the unofficial, yet widely accepted, definition of a recession.

Plugging the nominal and real GDP into the deflator formula, we obtain:

$$\text{GDP Deflator} = \frac{21.00}{17.20} = 1.22$$

This simple example indicates an inflation rate of 22% between years 1 and 5. Alternatively stated, the nominal GDP of year 5 has to be "deflated" by 22% to give us the real or inflation adjusted GDP.

In actual computations performed by the Commerce Department's BEA (Bureau of Economic Analysis) that calculates and releases GDP figures, all goods and services included in GDP, along with their respective prices, are included in calculating the deflator. In fact, until 1996 the BEA used a technique similar to the above example. However, with advances in technology, health care, and communications (to name a few sectors), it was found that many goods produced in the current year (5) were not in existence in Year 1. Or, alternatively, the base year counterparts of goods in Year 5 computers, mobile phones, etc.) were simply not in the same league in terms of productivity and performance.

To remedy this problem, the BEA has adopted a Chain Index for calculating real GDP with the base year now just one year behind the current year. In our simple example, the average of the prices of Year 4 and Year 5 would be used for computing the real GDP in Year 5, instead of the Year 1 prices, as done earlier. Presumably, Year 4 would have more of the items produced in Year 5, and these items would be closer in quality and performance to current items than those produced in Year 1. For the following year (6), a moving average of prices of years 5 and 6 would be computed as "base year" prices, and so on. Hence, real GDP is now often presented in chained dollars, and a chained-type price index for GDP is essentially the rectified equivalent of the GDP Deflator.

2.2.2 CONSUMER PRICE INDEX (CPI)

In marked contrast to the above index that includes all goods produced in the economy, the more familiar Consumer Price Index (CPI) tracks only the rate of change in price of a relatively fixed bundle of goods ("market basket") over time. This market basket is designed to represent the typical monthly consumption of urban consumers, and is also referred to as CPI-u.

Initially constructed during World War 1 as a benchmark for adjusting shipbuilders wages paid by the US government, the index is computed monthly by the Bureau of Labor Statistics (BLS). On a monthly and bimonthly basis, the BLS collects price information of around 96,000 goods and services—everything from mouse pads to mangoes is included. Every month, the Department of Labor sends a team of observers to more than 50 urban centers to record the most current prices. These items are then placed into seven major expenditure categories to finally produce one price index, the CPI, computed as follows.[6]

$$\text{CPI} = \frac{\sum P_i q_0}{\sum P_0 q_0}$$

Where P_i = current prices

q_0 = "fixed" market basket (consumption bundle)

P_0 = base year prices

In the following table, the first column represents the "fixed" market basket composed of 15 of X and 50 of Y. It is the change in price of this consumption bundle over time that will give us the CPI.

Table 4

Base year (Year 1)	Current Year (Year 5)	To get $\sum P_i q_0$
15 of X at $0.20 = $3.00 50 of Y at $0.22= $11.00	20 of X at $0.30 = $6.00 60 of Y at $0.25= $15.00	15 of X at $0.30 = $4.50 50 of Y at $0.25 = $12.50
$\sum P_0 q_0$ = $14.00	Total = $21.00	$\sum P_i q_0$ = $17.00

The denominator in the formula is simply the nominal value of the market basket in Year 1 dollars. The numerator is the price of the "fixed" Year 1 basket in Year 5 (current year) dollars. This is computed in the column on the extreme right.

Hence, the CPI is:

$$\text{CPI} = \frac{17}{14} = 1.21$$

This indicates 21% inflation in the fixed market basket from Years 1 to 5, in this simplified example.

The rigidity in the composition of the "fixed" market basket has always been known to cause the CPI to overstate the actual inflation rate. In fact, the 1996 Boskin Commission found this amount of overstatement to be as much as 1.1%.[7]

This overstatement is actually a very significant issue. In addition to measuring inflation, the CPI also measures the change in the cost of living for the urban population of the US, which accounts for approximately 81% of the total population. It forms the basis for annual benefits adjustments to recipients of Social Security benefits and food stamps, funding for school lunches and other programs, workers whose long-term wage contracts are determined by collective bargaining, and non-government sectors that use the CPI as a benchmark for future wage changes. Income tax brackets, interest on inflation-indexed bonds (I-bonds), and exemptions and deductions computed by the IRS are also distorted by overstated inflation.

The overstatement can be primarily attributed to four factors:

(i) Substitution Bias

The CPI does not capture the fact that when the price of a particular good increases, consumers quickly shift to a substitute good whose price may not have increased by as much.

(ii) New Product Bias

This occurs when new goods and services are introduced into an economy but not yet incorporated into the fixed weights of the market basket. Air conditioners in the 1950s, and mobile phones and laptops in the 1990s, for example, were included years after their introduction. These new products typically experience sharp drops in price within the first few years of introduction, with this initial price decline not captured by the CPI.

(iii) Quality Bias

It is increasingly difficult, especially in technologically advanced economies, to separate simple changes in price from changes in quality. New video equipment and new medical technology, for example, may be significantly more expensive in the current year, but may easily outperform the corresponding items that constitute a market basket from some earlier base year.

The BLS does indeed attempt to make adjustments for increases in quality. Inflation in the auto sector from 1967 to the present would have been far higher if this had not been done. Since 1992, the US has also been making quality adjustments for hardware in the information technology (IT) sector. Nevertheless, quality bias, which is linked to the new product bias, remains a challenge for the BLS.

(iv) Outlet Substitution

More and more consumers, both in the US as well abroad, are shopping in outlet malls.   Furthermore, sophisticated supply chain management has resulted in generations of discount stores such as Walmart that can sell significantly below standard retail prices.   If these stores are not fully represented in the CPI, an upward bias may result in the final inflation figure.

To remedy the bias problem, from 1998 the BLS has switched from updating the weights and composition of the market basket from every ten years to every two years. This shorter period should provide a more timely and flexible measure of consumer spending patterns that, in turn, should give us a more accurate measure of inflation. Mobile phones and auto leases were included in a new category in 1998, labeled "education and communication", and personal computers were given a greater role.

This more frequent revision of the composition of the market basket will, hopefully, ensure that the consumption bundle is more in line with current consumption patterns, thereby resulting in a more accurate measure of inflation.

The BLS also announces the "**core rate of inflation**" which is simply the inflation measured by the CPI minus price increases (changes) in food and fuel. This is done to sift away the exogenous factors causing inflation and to allow policy makers to focus on the component of inflation caused by domestic endogenous influences such as excess consumer and investor demand. We will discuss this endogenous inflation in detail when concepts such as "overheating" and "soft landings" are discussed in Chapter 5.

We now turn to discussion questions followed by simulated "media articles" in which concepts covered in this chapter will be presented in the form in which macroeconomic information is usually encountered in our professional and personal lives.

2.3 DISCUSSION QUESTIONS

The following Q&A section highlights some additional aspects of these inflation indexes.

(1) Since both the CPI and the chained-type price index (deflator) measure inflation, why do we often see a "spike" in one and not the other?

The deflator includes all goods and services that constitute GDP, but the CPI does not. However, the CPI includes imports, which are not included in the deflator. Typically when oil prices surge, for example, a spike in the CPI is observed while the deflator seems to be unaffected, at least during the particular period. Additionally, the two indexes are not always synchronized; the CPI is measured monthly, whereas the deflator is available only quarterly.

(2) Is one index superior to the other? Which index must one use?

The CPI suffers from substitution bias, while the deflator, better known as the Personal Consumption Expenditure (PCE) index, does not. While this bias has caused the US Federal Reserve to switch from the CPI to the PCE index as its primary gauge for measuring inflation and prescribing policy, the CPI still remains very much alive in that it determines adjustments to social security benefits, pension payments, etc. Furthermore, recent improvements to the CPI's market basket are designed to continuously reduce substitution and outlet biases and to align the CPI more closely with the deflator (PCE).

Generally, very rarely do policy makers examine just one index—CPI or PCE—in isolation. An array of more specialized indexes are also consulted, such as the PPI (producer price index), and the forward-looking CRB (Commodities Research Bureau) index. Other examples include the precious metals index, employment cost index, and the feed-and-seed index. Smaller economies such as Singapore, where foreign trade constitutes a significantly larger proportion of domestic GDP compared to that for the US, would have a greater role for exchange rate influences that affect the price of vital imports such as fuel and food.

(3) The PPI is another eagerly awaited number. Is it similar to the CPI?

The PPI is indeed calculated in similar fashion. It measures the wholesale prices of approximately 3,500 items and was, in fact, formerly known as the wholesale price index. However, its implications are quite different from those of the CPI and the chained-price deflator. The PPI includes many raw materials and semi-finished goods in the early stage of the supply chain. Therefore, movements in the PPI serve as leading indicators of future price movements at the retail level captured "later" by the CPI and the deflator. This often results in the PPI being one of the more eagerly awaited statistics when expectations of resurgent inflation are high. Another noteworthy index of future inflation is the monthly FIBER (Foundation for International Business and Economic Research). This index focuses on expected labor and raw materials shortages in the near future.

(4)   Should central banks strive for zero inflation?

Given the fact that—revisions to the market basket notwithstanding—most G7 economies' CPIs tend to overstate the actual cost of living, a zero percent inflation target as measured by the CPI may conceivably correspond to a negative inflation rate in reality![8] These economies would experience deflation with across-the-board average decreases in prices of real estate, stocks, manufacturing, wages, etc., reminiscent of the agony experienced by Japan in the 1990s and into the 2000s. In later chapters, we will examine how some central banks aim, instead, for stable inflation rates of 1-2%, rather than potentially deflationary absolute values such as "zero inflation".

Unfortunately, though, when banks adopt targets of, say, 2% (corresponding to actual inflation of, perhaps, 0.5%), unions and others often tend to misinterpret this as a sign that the central bank is prepared to tolerate a little inflation. They may then push for 2% wage increases, thereby actually contributing to actual future increases in inflation!

(5)   Finally, since measured inflation tends to overstate the actual cost of living in most economies, does this imply that there is some globally standardized index of measuring inflation?

While the technique of computing the price indexes in different countries is similar, the market baskets are, unfortunately, not. For example, unlike the other G7 countries, the UK's retail-price index includes interest payments on home loans. The former Soviet Union did not include many costs of services. Economies like Singapore, that have relatively large trade sectors, have proportionally greater emphasis on traded, exchange-rate sensitive goods such as water, fuel, and food, in addition to re-exports, compared to the US.[9] And Japan's CPI excludes many popular goods such as mobile phones and personal computers. Attempts at convergence are, however, gradually being made—China, for example, switched from using a retail price index to a more standardized consumer price index in 2000.

Article 2.2 provides more details pertaining to the choice of deflators in the US, France, and Germany which adjust for quality improvements, particularly in the information technology (IT) sector.

In the following simulated articles, please comment on/define/explain the underlined phrases/sentences with reference to material from this chapter.

ARTICLE 2.1   CHOOSE YOUR INFLATION TARGET

Fred Mandelstamm, The New York Ledger [10]

Last week's comments regarding the "right" level of inflation by the Chief Economist of the National Chapter of Certified Accountants have sparked what seems to be a national debate. Even talk-show hosts are in on the act, espousing their personal views on the subject! This newspaper decided to randomly interview some Americans from different walks of life, to get a perspective on what they are thinking on Main Street, USA.

"Why don't they just **(a)** aim for zero inflation? Seems straight-forward! Why argue over whether it (target inflation) should be 1% or 2%? Hey, zero is best!" was Sam Trivenni's comment, as he emerged from his police car in Houston, Texas. Sam is a police veteran of 17 years, and assists wife Judy when he can in her pet grooming business.

Mary Etawills of Wills Travels Agency in Blacksburg, Virginia, disagrees. "I'm no rocket scientist, but it seems like some

inflation would be good. We want the prices of houses and other assets to go up, don't we?"

The inflation debate affects individuals of all age groups. Edna Winterbauer, resident of Memories Retirement Home in Fayetteville, Arkansas, is con-cerned. **(b)** "The only increase I ever get in my social security check is cost-of-living. Will zero inflation mean no increases for us retired people? No, I don't like it!"

Mohit Sharma, an IT consultant in San Francisco, takes time out from his latte break at Starbird's to talk to us. He feels that "the indexes are quite confusing. I noticed that **(c)** often the CPI rises sharply, but the other major indicators do not. Just have one index and try not to confuse the public." His co-worker, Shifra Bergstrum, added, "I don't even think that the indexes are accurate. I mean, **(d)** if the inflation is 'low' as the indexes indicate, then why is it impossible to afford a house in the Northeast or here on the

20

West Coast? It just doesn't make sense!"

In Colorado, digital spectroscope manufacturer John Zalinsky, who imports electronic components from Asia, went on to say that, "the strong dollar makes my costs of basic electronic components imported from Southeast Asia much lower, and **(e)** hence, my final product, many steps down the supply chain, is cheaper. This has to decrease inflation. Is this figured in the inflation measurement?" Lots of opinions. Lots of ideas. The debate rages.

ARTICLE 2.2 **INFORMATION TECHNOLOGY AND MACRO-DATA**

Ernest Shlieffen, Frankfurt Business Policy Review

Comparing global growth figures has become even more of a challenge in recent years because of the different statistical methods employed by countries to account for changes in quality of output. One major component within this category is the **(a)** change in the quality of computers.

As the G7 economies have increased capital investment in information technology (IT) hardware, the magnitude of the potential statistical error in measuring **(b)** real GDP growth has increased proportionally.

"Measuring the real output of, say, crude oil or coal over time is relatively easy. With computers, however, the change in quality every year is so significant that it is really very hard to separate an increase in nominal output or spending between a change in price and a change in volume," remarked Prof. Eugenie Moulin of Tourainne Macroscience Labs, in Tours, France.

Given the massive increases in speed and memory in IT hardware, American statisticians have adopted techniques for adjusting for quality improvements in computers when computing GDP deflators. Within the eurozone, though, only France uses this adjustment technique; Germany does not.

"This adjustment for quality isn't just a matter for statisticians and macroeconomic purists", states Professor Moulin. "This makes a very significant difference."

From 1992 till the early 2000s, the **(c)** price deflator for IT equipment in the US has fallen by over 80%. In other words, nominal output in the IT hardware sector is deflated by 80% compared to the amount for 1992 to account for a bias in inflation measurement.

Since Germany does not adjust for this bias, the deflator for IT has shrunk by only 20%. The implication is that growth in the real IT investment in Germany is understated and so is its real GDP.

In fact, studies by the Macro Institute in Frankfurt (among others) find that if Germany's nominal capital investment in IT were to be deflated by the relatively smaller US GDP, then German investment has grown by an average of 29% a year since 1992. This is in stark contrast to the 6% growth figure reported in official government (German) statistics!

(d) "Japanese statistics in this area are, in fact, even more distorted. The Asian economies along with the eurozone economies need to be aware of the measurement differences that exist between their countries and the US, before they design macro-economic policy," states Lord Larry Duncan, a financial analyst an owner of WorldSoft, an IT consulting house based in London.

We find macroeconomic experts everywhere to be well aware of the measurement problems. "No wonder the French statistics (regarding capital investment in IT) look so good!" exclaims Victor Gulli, Senior Economist at Rome's Modigliani Center. "We should all be using the US method which the French have adopted—it just makes sense!" He waves expansively towards his computer sitting beside a window with an amazing view of the Eternal City. "Look, I just bought this last year, and already my teenage son's laptop, which he bought last month, can do more. And he paid less!"

In fact, if American statistical methods were to be applied to the entire eurozone, then its **(e)** annual growth rate might be at least half a percentage point higher than it has been since the late 1990s.

ANSWERS AND HINTS

ARTICLE 2.1 CHOOSE YOUR INFLATION TARGET

(a) Zero inflation may actually lead to deflation, since inflation is usually overstated. Deflation is usually symptomatic of an economy in collapse, with average prices of assets falling across the board. Mary Etawills in the following paragraph, has the right hunch.

(b) This is not just an academic exercise. An inflation-indexed increase is often the only source of increase for those on fixed incomes—correcting the overstated inflation actually "hurts" these folks.

(c) The CPI includes imports, namely oil. The deflator (CPE) does not. So when oil shocks slam into the economy, the CPI rises while the deflator remains dormant.

(d) This is average rate of inflation for the whole economy. In some cases, the overall rate of inflation may seem low but could mask high and rising inflation in certain specific sectors. Hence, the increased focus on the notion of speculative asset price (SAP) bubbles in sectors such as IT, the stock market, and in real estate. This will be discussed in Chapter 5.

(e) The PPI would be the relevant statistic here. Please refer to discussions pertaining to the "early-warning" potential of this inflation statistic.

ARTICLE 2.2 INFORMATION TECHNOLOGY AND MACRO-DATA

(a) Which bias is being discussed here?

(b) Business purchases of software are now included in capital investments (I). Clearly, rapid increases in technology and related IT products have unleashed a host of complications in measuring accurate GDP statistics—biases abound.

(c) This is a special deflator for the IT sector, primarily hardware. If the deflator for the US has shrunk by 80% this means that nominal IT output in the current year has to be deflated now by only 20% compared to 1992. Why?

(d) Please give an example of these Japanese "distortions" from earlier in the chapter.

(e) As discussed, the annual growth rate of an economy is simply the per capita growth rate of real GDP.

---

[1] The exact mechanism by which money growth is changed will be covered in detail in Chapter 11.

[2] The Great Stagflation is discussed in the context of the "second paradigm shift" in Chapter 10.

[3] A "model" is simply a well-articulated, theoretical macroeconomic framework. Typically a model includes descriptions (equations) of the goods, money, foreign exchange and labor markets. These markets can be represented and analyzed graphically or mathematically. The major focus of this volume will be on graphical analysis emphasizing the real-world policy aspects of macroeconomics.

[4] The discussion of the time-series generated Identification Problem in Chapter 10 explains how two very different models with drastically different policy prescriptions can legitimately co-exist and explain macroeconomic behavior equally well.

[5] For example, the boost in GDP obtained by harvesting every tree in the vast forests of the Pacific Northwest in the US would certainly be dwarfed by the ecological disaster that would follow. In fact, historically, economies experiencing phenomenal GDP growth have often also experienced accompanying increases in pollution; Dickensian England is an oft-cited example.

[6] The seven categories along with their general expenditure proportions are housing (43%), food and beverages (19%), transportation (18%), medical care (10%), apparel and upkeep (4%), entertainment (4%), and other (about 2%).

[7] Named after Stanford University Professor, Michael Boskin, chairman of the committee. While it was clear for some time that the CPI was overstating actual inflation, the Boskin commission systematically estimated this value.

[8] The G7 economies are Canada, France, Germany, Italy, Japan, the UK, and the US. With Russia included, we have the G8.

[9] Singapore's trade sector (imports plus exports and including re-exports) as a percentage of its GDP was in the 160-180% range by 2000, while the US had a trade/GDP ratio of 22-25%.

[10] All "articles" have been created by the author and, as discussed in Chapter 1, are designed to mimic actual reporting of macroeconomic events by the news media. The objective, as discussed earlier, is to allow managers and executives to relate concepts discussed in the chapter to macroeconomic news and analyses presented by the media on a daily basis. The names ascribed to the newspapers and magazines, and to the individuals "quoted" in the articles as well as listed as "authors" are purely fictional. Any resemblance to any existing publication or persons is coincidental. This endnote applies to all "articles" in all chapters of this book.

3. BUDGET DEFICITS, TRADE DEFICITS AND GLOBAL CAPITAL FLOWS: THE NATIONAL SAVINGS IDENTITY

In this cornerstone chapter, the vitally important **National Savings Identity (NSI)**, linking trade and budget balances to global capital flows, interest rates, and exchange rates, makes its first appearance. In many ways, this chapter, linking the "twin deficits" in a fundamentally intuitive manner, sets the tone for macroeconomic policies to be discussed in following chapters.

To some extent, this chapter will be "backward looking" in that past macroeconomic episodes in the US, Europe, and Asia, characterized by record budget and trade deficits, will be discussed here in the context of the NSI. For example, the 1980s US bond-financed budget deficits, the early 1990s post-unification German experience, and the Mexican and Southeast Asian currency crises of the mid- to late-1990s will be discussed in this chapter.

The current US trade and capital flows with China will also be highlighted here. An NSI analysis of the massive global capital inflows that, in varying degrees, helped fund the internet-driven economy in the US from the late 1990s to the present will be a prime focus of this chapter. Using the NSI, we will see how, despite record low national savings and record-high national consumption, the mammoth capital inflows, directly related to the unprecedented US current account deficits (loosely, trade deficits), may have helped finance the so-called "new" economy of the 2000s. In addition, we will examine the potential pitfalls of large global capital inflows as well as the sudden outflows of "hot capital" such as those that traumatized the Southeast Asian economies in 1997-98.

3.1 THE NATIONAL SAVINGS IDENTITY (NSI)

If Y is the value of domestic output (real GDP, from Chapter 2), and if imports of goods and services are denoted as "Imp", the total goods and services available in an economy will be (Y + Imp). This total output is equal to the sum of **(1)** the private consumption expenditure (C), which accounts for almost 70 percent of GDP in the US, **(2)** capital investment expenditure (I), **(3)** government expenditure on goods and services (G), and **(4)** foreign consumption denoted as exports (Exp).

Algebraically, this can be expressed as:

$$Y + Imp = C + I + G + Exp$$

Simplifying, we get:

$$\mathbf{Y = C + I + G + (Exp - Imp)} \qquad (1)$$

Where:
Y : National output
C : Private consumption expenditure (Personal Consumption Expenditure)
I : Capital investment (new plant and equipment)
G : Government expenditure on goods and services
Exp: Exports of goods and services (Foreign consumption)
Imp: Imports of goods and services

Capital investment (I) is not to be confused with investing in the stock market and in mutual funds, for example. This latter kind of investing falls under "savings" in macroeconomics. Instead, the "I" in equation (1) pertains to capital investment as in new construction, purchasing new hardware, and plant and equipment. Capital investment (I) in macroeconomics usually necessitates the borrowing of loanable funds, and we will soon see how it is closely linked to interest rates.

Since October 1999, the Bureau of Economic Analysis (BEA) has redefined capital investment to also include business purchases of computer software. This huge step, reclassifying software purchases as fixed capital investment, was a significant acknowledgement by the BEA of the undeniable emergence of the "new" internet-driven economy. By some estimates, including software purchases in (I) may have boosted annual real GDP growth by about 0.1 percent in the late 1990s and early 2000s.

If Y goods and services are produced and sold in this economy, the income obtained from the sale of goods of value Y will be Y dollars. This national income, in turn, is used for private consumption (C), part of it is saved (S), and part is devoured by net taxes (T), which are taxes paid minus transfers received.

This is represented algebraically:

$$Y = C + S + T \qquad\qquad (2)$$

Where:
Y : Income from sale of goods of value Y
C : Private consumption expenditure
S : Private savings
T : Net Taxes.

Simply put, expression (1) describes how the available output is distributed, while (2) above describes how the income from the sale of the output is divided between national consumption, savings, and taxes.

Equating (1) and (2) we obtain:
C + I + G + (Exp - Imp) = C + S + T

26

Simplifying further, we finally get the **National Savings Identity**:

$$(G - T) = (S - I) + (Imp - Exp) \qquad (3)$$

The term $(G - T)$, the difference between government spending and national tax revenues, represents the national budget balance. If $(G-T)$ is positive, then national budget deficits are incurred as government spending exceeds tax revenues, and if $(G-T)$ is negative, then the national budget is in surplus. [1]

The last term $(Imp - Exp)$, is defined as the current account balance. If $(Imp - Exp)$ is positive, this economy experiences a current account deficit, and a current account surplus if the balance is negative. The current account statistic is reported quarterly and includes trade (exports minus imports) in goods and services, along with global net investment income, and net unilateral transfers (foreign aid or transfers received from abroad). At this point, for notational convenience, investment income and transfers from abroad are subsumed by the term (Exp), while incomes paid (and transfers made) to foreigners constitute outflows of funds, and are included in the term (Imp).

It should be noted that the more familiar "trade balance" reported monthly includes only merchandise trade—goods that clear customs and require paperwork such as bills of lading at ports. The service sector, in which the US has a surplus, while included in the current account balance, is however not fully included in the more familiar trade balance.[2]

To appreciate the full potential of the NSI, the next logical task is to explore the fundamental macroeconomic intuition underlying it. The immediate observation is that the two balances—budget and current account—are inextricably linked. We begin by assuming that the domestic economy incurs simultaneous budget and current account deficits; $(G-T)$ and $(Imp-Exp)$ are both positive in (3).

Exactly what is the mechanism by which these "twin deficits" are linked? Furthermore, what is the direction of causality? Do budget deficits "cause" current account deficits, or vice versa?

The first step is to examine the left-hand-side of (3), and review how national budget deficits are financed. Three broad methods of deficit financing are:

1. Borrowing from domestic and foreign residents. Here the domestic deficit incurring government issues (sells) government bonds. In the case of the US, the Treasury is the bond-issuing entity, and the debt instruments (Treasury bills, bonds) are really discount bonds sold at below face value in national auctions. In this case, the interest rate is endogenous and determined by the market supply and demand for domestic government debt at each individual auction. (The concept of "endogencity" alluded to in the previous chapter, will be explained in the following section 3.1.1.)

2.   Monetization. Here the central bank is forced to "print money" to pay for outstanding government debt, or is said to "monetize" the deficit. This is clearly not a viable deficit financing option, and detailed discussions of high inflation and hyperinflation in later chapters will bear testimony to the disastrous consequences of rampant monetization.

3.   Debt repudiation. This is simply a national default on government debt, and, once again, certainly not a viable deficit financing option. (For the sake of completeness, another "option" is the one-time sale of national resources. One example is the sale of gold reserves and oil by Russia following the dissolution of the USSR in the early 1990s. This financing option would be a one-time measure at best.)

3.1.1   TWO CRUCIAL ASSUMPTIONS UNDERLYING THE NSI

(1)   Deficits are completely bond financed.

We restrict the following discussion and analysis to the case where national budget deficits are incurred by an economy with responsible fiscal and monetary policy and are <u>mostly if not entirely bond financed</u>, as in the case of the US deficits since the 1980s and the German post-unification deficits.   Monetization and debt repudiation are not viable deficit-financing options here. (The assumption of responsible macroplicy is relaxed in later chapters to cover the whole range of macroeconomic consequences.)

(2)   Fiscal and monetary credibility is sound.

The central bank has a long-standing reputation of monetary discipline, and will not be pressured by the government to monetize any runaway deficits caused by profligate government spending. The political climate is stable. The national debt is "risk free" or low risk.

At this stage, a short overview of microeconomics is in order. Specifically, the notion of endogenous variables and the shifting of demand and supply curves will be vital to fully appreciate the ISLM-ADAS model which is the 'engine room' of this book.

3.1.1.1   MICROECONOMICS REVIEW

The following **Figures 1a** and **1b** present simple demand and supply plots.   As an example, we use the market for the most technologically advanced household communications device—the Ultimate Phone. As prices increase, all other variables staying unchanged, quantity demanded of phones decreases in Figure 1a; as prices increase, quantity supplied increases in Figure 1b, and vice versa.   Both the plots depict changes in quantities demanded and supplied for a hypothetical range of prices.

Superimposing Figure 1b on to 1a, we get **Figure 1c**, a simple market-clearing diagram for Ultimate Phones. The market equilibrium price for these phones is given by the intersection of supply and demand—where supply equals demand—denoted by P_E, with Y_0 phones sold, and no unsold inventory or shortage.

This market clearing equilibrium price is determined "endogenously", or "from within the market" by supply and demand forces. For instance, if all conventional phones were to suddenly become inoperative, there would be an increase in demand for Ultimate Phones at all prices. In Figure 1d, this increase in demand results in a new demand curve located to the right of the existing curve, denoted 'Higher Demand'. Diagrammatically, the increase in demand translates to a shift to the right in the demand curve, while a decrease in demand causes the demand curve to shift to the left.

In **Figure 1d**, we have superimposed the original supply curve on this new demand curve, and as a result the equilibrium price (point of intersection) is now higher. Here, prices of Ultimate Phones increased endogenously due to the increase in demand characterized by the rightward shift in the demand curve.

Shifts in both supply and demand curves, or in either of them separately, will affect the endogenous prices of cellular phones. For example, an increase in supply resulting from a massive increase in Ultimate Phone production from global production or imports would shift the supply curve to the right, thereby endogenously driving down equilibrium prices, and vice versa.

While this is a purely "micro" example confining itself to the specific market for phones, in later chapters this concept of endogeneity will be extremely important. The notion that changes in market-clearing "prices" of equilibrium variables are driven by market forces, and not by central planning committees (as in the former Soviet Union), will be applied to macroeconomic variables such as interest rates, exchange rates, GDP, wages, employment, and inflation.

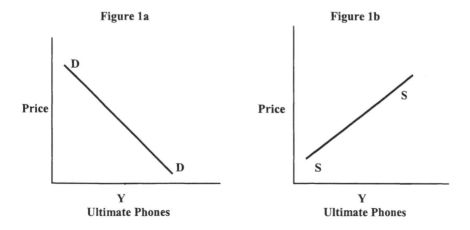

Figure 1a

Figure 1b

Price

Y
Ultimate Phones

Price

Y
Ultimate Phones

Figure 1c

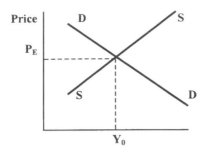

Ultimate Phones

Figure 1d

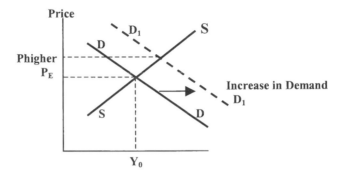

Ultimate Phones

3.1.2 LINKING THE TWIN DEFICITS

Coming back to the National Savings Identity, we now explore how the budget and current account balances may be linked by the NSI expression:

$(G-T) = (S-I) + (Imp-Exp)$.

By virtue of the assumptions of deficits being bond-financed in a safe haven economy, the left-hand-side of the NSI is in fact a demand for borrowing, while the right-hand-side, in equilibrium, constitutes a supply of lending, as presented below.

$(G - T) \quad =$	$(S - I) + (Imp - Exp)$
Demand for borrowing (Demand for loanable funds)	Supply of loanable funds

The following Figure 2, presents a market for loanable funds, with the initial interest rate i_0 obtained where demand for borrowing exactly equals the supply of lending. Here i_0 is the endogenously determined equilibrium interest rate prevailing in this economy. The interest rate on risk-free, short-term domestic government bonds could serve as a good proxy for i_0.

The following steps 1-7 present the macroeconomic intuition linking the twin deficits.[3] Steps 1, 2, 6,and 7 are also included in **Figure 2**.

1. As the central government incurs a budget deficit that has to be financed by borrowing (since we assume no monetization here), the demand for loanable funds increases and the curve DD accordingly shifts to the right to D_1D_1.

2. This increase in demand drives up domestic interest rates to the higher equilibrium, i_1.

Figure 2

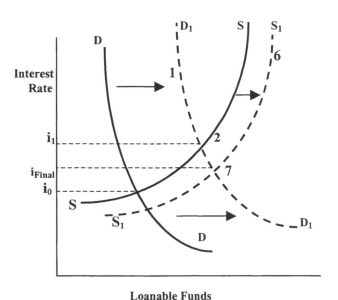

Loanable Funds

3. The time has come to extend our analysis to the global sector. As interest rates of these safe haven domestic government bonds exceed those of other countries, domestic and foreign investors now "switch" to the higher yielding and safe domestic government debt.[4] (Actually, interest rate differences are

31

not the only factors driving global capital flows. As we will discuss later in this chapter, an economy's long term macroeconomic outlook is vitally important in order to attract global capital.) These investors, who include individuals, life insurance companies, global investment houses, governments, central banks, etc., need to swap their respective currencies for domestic currency, e.g., yuan or yen or euro for US$, with the US being the "domestic" country in this example. This excess demand for domestic currency—US dollars—makes this currency "more expensive" in terms of foreign currency in the global foreign exchange markets. That is, the domestic currency appreciates (gets "stronger") relative to foreign currencies. A hypothetical example of US currency appreciation would be:

Before step (1)   1 US$ = 100 units of foreign currency.
After step (1)   1 US$ = 120 units of foreign currency.

4.   With the strengthening of the domestic currency, imports now become "cheaper" for domestic residents, while domestic exports become more "expensive" to foreign consumers who have to exchange more units of their currencies for one unit of domestic currency.

5.   Hence, as imports surge and as exports slow, the current account balance (Exp-Imp) decreases and the domestic budget deficit incurring economy eventually experiences a deterioration in its current account balance. In this scenario, the "twin deficits" are indeed linked. Here, the budget imbalance (G-T) drives the NSI and, by influencing interest rates and exchanges rates, results in a decrease in the current account balance and perhaps eventually in a current account deficit.

During the 1980s for the US and the early 1990s for Germany, for example, the twin deficits did indeed exhibit strong positive covariance for both these economies. Both countries had to resort to large bond issuances to finance their significant budget deficits: the Americans financing the mammoth Reagan-era deficits, and the Germans struggling to finance their post-unification outlays stemming from infrastructure demands of the former East Germany.

6.   As the domestic economy amasses cheaper imports, foreigners accumulate deposits of domestic currency. For example, the US accumulates imports from Japan and China, while these two current account surplus countries amass massive dollar deposits. These dollar deposits are then promptly re-invested in the safe haven, high yielding domestic economy (the US, in this example). That is, the domestic economy incurs a current account deficit but also experiences an inflow of capital—a capital account surplus. This is reflected in move (6) where the inflow results in an increase in the

supply of loanable funds, thereby causing the curve to shift to the right from SS to S_1S_1.

7. Finally, thanks to this capital inflow, equilibrium interest rates in the domestic economy are now lowered to i_{Final}. Capital inflows supplement domestic savings (supply of loanable funds), and thereby exert an important ameliorating influence on domestic interest rates.

Almost 40 to 60 percent of the US deficit in the 1980s era and virtually 100 percent of US interest expenses on government debt were funded by massive capital inflows associated with the US current account deficits.

The inflow is not just limited to absorbing additional domestic government debt. In fact, from the early 2000s, huge net capital inflows from Asia (mostly Japan and China) have financed auto plants, real estate ventures, and significant portions of the high-skilled labor-intensive manufacturing sector. In fact, one in eight US manufacturing jobs since the late 1990s is in a company owned by a foreign affiliate. In addition, an astounding number of startups in the information technology (IT) sector—particularly in the heyday of the new economy—were funded by mammoth capital inflows tied to the unprecedented US current account deficits.

Under the assumptions made earlier, a country incurring a current account deficit (loosely, trade deficit) will also experience a capital account surplus (net capital inflow). The capital account surplus and the current account deficit are two sides of the same coin.

This form of bond financing sounds extremely convenient. The budget-deficit-incurring country experiences a current account deficit but also benefits from capital inflows that serve to keep interest rates lower at home!

How long is this sustainable?

At this point, a "sustainable" bond financed deficit is defined as that which can be rolled over perpetually by issuing additional bonds when the current bonds comes due. As long as the inflation adjusted (or "real") rate on government bonds is less than the growth rate of the economy, deficits are defined to be sustainable and the NSI bond-financing model can be implemented with impunity.

A "non-sustainable" deficit, however, is that which has exploded out of control and cannot be bond-financed any longer; domestic and foreign investors refuse to absorb any more of this government's debt in their portfolios. A massive monetization becomes inevitable. Here the real interest "lost" on government debt exceeds the growth rate of the economy.[5]

A loose rule of thumb for G7 economies is that sustainability usually implies a budget deficit/GDP ratio of less than 5 percent. Even more stringent, however, is the criterion of the 1991 Maastricht Treaty to qualify for membership in the European Monetary Union (EMU) that specifies a budget deficit/GDP ratio of less than 3 percent. Emerging economics, which will be discussed later in the chapter on Keynes, typically have higher sustainability benchmarks with acceptable budget deficit/GDP ratios well in excess of those of their more developed G7 counterparts.

We now turn to some criticisms of large bond financed deficits.

3.2 POSSIBLE NEGATIVE ASPECTS OF BOND FINANCED DEFICITS

(a) Crowding Out

Large bond-financed deficits certainly have their detractors. The most prevalent critique leveled against this form of bond financing is that it "**crowds-out**" private capital investment by large government borrowing. Ignoring the foreign sector here, the NSI can be written as:

$(G - T) = (S - I)$

and re-written as:

$$[(G - T) + I] = S \qquad (4)$$

where the left-hand-side of (4) is the total demand for borrowing. This is now represented as a composite demand for borrowing comprising two components, (i) the government demand for loanable funds (G-T), and (ii) the private sector's demand for loanable funds for capital investment, denoted I and represented by the hatched line in **Figure 3**. The right-hand-side of (4) is the supply of loanable funds, which are national savings, S.

Figure 3

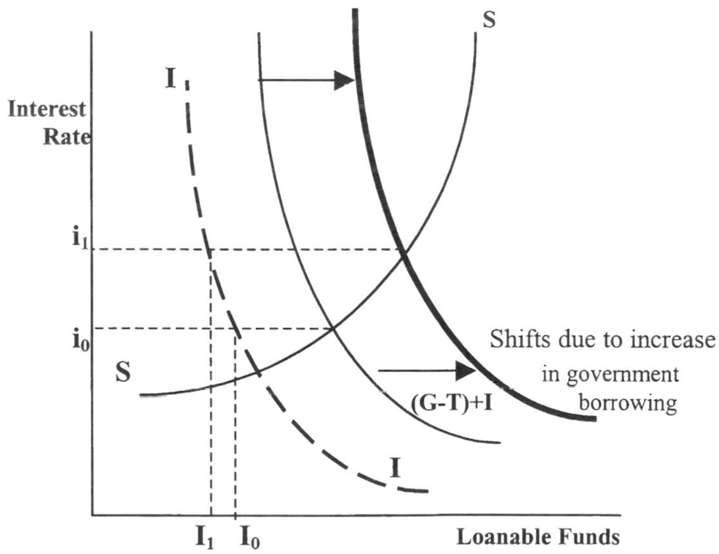

The equilibrium interest rate is determined at i_0, the intersection of the overall demand and supply of loanable funds. Initially, at these interest rates (arbitrarily assumed to be 7% here), the level of private capital investment is denoted I_0 in Figure 3. This is the private demand for loanable funds at existing overall interest rates i_0.

With the increase in government demand for borrowing to finance budget deficits, the total composite demand curve shifts to the right, as discussed earlier and depicted in Figure 3. This shift, in turn, drives up overall interest rates to i_1 (8.25% in this example). As borrowing costs rise, the quantity of loanable funds demanded by the private sector falls to I_1 in Figure 3. Here, private capital investment has been "crowded out" of the market place by the large government appetite for the finite pool of loanable funds. Due to the higher interest rates caused by excessive government borrowing, private borrowers are unable to afford the same high level of planned capital investment I_0, and consequently have to cut back to a lower level I_1. The amount by which private capital investment has shrunk, or been "crowded out", is simply (I_0-I_1).

Proponents of large bond financed deficits, however, counter that if the conspicuously absent capital inflows associated with the current account deficits are properly included in this analysis, interest rates would indeed be decreased by the capital inflow (as in Figure 2), and the effect on any crowding out ameliorated, if not eradicated.

(b) Trade Deficits

Another critique leveled at the NSI-type bond financing pertains to the so-called "deterioration" in the domestic country's export sector. It is argued that such a policy causes jobs to be lost to "foreign competition," not to mention loss of domestic output. In actuality, however, there is no positive correlation between national unemployment and increases in current account deficits.

In fact, episodes of soaring US current account deficits have been characterized by decreasing national unemployment. The then-unprecedented current account and budget deficits of the 1980s were accompanied by strong growth and a virtually full-employment economy. Later, in the early 2000s, the record US current account deficits (this time coinciding with budget surpluses, which we will discuss soon) were accompanied by 30-year lows in the rate of unemployment along with amazingly strong rates of GDP growth that characterized the "new" economy.

The inescapable fact is that free trade does indeed make all trading economies eventually better off. This accounts for the dedication with which many emerging economies (Chile, Mexico, China, Poland, India, to name a few) are intent on pushing for increased globalization by joining global trading blocks and unleashing the benefits of free trade *vis-a-vis* their memberships in the World Trade Organization.

What the critics often fail to acknowledge are the effects of free trade on the economy as a whole, and the positive effect of the capital inflows associated with current account deficits. Typically only the merchandise trade deficits (and not even the current account deficits which include more services) become the familiar headline grabbing statistics. Unfortunately, the crucially important attendant capital inflows are hardly mentioned, not fully understood, and usually relegated to the sidelines.

3.3   TWO CASES OF THE NSI: THE UNITED STATES AND CHINA

The following two polar cases pertaining to the early-mid 2000s will highlight the importance of the (S-I) term in the NSI.

A "US type" economy will be defined to include any relatively safe haven economy that incurs a decreasing fiscal deficit, balanced budget or budget surplus, and a significant and increasing current account deficit.

A "China type" economy will encompass all reasonably safe haven economies that have generally sustainable fiscal deficits (or even balanced budgets) and significant and increasing current account surpluses.[6]   In the following discussion, the main difference between the two "types" lies in the current and expected state of their current account balances.

3.3.1   US-TYPE NSI

We begin by plugging in some hypothetical representative numbers for this class of economies, into the NSI:

$$(G - T) = (S - I) + (Imp-Exp) \qquad (3)$$

Let $(G-T) = (0)$, a budget in balance, and let $(Imp-Exp) = 300$, a significant current account deficit. All numbers are assumed to be in billions of US dollars.

$$(0) = (S - I) + (300)$$

What is the value of (S-I)?

Quite simply, $(S-I) = (-300)$.

This implies that private demand for loanable funds in this economy outstrips the supply of domestic savings by 300 billion US\$. If S were given to be 250, this indicates that I would be 550, to yield $(S-I) = (-300)$

How is this shortfall in the supply of loanable funds financed?

Re-writing (3) we obtain:

$$(Imp - Exp) = [(G - T) + (I)] - S \qquad (4)$$

The first term on the right-hand-side, $[(G - T) + (I)]$, is the composite demand for borrowing, comprising government demand $(G-T)$ plus private demand, (I). S is the domestic supply of loanable funds.

Once again, plugging in the numbers into the right-hand-side of (4):

$(Imp - Exp) = [(G - T) + I] - S = [(0) + 550] - 250 = 300$

Here, the current account deficit, or more specifically the capital inflow associated with the current account deficit, amounts to 300 billion US$. It is this inflow of funds that finances the shortfall in the supply of loanable funds. While a "US Type" economy of the early-mid 2000s has no significant fiscal imbalance to fund as it did in the 1980s, it has, however, a strong excess demand for loanable funds from its private sector for which it remains vitally dependent on capital inflows.

3.3.2   CHINA-TYPE NSI

Here we let the hypothetical sustainable budget deficit be $(G-T) = 10$, and the current account surplus is given as $(Imp - Exp) = -347$. Substituting these values into the NSI we obtain:

$(G - T) = (S - I) + (Imp - Exp)$

$(10) \quad = (S - I) + (-347)$

Calculating the (S-I) term, we obtain:

(S-I) = 357 billion US$. This is symptomatic of most economies in Southeast Asia that are awash in domestic savings and, on net, are "exporters" of global capital. Given the current account surplus in this example, the outflow is computed to be 347 billion US$.

3.4 FACTORS INFLUENCING GLOBAL CAPITAL FLOWS

As stated earlier, two factors attract global capital flows to the domestic country:

(1)   Higher domestic interest rates relative to interest rates in the rest of the world.
(2)   Stronger long-term macroeconomic outlook for the domestic country.

Item (1) was discussed in the context of the NSI. The importance of (2) cannot be overstated. Global capital is often dispatched to economies, even regions, which may not necessarily have higher interest rates compared to other nations' domestic bonds, but instead may exhibit impressive growth that is expected to continue into future periods.

In the early to mid-1990s, for example, with the US recovering from its recession of 1990-91, with the European Union wrestling with the demise of its exchange rate mechanism (ERM) and sluggish growth coupled with persistently high unemployment, and with Japan in prolonged recession, the Southeast Asian countries captured the center-stage of global attention. Phenomenal growth rates of over 10 percent annually, low inflation, high employment, stable governments, and rapid increases in infrastructure development, all contributed to massive capital inflows into Malaysia, Indonesia, Taiwan, the Phillipines, Singapore, and South Korea. The impressive macroeconomic performance of this region coupled with the fact that the other traditional destinations for global capital were not factors in the early 1990s led to unprecedented (and destabilizing) global capital flows into these rapidly emerging economies.

3.4.1   HOT CAPITAL: SOUTHEAST ASIA (1997-98) AND MEXICO (1994)

Typically, a hot capital flow is defined as short-term capital flow into an economy, primarily for the purpose of speculative investment. The duration of investment is almost certainly under one year—in fact it could be weeks or even days. Unfortunately, huge amounts of global inflows, primarily of the "hot capital" variety, can become macroeconomic liabilities, as events in Asia were to demonstrate. As discussed in the context of NSI, the inflows were the "flip side" of the current account deficits, and partially helped fund significant portions of the budget deficit. However, the Southeast Asian economies (with the exception of Indonesia) had budget surpluses. Furthermore, most of them had high rates of employment set against a backdrop of almost an oversupply of electronics, automobiles, etc. That is, there was no deficit to finance, nor many huge new capital investments needed in manufacturing.

As capital inflow poured in during the early-mid 1990s, attracted by the impressive growth rates, much of it went into the stock market, real estate, and questionable infrastructure projects such as the longest bridge in the world, the tallest office building in history, or yet another automobile plant. These economies "overheated" (a term we will revisit in great detail in later chapters), with stock markets and real estate assets rising to astronomical prices. It was not uncommon to rent small, efficiency-type apartments in Hong Kong or Singapore in excess of US$12,000 per month by 1996-97. A dangerous speculative asset price (SAP) bubble developed.

By the late 1990s, the US recovery powered by the "new" internet-driven and productivity-enhanced economy shifted to a higher gear and was soon joined by signs of recovery in Western Europe. At this point, investors, already apprehensive about the overpriced "bubble" assets of the overheated Southeast Asian economies, pulled capital out from SE Asia and back into the US and Western Europe. This devastating and fairly sudden exodus of capital, referred to as a "hot capital" outflow, was a major factor in the

38

currency crises that traumatized the Southeast Asian economies in 1997-98.[7]

A similar hot capital crisis was experienced by Mexico in 1994. After embarking on an impressive privatization campaign in the 1990s, backed up by significant fiscal and monetary reforms that won global admiration, Mexico was "rewarded" by record capital inflows, primarily from the US. In fact its progressive macroeconomic policies were primarily responsible for enabling President Clinton to push through the North American Free Trade Act (NAFTA). The Mexican central banker, Mr. Miguel Mancera, was legendary in his intolerance for any form of monetization; he epitomized monetary prudence and discipline. The macroeconomic outlook looked rosy indeed, and more capital poured in.

In 1994, however, with the Chiapas Indians in Mexico demanding autonomy and disrupting national transportation, two political assassinations (including that of the prime opposition candidate on live TV), and financial scandals at the highest levels, any notion of Mexico's "safe haven" status was suddenly and fatally damaged. And "safe haven" is indeed a necessary condition for capital flows. With the status gone, so was the hot capital in a dramatic outflow in the last quarter of 1994.

To minimize the destabilizing effects of such flows, many emerging economies have placed restrictions on hot capital inflows. China, for example, has restricted purchases of its A-type stocks by foreign investors; inflows cannot be speculative. Instead, inflows aimed at long-term infrastructure spending within China (power plants, information technology, water purification plants, etc.) are encouraged. "Warm" or "cool" capital is desired, not the flighty "hot" kind.

The following **Figure 4** displays a hot capital outflow and its effects on domestic interest rates.

Figure 4

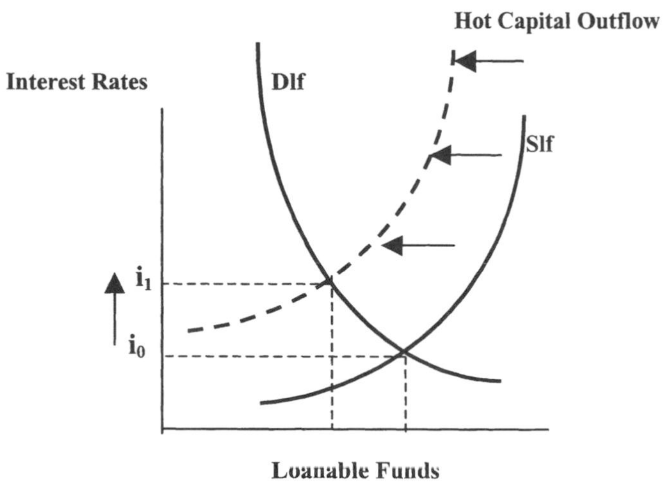

Hot Capital Outflow

Interest Rates   Dlf   Slf

i_1

i_0

Loanable Funds

In Figure 4, domestic interest rates spike sharply from i_0 to i_1 with the sudden exodus of hot capital. This has been clearly evident in Mexico following the outflow of late 1995, as well as in Southeast Asia in 1997-98. The sharp rise in domestic interest rates traumatizes domestic capital investment, as borrowing costs become prohibitive.

Furthermore, as speculators "dump" domestic assets in their race to unload their speculative investments, the reverse of the earlier NSI story occurs—the domestic currency collapses as exchange rates weaken. Imports become prohibitively more expensive as the currency gets progressively weaker, sparking increases in inflation (particularly in prices of vital imports such as food and medical supplies), and weakening confidence as the rout continues to escalate.

Singapore largely escaped the currency meltdown in 1997-98 by remarkably prudent monetary policy. Most of the Southeast Asian countries had "managed pegs", or relatively fixed exchange rates with respect to the US currency. (Actually, the Sing$ was pegged to a basket of currencies with the US being the major component). While the reasons for having "fixed" exchange rates will be discussed in a later chapter, the point here is that inflows in pegged exchange rate regimes translate to direct increases in the recipient country's money supply. If exchange rates were flexible, as in the NSI discussion, the domestic country would experience an appreciation (strengthening) of its currency that would act as a "pressure valve" of sorts and negate the volume of the inflow.

Singapore under the guidance of its renowned central banker, Dr. Richard Hu, the head of the Monetary Authority of Singapore, the nation's highly regarded central bank, prudently allowed its currency to float on two crucial occasions to mitigate the incoming flow of funds. In addition, the central bank also countered the inflow with offsetting domestic monetary contraction, thus minimizing the destabilizing effects of large inflows of funds overheating its stock market and its real estate sector.

3.5 DISCUSSION QUESTIONS

The following questions and answers will highlight and hopefully demystify aspects of budget and current account balances, and their relationships to capital inflows.

1. **Isn't the bond financing discussed here a risky proposition? Isn't the budget-deficit-incurring country essentially being "held hostage" to capital inflows?**

Yes, it is indeed risky if the country in not perceived to be a safe haven, or is simply experiencing a short term (hot) inflow for speculative purposes.

Such an economy could be crippled by sudden outflows and spiking interest rates. However, if the economy is perceived as a true safe haven, then it can be very resilient to temperamental outflows.

The best example, perhaps, is that of the now-famous US petrodollar inflows of the 1970s. In spite of an OPEC engineered embargo of oil exports to the US, most of the huge dollar revenues amassed by the oil exporting economies were, surprisingly, funneled back into the US! And this at a time when the US economy was in stagflation, characterized by double-digit inflation, high unemployment and recessionary output. So in spite of being in political disfavor with OPEC and undergoing a traumatic stagflation, the petrodollars still found their relatively safest-haven destination.

2.   Isn't the interest paid to foreign investors a source of net wealth loss for the domestic deficit incurring economy?

This "net wealth loss" has to be weighed against the fact that the capital inflows are indeed lowering domestic final interest rates from i_1 to i_{final} as we have discussed in Figure 2. Domestic rates certainly would be at the higher interest rate i_1 in a bond-financed deficit incurring economy that was closed to global trade and capital.

3.   There is no denying that while jobs at the national level may be created by capital inflows, specific industries competing with imports do indeed suffer job loss (textiles, steel, apparel, for example). In the context of the NSI, what would happen if the protectionists got their way and disrupted global trade?

In fact a similar scenario was almost played out in the US in the mid-1980s, and at various times since then attempts have been made to disrupt global trade meetings. In the mid-1980s, the deterioration in the US merchandise trade deficit prompted cries for restricting imports. The US Federal Reserve was keenly aware that any disruption in the trade balance would immediately disrupt the capital account. A sharp cut-back in imports due to trade disruptions would also mean a similar shut down in capital flows. Given the huge budget deficits that were dependent on global capital at that time, such a disruption in capital inflows would have spelled macroeconomic disaster. The supply of loanable funds (in Figure 2) would have rapidly shifted left, spiking domestic (US) interest rates i_{final} back to i_1, and traumatizing the economy. To preempt this, the famous Plaza Accord of G5 finance ministers (held at the Plaza Hotel in New York) attempted to artificially weaken the US dollar, shrink the current account deficit, and hence ward off the dangerous cries for protectionism.

4.   In the years following the inception of the Euro in 1999, why did the euro steadily weaken with respect to the US dollar (and British

Sterling) even though the difference in interest rates between the countries in the Eurozone and the US was fairly constant?

Once again, it is <u>not just</u> the interest difference but also the long term macroeconomic outlook that dictates the flow of global capital. The US macroeconomic performance characterized by productivity increases, low inflation, and relatively strong growth from the late 1990s through the early 2000s, clearly outperformed that of the eurozone with its rigid labor laws and high level of government regulation.

5. **Why are countries like China actively pursuing a policy of bond financed increases in government spending (in the early 2000s), when the US and other G7 economies have been actively trying to reduce their fiscal imbalances?**

In the Keynesian macroeconomic model to be discussed soon, an increase in government spending of $X may result in the final GDP increasing by more than $X—maybe even $2X! This "multiplier effect" propounded by Keynes was very effective from the 1940s to the late 1970s, but then, according to one group of economists discussed later in this book, ceased to exist in most of the G7 countries. This is why there has been a tendency to decrease government spending in the developed economies, while emerging economies (like China) can still pursue deficit spending policies since multiplier effects from government spending still exist. This will be the subject of the chapter on Keynesian macroeconomics.

6. **Isn't it puzzling that several Southeast Asian economies with national budget <u>surpluses</u> (Singapore, for example) began issuing national debt in the early 2000s?**

The market-determined interest rates on long-term government bonds (of duration 10 years, at least) are vital benchmarks that indicate the level of risk that investors take by purchasing long-term government debt. After discussing the Fisher Effect and the yield curve, we will find long-term interest rates on government debt to be invaluable forward-looking indicators of expected <u>future</u> inflation. This information is imperative in enabling the central bank to make effective current monetary policy decisions based on expected inflation in the future. This feature motivates Singapore's issue of 10-year government debt in spite of incurring budget surpluses.

7. **How is it that Japan incurs huge budget deficits through the mid 1990s into the 2000s, and has virtually zero interest rates for most of this period? Shouldn't rates rise at home by virtue of the NSI?**

In addition to bond-financing huge government outlays, Japan also indulged in very significant (albeit intermittent) increases in its money supply. In this chapter it was assumed that this was not the case and that large budget

42

deficits were fully bond financed without any accompanying monetization.

8. **This ties in with the following question. Where is monetary policy in the NSI? And what about tax rates, consumer confidence, wages, productivity, employment, and inflation?   All   these   are conspicuously absent.**

Yes, they are indeed absent from the NSI discussion presented in this chapter.   The NSI is an accounting identity that provides a wonderfully intuitive discussion of fundamental accounting relationships.   It is a "broad brush" explanation of the flow of funds and the mechanism linking the budget and current account balances as well as national savings and investments.   Its strength lies in the simplicity with which several macroeconomic scenarios can be intuitively analyzed. The equally important details—all the variables listed in the above question, plus some—will be presented in the "engine-room" model of this book, namely, the ISLM-ADAS model.   Construction of this fully articulated model beginning in the following chapter will add several layers of sophistication to the discussion presented in this intuitive chapter.

In the following simulated media articles, please comment on the underlined parts using material from this and the previous chapter.   Use diagrams wherever applicable.

Article 3.1   TRADE DEFICIT CLIMBS TO RECORD

Edward Poston, Chicago Business News

**Setting**: **This domestic safe haven economy has a national budget surplus and a very high current account deficit.**

The Commerce Department reported that the nation's trade deficit widened to a record of $31.4 billion in June. Factors cited ranged from the voracious domestic appetite for imports to the higher crude oil prices.   The trade gap was slightly larger than experts had expected; the trade deficit for May was $30.1 billion.

"We prefer to work with the broader **(a)** Current Account statistic," said Dr. Michael Grant of Intex Macro, in New Orleans. "The current account has flattened out over the last 3 months, and this is a **(b)** good sign regarding the long-run sustainability of this economy."

However, analysts at Matrix Labs in New Orleans were not nearly as sanguine. In their "Macro Watch" section, the focus was on the Commerce Department's number for national savings, a sharp drop to –0.25% in June, the lowest rate since the Commerce Department began keeping track in 1959. "You know, you can't consume and spend more than your income over the

43

long run", said Jackie Mello, CFO, "plain and simple!"

Others, such as Senator Paulina Kawolsky, remain unruffled. On last night's Face the World, the Senator first thanked all her well wishers for their cards while she was hospitalized and then she proceeded to discuss the macroeconomic report. She pointed to several shortcomings in the measurement of savings. "What about our pensions, our mortgages, the money we have socked away in investments to pay for our kids' education? All these are not captured fully in the 'savings' statistic. Include these and *voila*, the savings rate turns positive!"

Yet Dr. Grant remains unperturbed. "I hate not to get caught up in this fuss and let you guys down in this interview, but I have no dire doomsday predictions," he told this paper. "The whole commotion about whether savings are positive or negative is misplaced. **(c)** The real attention should be on the relative size of savings compared to the demand for borrowing from the public and private sectors". He pointed out that according to **(d)** a fundamental relationship in macroeconomics, a nation such as ours, with a budget surplus and a large current account deficit, would indeed face "a serious shortfall in the money available for borrowing."

This statement finds resonance with Faramroz Daruvalla, Senior Financial Analyst at Pernext Securities in Portland, Oregon, and well-known marathon runner. "The trade deficit adjusted for the present surplus in services **(e)** is basically the capital flowing back in. This finances the capital investment binge in technology." He adds, "How do you think the Ultimate Phone was made?"

Most individuals interviewed nationwide by this paper did not seem overly concerned with the low savings rate or the record trade deficit. As long as the economy moves along, employment stays fairly strong, and the investment finds a source of funds, Dr. Grant's macroeconomic relationship will hopefully make sure that that all will be well.

"I know all about the NSI," remarked Danielle Soler, an MBA student in Arizona, "but foreign investors **(f)** can still get spooked. A pull-out would mean problems here at home. In other words, I just hope that **(g)** interest rates on our government bonds here stay higher than those offered by foreign bonds". Danielle's parting wish was "everything should run smoothly till I finish my MBA and get my dream job!"

Yes, we all agree with that last comment---everything should run smoothly.

Article 3.2   AFTER EUPHORIA, GERMANS CONCERNED

Diana Hammerdorfer, Berlin Weekly Review

Setting: **Germany in the early 1990s, with the budget deficit increasing dangerously.**

It is now almost two years since that magical day when the wall came down. The wall is gone, but has the magic gone too? Today Germans are increasingly worried about the state of their economy. Projected infrastructure spending to modernize the former East Germany has far exceeded even the wildest and most extravagant estimates made just last year.   Massive infrastructure expenditures on new telephone lines, sanitation systems, power grids, environmental control, highway repair, nuclear waste disposal, and basic health concerns add up to make the German deficit a whopping 4.8 percent of its GDP.

"This is most worrisome. I see a problem," exclaims Peter Metz, of Madison Securities in Madison, Wisconsin. "If you were to include the Treuhandalstadt, a fund set aside for overhauling obsolete manufacturing Communist-era plants, the budget deficit, according to my numbers, **(a)** will easily be close to 8% of GDP in the very near future. This is not good," he mumbles, nervously fiddling with his tie.

This concern is felt by most Germans—it is most palpable in the former West Germany which will have to subsidize its Eastern half. To this end, the **(b)** Unity Bonds have helped tremendously, drawing in global capital to help fund the post-unification infrastructure expenses. In fact, the plan is to make Germany a sort of magnet for global funds.

However, Dr. Marie Heinkel, an economist with Bonn Bank, warns, "We Germans will have to understand that with these Unity Bonds, things will change. We have become used to having trade surpluses. **(c)** I will not be surprised to see German trade deficits very soon. This is bound to happen by the laws of macroeconomics." When asked if she felt that this was a problem, she nonchalantly (and enigmatically) replied, "Look at **(d)** the American experience with large budget deficits and learn—what is the expression? You can't eat your cake and have it too?"   And with that and an "auf wiedersehen", she jumped into a cab and was gone.

However, not all aspects of the bond financing by foreign lenders are worrisome to most Germans. "It is good that foreigners are pumping money into our economy. This is a good thing because there is a lot of cleaning up left to do," says Manfred Hartmann, as he takes orders in his third-generation delicatessen in downtown Frankfurt. "But **(e)** the country loses since we have to pay all this interest to these foreign lenders. I'd rather borrow at home and keep the interest at home," and then with an abrupt change of subject, "Here, try this bratwurst—family recipe".

The large and growing budget deficits just don't sit right with the Germans. We went to the countryside to interview the rural folks, and met Aida Spiegel, 78, happily retired with her four dogs in her glass-blowing studio 45 miles from Aachen. "My parents taught me never to go into debt. See, they were in the hyperinflation. So I have always balanced my checkbook. **(f)** <u>If I, a retired librarian, can have the discipline to do this, our government must—should—be able to balance its budget. I am never late with my house or car payments</u>. This big budget deficit now and borrowing from the people, I don't like that".

The predominant emotion two years ago was euphoria. Now it is replaced by uncertainty. Aida and her dogs, Manfred in his deli, Marie at her bank, and Peter in Madison all wait and hold their breaths.

ANSWERS AND HINTS

Article 3.1   Trade Deficit Climbs to Record

(a) Describe a fundamental difference between the trade deficit and the current account deficit, and also why Dr. Grant may prefer the latter statistic.

(b) A current account/GDP ratio over 5% is dangerously close to non-sustainability. While this is a general benchmark, it nevertheless implies that the economy has become dependent on an exceedingly large amount of inflow (relative to GDP). Hence, even a short-term disruption in inflows, for whatever reason, could prove disastrous. A 'flattening out' of the current account implies a similar flattening out of inflows, thereby indicating that the domestic economy may have attained some upper limit to its reliance on huge infusions of capital from abroad.

(c) The pertinent macroeconomic statistic is not the absolute measure of national savings but, instead, the magnitude of the (S-I) term as derived from the NSI. This is obtained after substituting in the fairly unambiguous (G-T) and (Imp-Exp) terms.

(d) The "fundamental relationship" is, of course, the NSI. Evaluate the validity of Dr. Grant's conclusion by plugging in appropriate values for the budget and current account balances into the NSI.

(e) Explain how an inflow is linked to a trade imbalance, using NSI with diagrams. Also, algebraically show how the inflow finances the difference between the <u>total</u> demand for loanable finds minus the total supply.

(f) Using diagrams, explain the phenomenon by which this would happen. Also be sure to explain the "problems" that would arise due to this "pull-out" of capital. Give examples.

(g) As we have discussed, it is not just interest rates that drive global capital flows. Explain, giving examples.

Article 3.2   After Euphoria, Germans Concerned

(a) This clearly refers to budget deficit non-sustainability. Please be sure to fully explain exactly what "sustainability" means.

(b) This is a classic NSI bond-financing of deficits. Please relate to the discussion in this chapter.

(c) Again, this sequence has been discussed in detail. What are these "laws of macroeconomics" cited by Marie Heinkel?

(d) One could conclude that Marie perceives the resulting current account deficits to be problematic. Critically evaluate her concern. Give examples.

(e) Discuss Manfred's concern. Use diagrams.

(f) Aida is comparing her personal financing with that of the government's bond financed deficits. Is she not incurring any personal "deficits"? Critically evaluate this comparison.

---

[1] Some examples of budget deficits are the unprecedented US budget deficits of the mid-1980s and the Japanese and Belgian budget deficits of the early 2000s. Examples of surpluses are the US surpluses of the early-2000s, as well as the national balances of most Southeast Asian countries in the late-1990s to the early 2000s.

[2] The current account balance is reported only quarterly unlike the monthly trade balance because services are often intangibles and take time to record accurately. Services do not pass through customs, are harder to measure, and are not reported as frequently as goods crossing international borders.

[3] The steps are purely for the purpose of pedagogic intuition. They loosely follow the direction of causality from budget deficits to current account deficits for one particular borrowing cycle.

[4] These are "real" or inflation-adjusted interest rates. At this point, given no monetization, we assume that the interest rates are indeed real rates. This will be discussed in detail while covering nominal and real rates in later chapters.

[5] Seminal work in the area of budget deficit sustainability was done by Sargent and Wallace in their influential "Some Unpleasant Monetarist Arithmetic", Federal Reserve Bank of Minneapolis Quarterly Review, Winter 1985.

[6] The huge generalization made here is only for the purposes of highlighting polar extremes of NSI applications. Each economy in East Asia as well as in the G8, certainly has its own specific labor skills, degree of monetary and political stability, widely different states of infrastructure, etc.

[7] One primary factor contributing to the meltdown was the nature of the pegged or quasi-fixed exchange Southeast Asian exchange rates.

4. AGGREGATE DEMAND: SETTING THE STAGE FOR DEMAND-SIDE STABILIZATION

This chapter marks the first step toward the construction of the ISLM/ADAS model which will power macroeconomic analyses in the chapters to come. At this stage we have completed an intuitive overview of the broad links between global capital flows, fiscal and trade imbalances, and their effects on interest rates and exchange rates.

The national savings identity (NSI), with its remarkable ability to provide an intuitive understanding of a range of diverse macroeconomic scenarios, was explored in the previous chapter. However, as highlighted in the discussion questions of Chapter 3, the NSI, in spite of its versatility and intuitiveness, suffers from a conspicuous lack of detail. The role of the central bank and monetary policy is completely missing. Similarly absent are tax rates and national tax policy, along with consumer and investor confidence. Key variables such as wages, employment, GDP growth and inflation, are also missing from our analysis in Chapter 3.

To incorporate the above, construction begins on a fully equipped, sophisticated, and well-articulated macro model—the "engine-room"—known as the ISLM-ADAS. The first step explains, derives, and explores the economy's aggregate demand (AD) curve which is the key component in macroeconomic demand-side stabilization.

4.1 DEMAND-SIDE STABILIZATION

In the economy depicted in **Figure 1**, aggregate demand at this stage is loosely defined as the total demand for all goods and services, and aggregate supply as "total output supply." Initially the economy is in equilibrium at some stagnant or recessionary GDP growth rate Y_{low} (presumably accompanied by high unemployment) and rate of price increase P_o.

From a purely diagrammatic perspective, how can this GDP growth be jump-started?

In figure 1, if the aggregate demand curve could somehow be shifted to the right by designing and implementing the right combination of fiscal and monetary polices, we could stimulate the economy to get to Y_{high} (presumably with lower unemployment). The "cost" of this policy involving a rightward shift in AD is a higher equilibrium rate of inflation (P_{high}), with the obvious benefits being greater GDP growth and more jobs.

This is the first example of demand-side stabilization. The emphasis is on combinations of fiscal and monetary policies that shift the aggregate demand curve (AD) to the right, in this simple example.

Figure 1

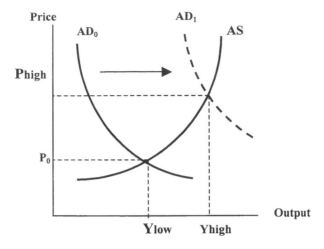

Another scenario is depicted in **Figure 2** where we find an economy suffering from high inflation and GDP growth racing out of control. Here, the "problem" is one of high inflation, and to alleviate this situation we resort to another diagrammatic exercise.

In this case, appropriate fiscal and/or monetary polices would result in a leftward shift in AD, taking the economy to $P_{moderate}$ and to a lower, and perhaps more manageable, rate of GDP growth. In this example, unemployment, presumably very low or non-existent to begin with, will actually increase as the GDP growth is deliberately slowed down to $Y_{moderate}$.[1]

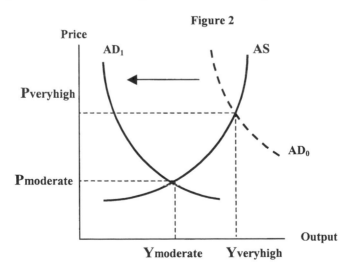

Figure 2

Both these shifts in the AD, caused by fiscal and/or monetary policies, constitute macropolicies that attempt demand-side stabilization. These polices primarily came into effect following a paradigm shift after the Great Depression and were later labeled as mainstream Keynesian stabilization policies. It was John Maynard Keynes who in the 1930s first propounded the idea to use combinations of discretionary fiscal and monetary polices to fine-tune the economy by shifting the AD curve.

An ideal situation would perhaps lie somewhere between the extremes depicted by Figures 1 and 2 with the economy characterized by moderate inflation and sustainable GDP growth. This scenario will be discussed in Chapter 5.

4.2 BUSINESS CYCLES

A stylized business cycle is presented in **Figure 3**. The peaks are, of course, periods of recovery and the troughs are recessions. The trend rate of growth is the inflation-adjusted real rate of growth of average GDP.

Figure 3

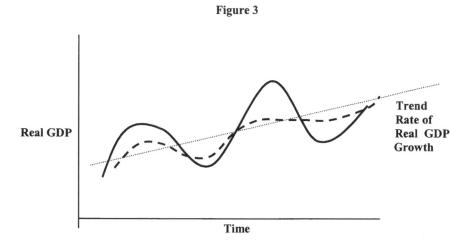

The objective of demand-side stabilization is to "flatten" business cycles by attempting to make periods of recovery less vigorous, and by making recessions less severe. A more stable planning horizon is preferable to a wildly fluctuating economy, especially when it comes to making long-term capital investments that come "on line" many years into the uncertain future.

The next step is to determine exactly how the AD can be shifted to accomplish demand-side stabilization and flatten business cycles by increasing growth in recessions or slowing down growth and, hence, bringing inflation down, as presented in **Figure 4**.

51

Figure 4

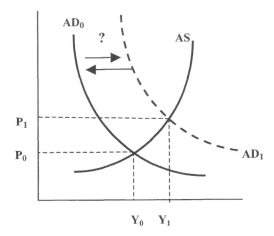

In order to <u>shift</u> the AD to implement demand-side stabilization, we must know exactly <u>what underlies this curve</u>, and how it is derived. The next few pages pertain directly to attaining this objective.

4.3 VARIABLES UNDERLYING THE AGGREGATE DEMAND: INTRODUCING THE GOODS MARKET

This process begins with an examination of the goods market. The condition for equilibrium in this market is actually an expression that we are familiar with:

Y = C + I +G + (Exp - Imp)

In **Table 1**, three scenarios in a hypothetical goods market are presented.

In row 1 (scenario 1), the value of output produced is 625, while the total planned expenditure composed of all the components, namely domestic consumption (C), domestic capital investment expenditures (I), government consumption (G), and net foreign consumption (Exp-Imp), add up to 675.

C + I + G + (Exp-Imp) = 675

In this case, since planned expenditure (675) exceeds the value of output, (625), suppliers respond to this excess demand in the goods market by increasing output and, hence, employment.

In the second row, the value of output in the goods market is 750, which equals total planned expenditure.

C + I + G + (Exp-Imp) = 750

Table 1

Y Value of output	C	I	G	(Exp-Imp)	Total planned expenditure and change in output and employment
625	475	50	125	25	675 Increase
750	550	50	125	25	750 No change
875	625	50	125	25	825 Decrease

In this case, the goods market is said to be exactly in equilibrium. Y is indeed equal to C+I+G+(Exp – Imp), there is no excess supply or demand, and there will therefore be no change in output supplied or employment.

Finally, in row 3, planned expenditures (825) are less than the value of output supply (875). Here suppliers respond to this excess supply condition by reducing output and, hence, employment.

These three goods market scenarios constitute the goods market, a crucial component of the fully-articulated model. Plotting output (Y) along the horizontal axis and the components of expenditures, C + I + G + (Exp – Imp), along the vertical axis, we find that all the points where Y will equal C + I + G + (Exp-Imp) must lie on the hatched 45 degree line. In fact, the hatched line is simply the locus of all possible points of equilibrium in the goods market.[2]

We now plot the three scenarios, 3 points on the vertical axis being 675, 750 and 825, and the 3 corresponding points on the horizontal axis being 625, 750, and 875. Plotting these three sets of points we obtain the expenditure line in **Figure 5**. This line intersects the hatched 45^0 line at E_o which represents the goods market equilibrium at 750.

The goods market equilibrium simply indicates that 750 units of goods produced would be exactly bought-up by 750 units of planned expenditures. At E_o there is no shortage of goods or unsold inventory. But E_o, by itself, <u>tells us nothing about the overall level of unemployment in the economy.</u>

At this point, a simple yet extremely important hypothetical exercise is in order. We are given that at E_o, in spite of the goods market being in equilibrium, the unemployment rate is a hefty 25%. What could be done to alleviate this unemployment?

According to the classical paradigm, the model in operation at the time of the Great Depression in the US, nothing could or should be done.[3] The classical economists believed in "natural" rates of output and unemployment which were not amenable to any sort of discretionary macropolicy.

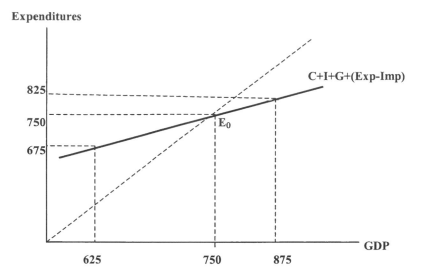

Figure 5

It was Keynes who threw a cat among the classical pigeons by propounding an actual discretionary role for fiscal and monetary policy in influencing the key macrovariables.

In our example, this would diagrammatically translate to moving the expenditure line up (using fiscal and/or monetary policies) so that it would intersect the 45^0 line at some higher point. As displayed in figure 6, this shift would take the goods market to a new and higher equilibrium at E_1, corresponding to a lower unemployment rate.

Keynes pointed out that E_0 was just one equilibrium point in the goods market, and not necessarily the only one, and <u>certainly not the optimal one</u> given the high unemployment in existence at E_0. Instead of assuming E_0 as fixed and inviolate, he proposed activist macroeconomic policies that would shift the expenditure line upward to yield a new and higher equilibrium E_1, resulting in a higher level of employment.

An increase in any of the components of the expenditure line C, I, G, Exports, or a reduction of Imports, can shift the line up. However, as discussed in Chapter 2, the only three policy instruments we have at our disposal are changes in government spending, tax rates, and changes in the money supply which in turn affect interest rates.

By increasing G, for example, the expenditure line moves up and a new equilibrium is established at E_1, as presented in **Figure 6**. In this situation, large government outlays "jump-start" economies out of recessions.

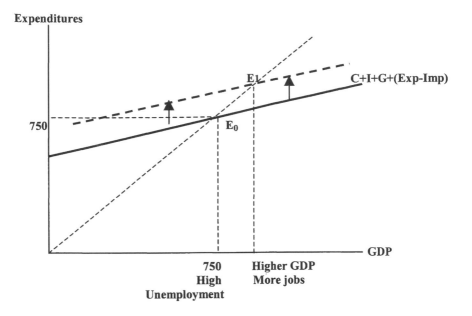

Figure 6

The shift in the expenditure line presented in figure 6 will translate to a rightward shift in (P, Y) space discussed earlier in figure 1 and later in this chapter and the following one.

China from the late 1990s well into the 2000s had to aim for around 8% GDP growth to absorb the increase in the number of new workers entering the job market.[4] This policy of **bao ba** (guaranteed eight percent) was de-emphasized in the early 2000s by Premier (and former central banker) Zhu Rongji , when it was found that some state and local officials may have been tempted to doctor final statistics under pressure to hit the target.

Another example of large government spending to move the expenditure line to some higher equilibrium E_1 is the US infrastructure spending on dams, power generation, roadways, etc., in the post-Depression years and well into the 1970s. We will discuss both these cases and others in Chapters 5 and 7.

4.3.1 ANALYZING THE COMPONENTS OF AGGREGATE DEMAND

The next step is to formally link the goods market to demand-side stabilization policies. We begin by moving to a higher level of sophistication to determine the specific composition of the variables that constitute the individual components of aggregate demand, C, I, G.[5]

The consumption function is described by the expression:

$$C = \underline{C} + bY + dW$$

Where:

C = private consumption expenditure

$\underline{C}$ = The autonomous component of consumption, "autonomous" in that this term is independent of income (Y). In this book, $\underline{C}$ will also be the term that includes tastes and preferences and, most important, $\underline{C}$ will be the term that captures consumer expectations. In the upcoming macroeconomic analyses, changes in consumer confidence pertaining to the economic outlook in the near-term will be proxied by this term.

For example, a collapse in consumer confidence in anticipation of an impending macroeconomic downturn is represented by a drop in $\underline{C}$. A surge in consumer confidence, on the other hand, translates to an increase in $\underline{C}$. (Later in this chapter we will discuss how confidence is measured.)

Consumer confidence, like investor confidence, is very sensitive to planned increases in future taxes or signs of unemployment. Even a whiff of impending tax increases or indications of impending or actual lay-offs causes consumer confidence to be adversely affected.

b = The marginal propensity to consume (MPC). This is defined as the increase in consumption, C, arising from a unit increase in national income Y. A value of $b = 0.8$ for the US means that if average national income were to increase by \$1, consumers would spend 80 cents of this increase in income and save 20 cents. The MPC is a stable statistic and inherently captures national as well as cultural spending and saving tendencies. While long-term and gradual changes in the MPC do indeed occur, we will hold b fixed in this book for expository convenience.

Values of MPC, while held fixed for individual economies, do vary significantly across countries. Japan's MPC (around 0.3) is significantly less than that of the US which is at the high end (around 0.85). Even within economies, the values of MPC may vary substantially by generation, race, or region. For example, some studies have found the Northeastern States in the US to have a higher MPC compared to the Midwest. In Japan, post-war generations have been found to exhibit greater tendencies to consume. This behavior is in stark contrast to that of those who witnessed the trauma following World War II and the virtual eradication of household savings. In fact, by the early 2000s, single Japanese women were at the very high end of the MPC spectrum, practically keeping the economy afloat with their formidable levels of consumption!

Y = National income and used synonymously with national output and GDP at this point.

d = The amount of an increase in planned consumption stemming from a unit increase in wealth (W) defined below. Here, d is a small number, unlike the MPC for the US. It may even be as low as 0.2; a $1 change in wealth does not result in a significant accompanying change in consumption, since investors (consumers) understand the enormous variability in the values of their wealth holdings.

W = National wealth holdings. This term includes stock market/mutual fund portfolios and other financial assets. Real estate holdings may also be included.

The celebrated and controversial "wealth effect" takes place when huge increases in the values of individuals' stock market portfolios and stock options coupled with, perhaps, significant appreciation in property prices inflate wealth holdings W. This expectation of future gains may induce individuals to increase consumption in the current period, and to lead a more extravagant lifestyle than their current disposable income would prudently allow. In a sense, the security afforded by future expected income (upon retirement, perhaps), may induce individuals to consume this "future income today". Conversely, a sharp correction in the stock market or a sudden bursting of a real estate price bubble may have the opposite effect—a negative wealth effect of sorts.

At this stage, we abstract from the wealth component for notational convenience and operate with the simpler version of the consumption function:[6]

$$C = \underline{C} + bY$$

We now examine capital investments, I, in similar detail. The investment function is:

$$I = \underline{I} - fi$$

where:

I = Private capital investment (necessitates borrowing) for items such as new plant and equipment, housing, and the growth of new capital stock.

I = Investment confidence. Along the lines of consumer confidence, this index captures the sentiment of business. The Dun and Bradstreet CEO Index as well as the Index of Leading Economic Activity (LEA) may be considered good proxies for investor confidence. Once again, a positive business (macroeconomic) outlook causes $\underline{I}$ to increase, thus driving up private capital investment and eventually the demand for loanable funds. Conversely, the opposite holds true—a crash in investor confidence sends private capital investment into a free-fall as in the case of Japan from the late 1990s through the early 2000s (please see box).

It should be stressed here that $\underline{I}$ is <u>extremely</u> sensitive to future tax increases, and news pertaining to unemployment, even more so than consumer confidence.[7]

f = The sensitivity (elasticity) of private capital investment to a unit change in interest rates, i. Again 'f' will be held fixed when we begin our ISLM analyses in Chapter 6. Here a unit increase/decrease in interest rates causes private capital investment to *fall/rise* by f, and hence the negative sign.

i = Interest rate as defined above. These are assumed to be short-term interest rates, and not to be confused with long-term rates introduced in the following chapter. Here, as interest rates fall, capital investment (private demand for loanable funds) increases, and vice versa.

The main determinant of change in capital investment I is $\underline{I}$ and not interest rates *per se*. If the business outlook looks dismal 1 to 5 years into the future, irrespective of how low interest rates may be, investors will be unlikely to pump more funds into private capital investment. Low interest rates—even zero, as in the case of Japan in the late 1990s-early 2000s— against a backdrop of gloomy business forecasts will not result in an increase in private capital investment.

While short-term rates are exogenously determined by monetary policy, investor confidence $\underline{I}$, like its counterpart, $\underline{C}$, is endogenous, and determined by investors and consumers who process all current and past information. Both $\underline{I}$ and $\underline{C}$ are very difficult, if not impossible, to change by policy. A recurring them of this book is that consumer and investor confidence, which may have taken years to build, can indeed be lost "in an afternoon" and policy makers would be unable to stop the collapse.

G = Government spending (used synonymously with government outlays and government consumption.) This is a policy variable.

Exp = National exports of goods and services

Imp = National imports of goods and services.

Before introducing the money market and prior to the derivation of the aggregate demand, an overview of the description and measurement of consumer and investor confidence is in order.

Measuring Confidence

Two major measures of consumer confidence, derived from large-scale surveys of households, are available in the United States. These are the University of Michigan's Index of Consumer Sentiment and the more familiar Conference Board's Consumer Confidence Index.

The Consumer Sentiment Index, developed by Katona and Mueller (1953), is constructed to measure "those factors which are capable of giving rise to independent variation in the rate of consumer spending and saving, namely, changes in people's perceptions, attitudes, motivations, and expectations".

This index is calculated by processing information from a survey of about 500 households. Survey respondents provide qualitative answers to questions pertaining to current family financial situations, expected financial outlook one year into the future, expected one-year-ahead business conditions, long-term (5-year) expectations of the business environment, and current buying plans for large household durable goods (defined as appliances with a service life greater than 3 years).

The Conference Board's Consumer Confidence Index is constructed in similar fashion. In this case, information is obtained from surveys mailed to about 5,000 households every month, with an average response of about 3,500 surveys. The questions include topics that pertain to current general business conditions, expected business conditions 6 months into the future, current employment opportunities, and expected household income 6 months into the future.

Comparing the two indexes, the Conference Board survey focuses on shorter-term expectations relative to the Michigan index; participants respond to queries about their perceptions of the economy over the next 6 months as opposed to 5 years. In addition, the Conference Board specifically includes questions pertaining to the respondent's employment and income prospects, instead of the more general "financial condition" questions in the Michigan survey. Basically, labor market news has a greater effect on the Conference Board's index, while the Michigan index is more sensitive to news from the financial markets. For these reasons, the two indexes are not always identical or perfectly correlated.

The Japanese Tankan Index

Confidence is measured along similar lines in most G7 countries. The closely watched Japanese Tankan index, initiated in 1961 by the Japanese central bank, is a key quarterly measure of business sentiment and is obtained by surveying 10,000 businesses. The index subtracts the percentage reporting an unfavorable business outlook from those who say that conditions are indeed favorable. Ambivalent ("so-so") outlooks are discarded. A net positive Tankan score indicates an overall optimistic outlook while a net negative score indicates the opposite.

From the bleak 1990s through the serial recessions of the early 2000s, a negative Tankan was, unfortunately, a recurring theme. The bursting of the Japanese stock market and real estate bubbles, the East Asian currency crisis, and the state of large non-performing financial institutions all contributed to the demise of confidence.

The respondents are divided into several categories such as large manufacturers, large non-manufacturers (retailers, builders, realtors, etc.), and small manufacturers. As bank credit for small manufacturers evaporated, and when a 33% plunge in expected profits was projected, the Tankan went into a record free-fall. At one point, in October 1998, this category's sub-Tankan score fell to an amazingly low level of –57, at that point a record low.

A Singaporean Proxy for Confidence

Some economies resort to commonly observed indicators that act as excellent unofficial proxies for formally measured confidence. In fact, these indicators are very readily available and are often extremely accurate. One such example is the use of the Certificate of Entitlement (COE), in the case of Singapore.

The COE is a legal document that must be obtained from the Singaporean government when a vehicle is purchased in the country. Just buying a new car by paying the car dealer the grand total inclusive of taxes, transportation charges, etc., is not enough. In Singapore, one must also obtain "permission" from the authorities to be able to drive this car on Singapore's highly "rationed" roads. The Ministry of Transportation determines the optimum number of vehicles that will operate on the nation's roads without causing the gridlock, pollution, and crippling congestion that plague so many other Asian economies. The "permission", or license, to actually entitle an individual to place another automobile into circulation is the Certificate of Entitlement (COE).

Every month, the government makes a quota of certificates available to the public. The quota is divided into vehicles of different categories and functions. The number of certificates in each category is determined by the ministry and is based on some pre-determined accepted growth rate of new cars on Singaporean roads, and presumably matched to the rate of growth of new roads, parking spaces, and emissions levels.

Individuals participate in an "auctioning process" and bid on the monthly COE tender either through ATM machines or through car dealers. In this highly regulated environment, obtaining a COE is a significant and non-trivial cost running into thousands of dollars; the average total COE price for a mid-size family car was in the Sing$30-35,000 range in the early-mid 2000s. Circumventing the law by purchasing a car and driving without the COE in this island economy where enforcement is a reality is not an option.

The final market-clearing market price of each quota (in the several different classes of automobiles) is, of course, influenced by the existing demand, <u>given a fairly stable growth in supply</u>. COEs become more expensive as demand for new cars increases, and vice versa.

Singaporeans, savvy to the notion of business and personal confidence, have concluded that the price of Certificates of Entitlement (released monthly) is indeed a good proxy of economic outlook and of confidence in the shape of things to come. An expected slow-down, such as the period following the East Asian currency crisis in 1997-98, resulted in a drop in prices of COEs as demand slumped, and the monthly quota (determined by the government) sold at a significantly lower price. As the economy bounced back after weathering the Asian crisis by 1999, and as confidence in the strength of the economy rose, demand for new cars increased. Given the relatively fixed supply (quota) of available COEs, this increase in demand caused prices of COEs to rise.

Of course, if the supply of licenses (certificates) were to also change, then any change in the final price of COEs has to be interpreted with caution. An increase in the price could either be due to higher demand stemming from increased confidence or, quite simply, to a cut in the supply of new licenses.

An examination of the money market is required so that we can proceed with the derivation of the AD curve in order to eventually shift the aggregate demand and enact stabilization policies.

Money supply in macroeconomics is defined in real terms, in units of goods. This is done to sift out inflationary effects of currencies of different countries and to reduce money supply to one common denominator, namely, the purchasing power of the money.

The real money supply is defined as:

M/P = Nominal Money Stock/Price level

M is in units of currency ($) in circulation and P is in units of $/good (the price of a typical market basket). For example: $M/P = \$100/\$20$ per good = 5 goods (market baskets)

The central bank (Federal Reserve), controls M, defined as the "nominal money stock". The real money supply M/P is a combination of M and P, with M being an exogenous policy instrument, and P determined endogenously by the economy. The real money supply, being independent of the interest rate, is represented by the vertical line in figure 8.

Money demand is defined as the demand for cash for transactions purposes.

Money Demand = kY – hi

Where:
k and h are constants
Y = national income, GDP
i = interest rate

The intuition underlying this equation is that, with higher national income Y, the average demand for cash for transactions balances increases. As interest rates rise, however, the "cost" of holding cash balances is the interest rate forgone by not placing this cash in an interest-bearing account. As interest rates rise, the demand for the amount of cash for transactions decreases, and vice versa. This accounts for the negative sign before the term with the interest rate.

Figure 7 displays a money market equilibrium with the equilibrium interest rate at i_0, and real money supply initially at M_0/P_0.

Figure 7

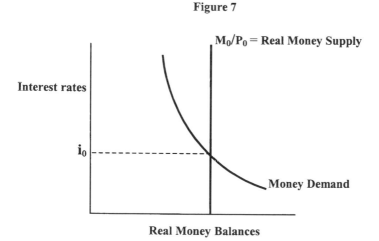

Real Money Balances

We now perform a simple yet very important experiment; if P_0 were to increase to P_1, with the nominal stock (M) held constant, what would be the effect in the money market presented in Figure 7?

As the price level increases to P_1, the new real money supply falls.

$M_0/P_1 < M_0/P_0$

A drop in real money supply is tantamount to a leftward shift (decrease) in the real money supply curve.[8] As real money supply shifts to the left, equilibrium interest rates increase from i_0 to i_1 as depicted in **Figure 8**. The result of this simple exercise will be crucial in the aggregate demand derivation that follows.

Figure 8

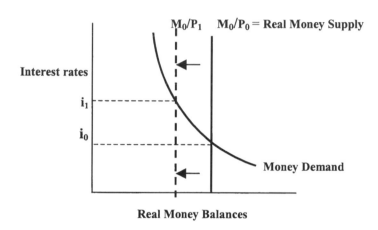

Real Money Balances

4.3.2   DERIVING THE AGGREGATE DEMAND

Figure 9 presents all the components pertaining to the derivation of the AD, developed up to this point.

We start by observing that the goods market is initially in equilibrium at Y_0, the initial equilibrium interest rate is i_0, and the initial price level is P_0. The aggregate demand will be derived in the space bordered by the P and Y axes, henceforth referred to as (P,Y) space. The step numbers (in bold below) are also referenced with corresponding numbers in figure 9).

(1) We begin by plotting the "given" initial point P_0 and Y_0 in (P,Y) space. (The steps numbers are matched in figure 9).

(2) P_0 increases to P_1. We now need to determine the final equilibrium Y_1 in order to obtain the second point in (P,Y) space. The 2 points in (P,Y) space can then be connected to give us the AD curve.

(3) As prices increase to P_1, real money supply falls (see the money market diagram) and equilibrium interest rates consequently rise to i_1 as discussed in the simple exercise in Figure 8.

(4) As interest rates increase, capital investment falls, as per our earlier discussion (no change in investor confidence here).

(5) This results in a drop in the expenditures line and a new equilibrium in the goods market at Y_1 that is a lower equilibrium relative to Y_0.

(6) Plotting this point (P_1, Y_1) and joining it to (P_0, Y_0), we obtain the aggregate demand (AD) curve. (In reality, the aggregate demand is a non-linear function, a rectangular hyperbola, to be exact.)

Figure 9

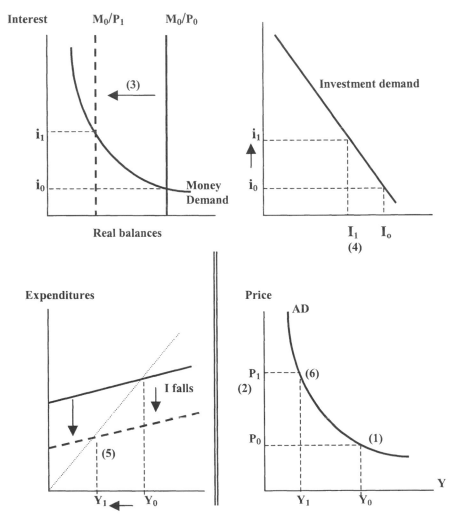

All points along this AD curve are points obtained by synthesizing the goods and money markets; in fact, each and every point on AD is one where both goods and money markets are simultaneously in equilibrium. Specifically, in figure 9, The points (P_0, Y_0) and (P_1, Y_1) are simply simultaneous goods and money market equilibria transposed into (P,Y) space. Both these points on the AD have corresponding points of equilibrium in the goods and money markets.

Although the AD reproduced in **Figure 10** appears to be just another downward sloping demand curve, it is a whole lot more. There is a tremendous amount of macroeconomic structure underlying this apparently innocuous demand curve. Embedded in the AD are: consumer confidence, investor confidence, government spending, private consumption, capital investment, monetary policy, and tax rates, not to mention a host of global variables such as imports and exports, and foreign GDP, that have been suppressed here.

Figure 10

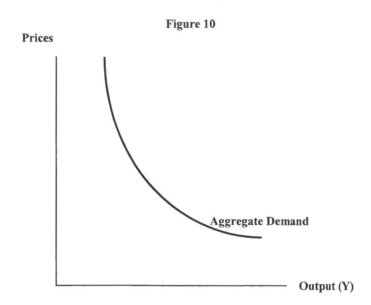

With the derivation of the AD, a very significant milestone in the analysis and design of macroeconomic policy has been reached. The stage is now set to explore how we can now shift this AD to implement demand-side stabilization in the following chapter.

The following section will highlight as well as supplement the information presented in this chapter.

4.4 DISCUSSION QUESTIONS

1. We have suddenly gone from a very intuitive plane to a more theoretical model. Is this the shape of things to come?

We have indeed moved to a more theoretical mode. In doing so, however, we have increased our level of sophistication. For instance, consumer and investor confidence, the wealth effect, the marginal propensity to consume, monetary policy and the money market, and tax rates (to be discussed soon) were all conspicuously absent in the NSI framework.

The NSI was a "broad-brush" accounting framework with tremendous relevance in analyzing international flows of funds, etc., but lacking the domestic details, and particularly missing the existence and role of monetary policy.

In this chapter, we are essentially converging to our final ISLM analysis. With the construction of that model, the "real world" benefits and the practicality of our final model will be evident.

2. Are most measures of confidence adopted in different economies based on survey-generated results? Are the indexes constructed in similar fashion?

Yes, the method is similar but not identical. We have discussed the Japanese Tankan index in this chapter. Germany's eagerly awaited index for consumer confidence is published monthly by the Munich-based research institute Ifo, referred to simply as the Ifo index. France has a similar index that is released once every other month that includes intangibles such as "quality of life".

In emerging economies, the confidence index may be skewed toward cities and may not be representative of the entire economy. In China, for example, a confidence survey conducted in Beijing or Shanghai, both on the fast-growing Eastern seaboard, may be at odds with the state of the economy in the more agricultural and rural central and western parts of the country. A single confidence survey may not be appropriate for these two structurally different sectors that exhibit vastly different hopes and aspirations, and, most importantly, consumption patterns.

3. What is the "triple whammy" effect on private consumption?

Private consumption (C) comprises three elements: consumer confidence, income (actually after-tax income), and wealth holdings (assuming MPC and "d" to be constant).

If the stock market were to undergo a very significant correction, then, according to the much-feared "triple whammy" effect, confidence would fall as wealth holdings collapse with the stock market. Further, if the factor(s) causing the stock market crash were to result in a slowdown in real GDP growth, Y would also fall.

Thus, there is concern that the "triple whammy" of decreases in national income (Y), consumer confidence $\underline{C}$, and wealth (W) would all rapidly conspire to severely curb private consumption.

4. Are economists in agreement regarding the importance of the role of confidence in designing and analyzing macroeconomic policy?

Unfortunately, they are not. Those who believe in the importance of the confidence statistic attribute its importance to:[9]

(a) Confidence being a causal factor capable of influencing macroeconomic activity in the near future.

(b) The ability of the confidence term to forecast macroeconomic fluctuations.

(c) The ability of confidence to act as a catalyst, magnifying the effects of macroeconomic shocks.

(d) The confidence index exclusively captures information pertaining to individual's expectations.

Those that do not subscribe to the above sentiment (Fuhrer, 1993, for example), find that aside from some idiosyncratic information, the variation in the Michigan Consumer Sentiment Index can be explained by readily available macroeconomic data. That is, any information content provided by the confidence index is already subsumed in the readily available macroeconomic data.

The fact is that while macroeconomic academics remain divided, the confidence indexes, both here and abroad, remain eagerly anticipated by individuals, central bankers and, most importantly, policy makers.

5. Can confidence be influenced by appropriate macroeconomic policies?

Both consumer and investor confidence are endogenous, and technically cannot be manipulated by macroeconomic policy. In rare and isolated cases, however, it may be possible to influence confidence with appropriate monetary policy only in the very early stages of a crisis in confidence. (Please see Chapters 8 and 9 of Burdekin and Langdana, 1995, for theoretical details.)

A good example may be Alan Greenspan's prompt action in decreasing interest rates twice in a 2-week period following the collapse of Long Term Capital in Fall 1998 and in the wake of the Asian currency crisis. There is a sense that this preemptive action prevented confidence in the US from collapsing along the lines of the indexes in the stricken East Asian economies.

Article 4.1   SCIENTISTS RATE MACRO CAMP A SUCCESS

By Mike Perron, <u>World Business Review</u>, New York.

Nestled on a hillside with a panoramic view of the Atlantic Ocean, the Macro Retreat conducted by New Jersey based Policy.Com is getting rave reviews. Designed exclusively to give professionals with non-business backgrounds a hands-on, working knowledge of macro-economic policy analysis, the program has been swamped by an unexpected number of applicants.

Prof. Steve Fountelroy, director of the program, said, "Professionals who have no business background are des-perately in need of information pertaining to how the economy works. Should they pull out of the market? Should they invest some more? This course will give them a very focused yet fundamental working knowledge". He adds, "individuals with non-business backgrounds are having to make very major business decisions today, both at work and in their personal finances. They need to know how the macroeconomy works, and this is where they get the necessary practical infor-mation."

Participants attend a 1-week course every 2 months over a 2-year period. "Most of our participants are either engineers,

doctors—we have every kind of doctor, even veterinarians—physicists, biotechnologists, rocket scientists, high-technology types, you name it," says general manager, Shelda Megan Wills.

We interviewed some of the participants, and here is a sampling of their comments following the first week's macro course.

Dr. Lenny Hartley, from Omaha, Nebraska, remarked, "I finally understand **(a)** <u>why consumption does not fall in proportion to a correction in the stock market</u>! And I'm a cardiologist who, until last week had no idea how the economy worked!" He adds, "I am worried about the **(b)** 'triple whammy', though…"

Gerhard Muller, a bona fide Austrian rocket scientist from Vienna, was confused about investment. "If capital investment increases with lower interest rates, **(c)** <u>why then did Japan's capital investment not soar when they had those zero rates</u> for all those years in the late 1990s and early 2000s?"

"This confuses me too", concurs Meadow Pellagrino, a marine biologist from Daytona, Florida, "and I am also puzzled as to why the **(d)** <u>classical econ-</u>

omists could not come up with Keynes' policies much earlier? Also, if we have equilibrium in the goods market at E_0, **(e)** <u>shouldn't there be no unemployment at this point, too?</u>"

Jasmine Bhargava, a consultant in the biotechnology sector in Morristown, New Jersey, loved the design and content of the course. But she feels that she is still not sure "how we can simply 'move up' from one equilibrium point to another. I understand this occurs by increasing government spending. But doesn't this mean that the government borrows x dollars from one group of people and pays the same x dollars to another group?"

At this point, Dr. Fountelroy, interjects, "Excellent question! Store this away as it forms the **(f)** <u>beginning of our session next time!</u> Superb!"

(g) "<u>China clearly enacts such polices</u> and maybe now I'll understand the mechanism," exclaims Yong-Suk Choi, a lawyer from San Francisco specializing in US-Far East trade, "but I guess I'll have to wait till next class!"

"You've got us all worked up," laughed Meadow, the marine biologist. "We want to know now!"

Now this reporter can see why the Macro Retreat has been so successful.

HINTS AND SOLUTIONS

(a) This is because 'd', the marginal propensity to consume with respect to a unit change in wealth holdings, is a small number in the consumption function.

(b) The "triple whammy" stems from the extended consumption function (including wealth) and is discussed in the text.

(c) This is because investor confidence, $\underline{I}$, was dead in the water, and $\underline{I}$ is the main driver in the investment function.

(d) They had no reason to come up with a Keynesian prescription because the classical model was performing well till the early 1930s. Remember, as discussed in Chapter 2, macroeconomic models are designed to reflect the reality of the economy they are based in. They are contingent on their particular backdrop and are functions of expectations. As these expectations change, macroeconomic models, unlike the models in physics or engineering, also change, and these transitions are known as paradigm shifts. As these changes occur, new paradigms are ushered in, such as from the classical model to the Keynesian model in the mid-late 1930s.

(e) The goods market equilibrium says nothing about the overall level of employment or unemployment. It simply indicates that the amount produced is exactly equal to planned expenditure, C+I+G+(Exp-Imp), with no excess demand or supply.

(f) Chapter 5 will cover the essence of Keynesian policy prescription. Large infrastructure spending will be advocated to reach E_1. The ongoing Three Gorges project in China, as well as the Tennessee Valley Authority (TVA) and the Civilian Conservation Corps (giant infrastructure projects in the US in the years following the Great Depression) are good examples. Massive increases in US government spending on reconstruction and defense, in the wake of the September 11, 2001 terror attacks, could also fall into this category.

(g) Beginning in the late 1990s, China has embarked on an ambitious infrastructure spending campaign on hundreds of miles of new roads, upgraded rail lines, new subway systems and airports, increases in power generation and, of course, the mammoth Three Gorges Dam on the Yangtze river.

---

[1] In the following chapter, the concepts of engineering soft-landings for overheated economies, and of jump-starting moribund output will be discussed.

[2] We assume here that both axes have the same scale.

[3] This classical belief is not nearly as preposterous as it sounds. Their paradigm was successful, well articulated, and did in fact represent the pre-Depression era quite well. It was the paradigm shift ushered in by mistakes made in the Great Depression that rang the death knell of the classical model with its notions of natural rates of employment and output growth.

[4] This included farm workers as well as former employees of state owned enterprises (SOEs).

[5] At this stage, we temporarily suppress the term (Exp-Imp) to focus primarily on the closed economy.

[6] Changes in wealth holdings will enter our analysis via accompanying changes in confidence. The confidence term acts as a proxy for changes in wealth holdings such as stock market corrections and run-ups, large swings in real estate prices, etc.

[7] "Taxes" here, include all taxes—federal, state, property, etc.,

[8] Shifts in curves were discussed in the microeconomic digression in Chapter 3.

[9] Please see Confidence, Credibility and Macroeconomic Policy: Past Present and Future, by Richard C.K. Burdekin, and Farrokh K. Langdana, for an in-depth discussion of this subject (Chapter 7).

5. DEMAND-SIDE STABILIZATION: OVERHEATING, HARD LANDING, AND EVERYTHING IN BETWEEN

In the previous chapter we examined the possibility of a shift in the goods market equilibrium from E_0 to a higher equilibrium E_1, which equated to an equivalent rightward shift in the AD curve. This chapter continues the analysis with a discussion of the specific fiscal and monetary policies by which the aggregate demand (AD) curve can be shifted to enact demand-side stabilization. This will be followed by an in-depth description of overheating, soft landings and hard landings.

In later chapters, we will examine why a significant body of expectations-based research finds demand-side stabilization to be an ineffective policy prescription in some economies since the 1980s.

The following section discusses the first method of shifting AD, namely, a change in the rate of growth of government spending.

5.1 SHIFTING THE AD: CHANGING GOVERNMENT SPENDING

Using the example of the goods market from Chapter 4, we now increase government spending from $G = 125$ to $G_1 = 175$, an increment of $50 billion as depicted in **Table 1**.[1]

Table 1

	Y Value of output	C	I	G_1	(Exp–Imp)	Change in output and jobs
1	625	475	50	175	25	725
2	750	550	50	175	25	800
3	875	625	50	175	25	875

With the higher level of government spending, the new equilibrium in the goods market is:

$C + I + G_1 + (\text{Exp-Imp}) = Y$.

From Table 1, this new higher equilibrium, E_1, is now 875, in row 3. The interesting and important observation here is that a $50 billion increase in government spending has resulted in an increase in equilibrium GDP in the goods market from 750 (equilibrium from Chapter 4) to a new higher equilibrium of 875, an increase of 125 billion.

This is the essence of a Keynesian stimulus. The final increase in GDP is significantly higher than the government's injection of the additional $50 billion into the economy. The end result, an increase in GDP of 125, is therefore, a multiple of the injection of G.

This multiplier effect is defined as:

Multiplier effect = change in GDP/change in components of AD
$$= 125/50 = 2.5$$

This is a very powerful (and convenient) result, with strong and obvious implications for government spending. All the government has to do to jump-start an economy is to spend more G, and the whole economy (in this example) experiences an increase in GDP of two and a half times the amount of the increase in government spending!

The next logical step is to determine the mechanism by which this intriguing multiplier effect is generated.[2]

5.1.1   THE MECHANISM OF THE MULTIPLIER EFFECT

The first step is to calculate the marginal propensity to consume (MPC), defined again as the change in national private consumption expenditures stemming from a unit change in national income.

MPC = Change in Consumption/Change in National Income, denoted Y
    = (550-475)/(750-625) = 0.6

This value of the MPC indicates that in this economy, for every unit increase in national income (Y), consumers increase their spending by 0.60, and vice versa. Thus, 60% of the initial injection of $50 billion will be spent, i.e., pumped back into the economy. If the initial increase in G were to be on a high-speed hi-tech transportation system designed to reduce congestion on the highways, then workers in this industry would spend—re-inject into the economy—60% of the $50 billion, which amounts to $30 billion. If this amount were to be spent on real estate, for example, then individuals in the real estate sector would, in turn, "recycle" 60% of $30 billion back into the economy, and so on.

This sequence of progressively decreasing transactions following the initial infusion of $50 billion is presented in **Table 2**. As the recipient of each transaction re-injects 60% back into the economy, this amount is added to the flow of national income. Over successive transactions, by the time the multiplier effect runs its full course, the total addition to the flow of national income should be $125, the multiplier effect.

The larger the marginal propensity to consume, the greater is the multiplier effect. Conversely, economies with low average marginal propensities to consume (rural China, for example), will experience weak multiplier effects. As we will discuss later in this chapter, large increases in G in such an economy may barely yield any larger increase in GDP.

Table 2

Time	Addition to the Flow of Income	Expenditure
1	50 (initial injection)	(50)(0.6)=30
2	30	(30)(0.6)=18
3	18	(18)(0.6)=10.8
4	10.8….	..
Event-ually	…	…
Sum:	50+30+18……=125	

The multiplier effect relates to the goods market as depicted in **Figure 1a**. The former goods market equilibrium from Chapter 4, $E_0=750$, is increased to $E_1=875$. This increase of \$125 billion in equilibrium output (national income) is due to the multiplier effect generated by the \$50 billion increase in government spending.

The relationship **Multiplier = 1/(1 – MPC)** conveniently links the MPC to the magnitude of the multiplier effect. Economies with relatively higher MPCs would benefits from larger multiplier effects compared to those with lower MPCs, even though both economies may have experienced increases in government spending.

The increase in national expenditures, denoted by an upward shift in the expenditure line in the goods market in **Figure 1a**, translates to a shift to the right in the AD curve **(Figure 1b)**, as national income increases across the range of prices.

Figure 1a

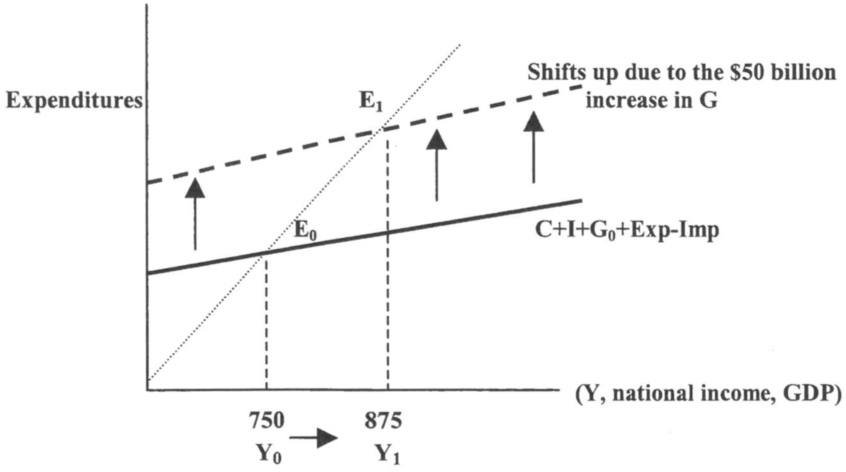

Shifts up due to the \$50 billion increase in G

Expenditures E_1

E_0

C+I+G$_0$+Exp-Imp

(Y, national income, GDP)

750   875

Y_0 → Y_1

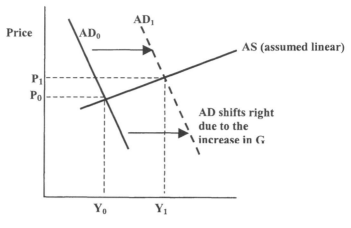

Figure 1b

Output (National Income)

Figure 2 represents a simple economy with the clockwise flow composed of nominal variables and the counter-clockwise flow consisting of real goods and services.

In the counter-clockwise cycle, consumers provide labor in labor markets. This labor constitutes a resource (input) supplied by the labor markets to firms that then supply goods and services to the product markets. These products and services are eventually consumed, thereby completing the counter clockwise circle.

The clockwise (nominal) cycle is explained as follows. Consumers incur expenditures on products in the product markets. These expenditures, in turn, are receipts to firms who then incur labor costs in the labor market. The labor costs to firms are incomes to the workers who are also the consumers, thereby completing the cycle.

The more vigorous these clockwise and counter clockwise flows (also referred to as the "income expenditure stream"), the stronger this "engine" runs, thereby keeping macroeconomic growth strong.   Conversely, when clockwise and counterclockwise flows become anemic, the "engine" begins to sputter, leading to a macroeconomic slowdown, or, worse, a recession.

The reservoir affixed to the right of the engine in figure 2 is a container of "idle" loanable funds. These are potentially loanable funds that, for some reason, have been pulled out of the income-expenditure flows of the economy. The greater the amount of loanable funds in this reservoir, the less vigorous the running of the engine, and the more sluggish the growth of the economy.

During the Great Depression, as banks failed and as entire family savings suddenly evaporated, individuals made "runs" on banks to withdraw whatever

74

savings they could before their banks failed. Liquidity was sucked out of the economy by understandably nervous households.[3] The reservoir was almost full of "idle" funds that were not being injected back into the economy.

At this critical time, Keynes introduced his model. He advocated a

Figure 2

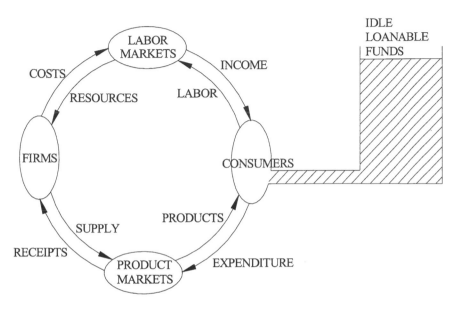

The author is grateful to former Rutgers MBA students Wenjeng Lee and Amir Razzaghi for digitizing the classroom version of this diagram.

strong increase in government spending funded by borrowing idle loanable funds from the general public.[4] In other words, if households and businesses were reluctant to invest in the economy (justifiably, perhaps, given the state of the economy during that period), then the government would do it for them. And most importantly, the injection of government spending would not simply be a one-for-one transfer from lenders to borrowers, but would, instead, jump-start the economy by unleashing multiplier effects. GDP would increase disproportionally, along with employment growth.

This was a shocking policy prescription for that time. Advocating an increase in government spending and even a budget deficit was anathema to the classical economists. As we will discuss later, there was no role for government spending in macroeconomic stabilization in the classical model that existed at the time of the Great Depression. In fact, there was no role for any fiscal and monetary policy in stabilizing output and employment whose rates of growth were referred to as "natural" rates by the Classicists. The very

75

notion that unemployment could be involuntary was incomprehensible in the classical paradigm.

Does this mean that Keynes advocated a string of fiscal deficits every time the economy slowed? Was his policy prescription fiscally irresponsible?

Simply put, Keynes did not advocate continuously increasing deficits. Rather, he advocated a cyclically balanced budget. **Figure 3** presents a stylized business cycle with the periods of recovery as peaks and recessions as troughs. As the rate of GDP growth begins to decrease, and as the economy goes into recession at point A, Keynes would prescribe an expansionary fiscal policy to jump-start the economy. Government spending would increase and the economy would experience an increase in national bond-financed budget deficits (or decreases in any existing budget surplus). [5]

Figure 3

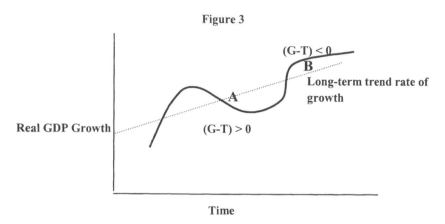

At point B on the business cycle in Figure 3, once the multiplier effect is well under way and the economy is in recovery at B, government spending is to be cut back to its original rate of growth. This reduction in government spending, coupled with the increase in tax revenues due to the recovery, results in a budget surplus at point B. With a budget deficit at A and a surplus at B, on average the budget would be in balance over the business cycle.

In fact, at point B, it is indeed imperative that government begins to phase out the new additional spending that it injected at point A. Failure to do so would result in both the government as well as the rejuvenated private sector competing for a relatively finite supply of loanable funds at point B. This competition would drive up interest rates and crowd-out some of the healthy private capital investment at stage B in the business cycle.

While the deficit did not disappear completely—that is, it wasn't cyclically balanced—over successive business cycles in the United States, the deficit/GDP ratio hovered in the 2.2 to 2.4% range from World War II until the mid-1980s. During the mid to late 1980s, however, the deficit burst from this range and rose to 6.1% of GDP by 1986. A reduction, due to the Gramm-

Rudman legislation that stipulated a timetable for automatic spending cuts in very late 1989, was negated by an increase in deficits during the 1990-91 recession (see footnote 5). By the early 2000s, as tax revenues burgeoned due to strong growth in the late 1990s and as government spending decreased, deficits shrank to finally yield budget surpluses by late 2000-early 2001.

Keynesian fiscal expansions and contractions will be revisited in detail in the context of the ISLM model in chapter 7. We now move to the second method of shifting the AD curve to enact demand-side stabilization—monetary policy.

5.2 SHIFTING THE AD: CHANGING MONETARY POLICY

An increase in the rate of growth of the money supply causes interest rates to fall from i_0 to i_1 (Figure 4a), causing capital investment to rise from I_0 to I_1 (in Figure 4b). As capital investments increase, the expenditure line in the goods market shifts up (4c) and this translates to a rightward shift in the aggregate demand (depicted in 4d).

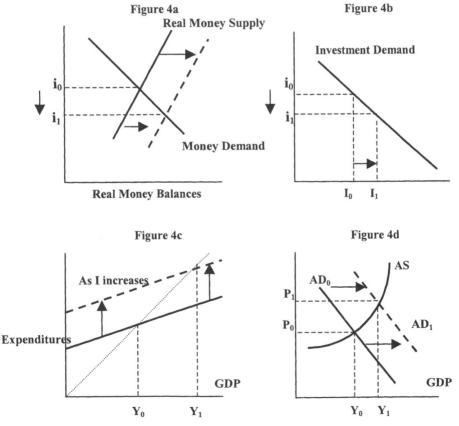

The opposite holds true as well. A contraction in monetary growth results in higher interest rates that act as brakes for interest-sensitive sectors such as construction, and cause capital investments to fall.

There are basically three processes by which the rate of growth of the money supply is changed by the central bank. These will be covered in Chapter 11.[6] At this early stage, we assume that monetary policy is conducted by implementing the most frequently used method in the US—open market operations.

All institutions that transact money are required by law to place a certain percentage of their deposits as "reserves" with the central bank. This percentage is known as the reserve ratio. To increase money growth, the central bank (Federal Reserve) in this highly simplified early example, essentially buys government bonds from financial institutions and credits their reserves with this amount. Banks have a greater lending ability thanks to these additional reserves, and competition between banks to make loans quickly results in a decrease in interest rates. To tighten monetary growth, the Fed sells bonds to the financial community, taking in reserves from commercial banks, thrifts, credit unions, etc., and consequently decreasing their ability to make loans. This dearth of loanable funds causes interest rates to rise. (In Chapter 11 we will also discuss how and why in reality, changing monetary growth in most developed economies is actually a lot more complicated than outlined above.)

5.3 SHIFTING THE AD: TAX POLICY

We now introduce the tax rate "t" into our analysis. At this stage this is taken to be one nationwide (income) tax rate of t percent.

The consumption function with the introduction of this tax rate t can be written as:

$$C_T = \underline{C} + bY_D \qquad (1)$$

where:
C_T is the consumption function in an economy with tax rate t.
$\underline{C}$ = consumer confidence as defined earlier
b = the marginal propensity to consume (defined earlier)
Y_D is the disposable (after-tax) income.

This disposable income can be expressed as:

$$Y_D = Y - tY \qquad (2)$$

This simplifies to: $Y_D = (1-t)(Y)$

Plug this expression for Y_D into the consumption function:

$$C_T = \underline{C} + b(1-t)Y \qquad (3)$$

From expression (3) we observe that an increase in the tax rate t to some higher tax rate t_1 causes private consumption expenditure C_T to decrease. This decrease in consumption causes a drop in expenditures in the goods markets. This, in turn, results in a drop in the goods market equilibrium, and a leftward shift in the aggregate demand.

5.4 SUMMARIZING THE THREE METHODS OF SHIFTING AD

The following three policies are designed to shift the AD to the right. In all three cases, expenditures increase, thereby increasing equilibrium output in the goods market and consequently shifting the AD to the right.

Policies that Shift the AD to the Right (presented in **Figure 5**)

Fiscal Policy
(1) Increases in government spending.
(2) Cuts in tax rates.

Monetary Policy
(3) Increases in monetary growth and hence decreases in short-term interest rates.

Figure 5

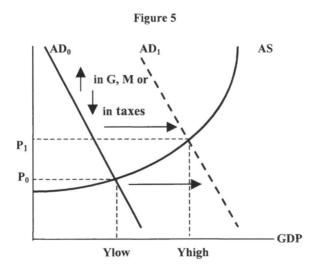

79

The opposite holds true for policies designed to shift AD to the left: decreases in government spending and monetary growth, and increases in tax rates.

5.5 UNEMPLOYMENT

The next step is to define the **unemployment rate, full employment** and **full capacity**, in order to fully understand frequently encountered macroeconomic phenomena such as **soft landings** and **overheated economies**.

One of the most frequently encountered and discussed macroeconomic statistics is the unemployment rate. In the US, the unemployment rates are released on the first Friday of each month. The Bureau of Labor Statistics (BLS) constructs a sample of some 65,000 households each month, and interviews them. (An allowance of a maximum of 2,500 incomplete interviews is allowed). Each household responds to work-related interview questions pertaining to all family members age 16 or older. The interview is always conducted during the calendar week that contains the 12th of the month to allow for cross-sectional intertemporal comparison. Every month, 25 percent of the households are replaced; thus no household is interviewed for 4 weeks in a row.

A household member is considered **employed** if (i) he/she has worked for at least one hour per week as a paid employee either for someone else or in his/her own business venture, (ii) the individual has worked for at least 15 hours per week without pay in a family enterprise, and (iii) the individual is temporarily absent from work due to illness, vacation, legal dispute, etc., even though this may be an unpaid absence.

A person 16 years or older who is not working but is indeed actively looking for work and has made specific attempts to find work during the past four weeks is considered an **unemployed** individual.

Persons not actively looking for work, either because they are discouraged and have given up looking for employment, or simply because they do not want a job, are classified as not being part of the work force. These individuals are not included in the unemployment statistics.

With these criteria, the Civilian Labor Force (CLF) is defined as the population over 16 years of age minus individuals who are, for whatever reason, not actively seeking employment. Alternatively, another definition for the CLF is the total number of individuals employed plus the number unemployed.

The frequently encountered "unemployment rate," is defined as the percentage of the labor force that is characterized as unemployed.

This can be expressed as as:

Unemployment Rate = Unemployed / (Employed + Unemployed)

In terms of the CLF, this is:

Unemployment Rate = Unemployed/Civilian Labor Force.

The definition of the unemployment rate is fraught with deficiencies and limitations similar to those affecting the GDP. Since discouraged workers do not "show up" in the reported unemployment rate as they are not included in the CLF, some analysts believe that the final unemployment rate may not be truly representative of the overall level of job-creation in an economy.

The number of discouraged workers is indeed a significant number. In the United States, this number is around 1.5 percent of the labor force during recessions and slightly below 1 percent in normal times. To capture this information and to provide a more accurate assessment of the level of national job creation, there have recently been calls for discouraged workers to be included along with those classified as unemployed.

Another important definition is the **labor-force participation rate**. This is defined as the percentage of the <u>total population</u> over 16 that constitutes the civilian labor force:

Participation Rate = Labor force / Population over 16.

The participation rate for the US has been steadily increasing. From around 59% in 1953, the rate had increased into the 75% range by the early 2000s. The participation rate in the Eurozone has been a different story. The goal is to increase this rate from its relatively low rate of 60% at the turn of the century towards the higher American rate. The role of labor market deregulation as well as tax incentives to endogenously induce more individuals, mainly women and early retirees, to re-enter the labor force and drive up the participation rate will be the focus of Chapter 10.

Interpreting the Unemployment Rate

The fact that discouraged workers are conspicuously absent from the calculation of the unemployment rate is not the only reason that movements in the announced unemployment rate have to be interpreted with care. Another key factor that needs to be considered is the variation in the participation rate and its effect on the unemployment rate.

During periods of strong economic recovery, economies typically experience increases in the participation rate due to surges in the labor force. Longer-term prospects of better, more stable jobs may induce homemakers, for example, to enter (or re-enter) the labor force. In periods of growth, companies facing labor shortages may offer better medical benefits, child-care, pension plans, prescription drug programs, etc. In this case, the after-tax income along with the benefits may outweigh the cost of staying at home.

Lucrative job openings may also induce some individuals to postpone higher education or make it attractive for retirees to accept part-time (or even full-time) employment, thereby increasing the participation rate.

While this surge in the number of people entering the labor force and actively looking for employment may be indicative of a strong economy, the unemployment rate may paradoxically rise if these new entrants do not immediately find jobs! The new additions to the labor force have suddenly gone from not being included in the unemployment rate to being classified as unemployed individuals, by merely actively looking for jobs.

However, as the economy continues to prosper, the unemployment rate should decrease as these individuals eventually find jobs.

There are also episodes when individuals enter the labor force and leave quickly if they do not find the "right" job soon. In these cases, a surge in the labor force is followed by a sharp decline, with the unemployment rate mirroring the participation rate.

For emerging economies, measuring and tracking changes in the unemployment rate is a challenge. Performing a sophisticated sampling of households and conducting monthly interviews may not be possible. These countries may not have the necessary tools to accurately track the nationwide civilian labor force. This problem is particularly acute in agrarian economies characterized by small and widely dispersed family farms. Hence, these economies often resort to surveys of demanders of labor—employers—by interviewing small to large businesses. Fluctuations in the level of labor demand for skilled as well as unskilled workers often serve as proxies for the strength of an economy.

In summary, while the unemployment rate is an important indicator of the strength of an economy, its monthly fluctuations need to be interpreted carefully with special emphasis on the underlying factors causing the changes. In addition, caution must also be exercised while comparing unemployment rates globally, as different countries may resort to different measurement tools, similar to the case of the GDP discussed in Chapter 2.

Unemployment is characterized as either frictional, structural or cyclical.

Frictional unemployment is defined as that rate of unemployment associated with the "normal" working of an economy. This is the residual unemployment that includes individuals currently between jobs or looking for new jobs after being laid-off, or even those who have just entered the work force—after graduating from college, for example—and who may be taking some time to find the job that best matches their interests and qualifications.

Structural unemployment is typically unemployment caused when entire sectors of the local economy shut down—steel, textiles, etc. In this case, there is a serious mismatch between the skills of the workers and the labor demand of a changing economy. Often it is difficult to separate frictionally unemployed workers from structurally unemployed ones. For example, highly skilled laid-off textile workers may be reluctant to accept the jobs that are currently available in the low-wage, manual labor sector.

Cyclical unemployment is that unemployment that fluctuates with the business cycle. Individuals in sectors such as consumer durables, construction, real estate and jewelry may be good examples.[7] Typically the increase in unemployment that occurs during recessions or depressions is described as cyclical unemployment.

Full employment occurs when the unemployment rate is composed mostly of frictional unemployment—cyclical unemployment is not included. Until the mid-1980s, full employment in the US was defined as 6 percent unemployment in the labor force. With the dramatic decreases in unemployment to around 4 percent by the late 1990s and early 2000s, this number has been lowered to 4 percent by many economists. Later in this chapter, the enormous consequences of this definition will be apparent when controversial issues such as "soft-landings" and "overheated economies" are discussed.

Involuntary unemployment imposes huge costs to society. The value of forgone output resulting from fewer workers is best illustrated by the Great Depression, when GDP fell by 30 percent from 1929 to 1933 with unemployment hitting a high of 25 percent! In addition to lost output, unemployment imposes serious social and personal costs. Prolonged spells away from work make it hard to get back into the work force and may permanently damage the applicant's job prospects. Unemployment constitutes a waste of resources; experience obtained at the prior job may now be lost to society. Unemployment is also found to be positively correlated with social problems such as alcoholism, theft, drugs and domestic violence.

Hence, it is hardly surprising that the Congress enacted the Employment Act of 1946, declaring that it was in fact the responsibility of the Federal government to "promote maximum employment, production and purchasing power". Full employment had become a formal policy objective in the US.

5.6 INFLATION

In Chapter 2, methods of determining the percentage change in prices were discussed in the section on the GDP deflator and the CPI. In this section **inflation** is defined as a percentage increase in the overall general price level. A **deflation** is an average decline in general prices, as evidenced in the Great Depression in the US in the early 1930s, and in Japan in the late 1990s. **Disinflation** is basically declining rates of inflation. Here prices are, in general, increasing, but by declining successive rates of growth. Examples are the disinflation in the US in the 1980s when the inflation rate fell from slightly over 10% in 1980 to around 3% by 1987.

We are now in a position to link changes in the price level with demand-side stabilization which pertains to policies that can shift the AD back and forth, to either stimulate an economy or to bring down dangerously high inflation and growth. This, after all, is the pre-requisite to understanding macroeconomic phenomena such as **overheating** and **soft landing**.

The first step is a discussion of the different kinds of inflation, namely, **Demand-pull, cost-push,** and **hyperinflation**. We begin with a discussion of demand-pull inflation, the most frequently encountered form of inflation, in the context of the following policy exercise.

5.6.1   DESIGNING MACROECONOMIC POLICY: AN EXERCISE

Two macroeconomic cases or scenarios, A and B, are represented in **Figures 6a** and **6b**. Both diagrams assume positively sloped AS curves, which will soon be labeled as "Keynesian" AS curves in the following chapters. This is a major assumption—entire macroeconomic paradigms will be differentiated solely based on the shape of the AS curve in later chapters.

Objective:
In Case A you are to prescribe a set of macroeconomic demand-side stabilization policies designed to move the economy in A from 1 to 2. The starting point 1 represents an economy with a low GDP growth rate accompanied by high unemployment. Essentially, the economy in A is in recession at 1. At 2, you are given that the GDP growth rates is Y_{max}, the strong rate of growth that exists when the labor force is at full employment, and where unemployment is mainly of the frictional type. At this point the economy is also operating at "full capacity," the maximum effective rate of factory utilization.

If policies designed to take the economy to 2 **continue to remain in effect** even after point 2 has been reached, what would be the effect on the economy? Here we explore the ramifications of demand-side policies that cannot be "turned off" and relentlessly continue to influence the economy long after the targets, Y_{max} and full employment, have been attained.

In Case B, the objective is to design a fiscal/monetary policy mix to move this economy in the reverse direction, from 2 to 3. The inflation rate at point 2 is a torrid P_{high} corresponding to a very high rate of GDP growth, high capacity utilization, and a very low unemployment rate. Point 3 represents an economy growing at a sustainable GDP rate, with moderate inflation.

Figure 6a   Case A

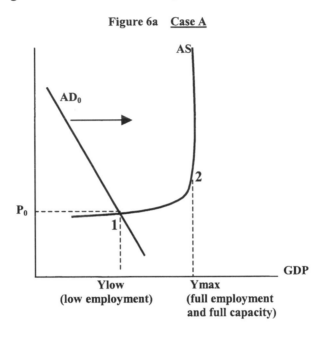

Figure 6b   Case B

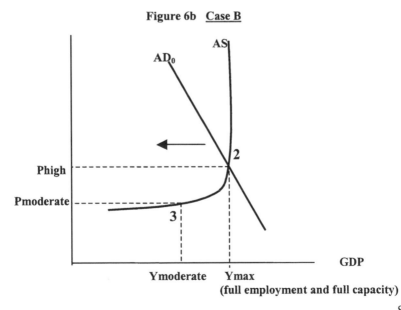

85

Case A

In Case A, the economy can be made to hit the target 2 by a combination of the following policies:

(i) **Government spending (G) could be increased.** Here, as discussed earlier, this fiscal stimulus generates a multiplier effect that takes the economy to point 2.

(ii) **Tax rates (t) could be cut.** As disposable income (Y_D) increases due to this fiscal stimulus, consumption (C) increases, and this, in turn, drives the economy to point 2.[8]

(iii) **The rate of monetary expansion (M) could be increased.** This monetary stimulus lowers interest rates, spurs capital investment (I), and stimulates growth to reach point 2.

Using Case A, the stage is finally set for a discussion of **demand-pull inflation** by examining the policies prescribed for Case A in **Figure 7**.

5.6.2   DEMAND-PULL INFLATION

We begin at point 1 in case A with an economy given to be in recession, with low GDP growth (Y_{low}), low inflation rate (P_0), and a high unemployment (low employment) rate which is not explicitly pictured in the diagram. As demand-side stabilization policies, such as increases in G, cuts in tax rates or increases in M, are put into effect, the economy gets "jump-started" and the AD curve begins to shift to the right along the positively sloped aggregate supply curve as shown below.

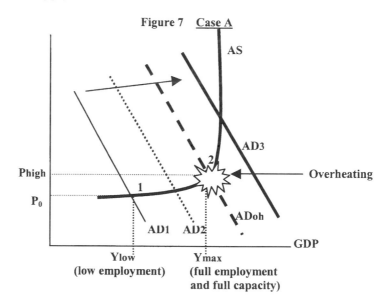

Figure 7   Case A

Stage One of demand-pull inflation (represented by the intersection of AD_1 and the AS curve in Figure 7) is described as the period in which the economy emerges from its recession. Workers are recalled from lay-offs and slowdowns, and plant and equipment roars back to life as the economy begins to revive. While rate of GDP growth is strong, inflation in stage one is very low. There is little or no price pressure, as evidenced by the gentle slope of the AS curve in the blue denoted as "stage 1" in Figure 7. The intuition supporting little or no acceleration in price growth is that laid-off workers returning to their previous jobs or re-entering the civilian labor force do not push for higher wages at this time. The excess capacity of the economy and the abundant supply of raw materials at this early stage also contribute to inflation being fairly dormant in Stage 1.

As the economy continues to grow due to some combination of expansionary fiscal and monetary policies, **Stage two** of demand-pull inflation is reached. As the AD continues to be shifted to the right (AD_2 in Figure 7), due to some combination of government-spending-induced multiplier effects, increases in consumption from tax cuts, or increased capital investment due to lower interest rates, the labor market begins to tighten causing wages to rise. Raw material and real estate costs also increase. In this climate, producers pass on these higher costs in the form of higher prices to consumers. Consequently, strong growth is now accompanied by increasing inflation in Stage two.

In many ways, stage two, given the nature of the AS assumed here, is symptomatic of a healthy, vibrant economy, growing at a sustainable rate, creating new jobs, and incurring moderate accompanying inflation.

However, if AD is pulled still further to the right by ongoing stimulative fiscal/monetary policies, we approach Y_{max} at "full employment" and full capacity. Bottlenecks begin to develop, and the highly skilled and specialized labor market is often the first to exhibit wage pressure. Retaining experienced workers in this climate becomes a challenge. Qualified workers become increasingly harder to find. Larger sign-on bonuses now become necessary along with a host of other perks such as stock options, and so on. And all this occurs despite the fact that newly hired workers may not be as productive as the "first picks" hired in stages one and two.

Raw materials and commodities, beginning with specialized inputs, now also come under excess demand pressure. Overall costs begin to escalate. The output growth for the economy starts rattling against the maximum possible growth, Y_{max}, at "full employment" and close to operating at "full capacity". The growth rate of GDP begins to slow down due to this combination of operating at (or close to) full capacity with fewer and less-productive new workers.

Accompanying this slowdown is an alarming rise in the inflation rate, driven by higher labor, real estate and raw materials costs. This increase in inflation could be evidenced either in conventional indices such as the CPI and the GDP deflator discussed earlier, or, more insidiously, in "proxies" of inflation called speculative asset price (SAP) bubbles (described in the following box).

The combination of rapidly increasing inflation against a backdrop of high employment and capacity utilization, and a recently strong period of GDP growth, characterizes an **overheated economy** (at the intersection of AD_{oh} and the AS curve in Figure 7).

For the developed economies, an overheated economy may have a GDP growth rate in the range of 4-7%, with unemployment as low as perhaps 4% and overall plant capacity in the range 85-88%. Typically, in the US, a benchmark used by economists as a sign of a tight labor market is the point when the number of first-time applicants for unemployment insurance falls below 300,000 per week. (This was indeed the case in the late 1990s, but then as the economy slowed by 2001, the number increased to well above 300,000.)

Emerging economies usually have higher sustainable rates of growth given their lower initial levels of output, employment, and effective capacity utilization. In the case of China and Southeast Asia in the mid- to late-1990s, for example, GDP growth over 10% would just be considered comfortable Stage 2. Overheating in China finally occurred in 1995, when GDP growth roared to over 15% with inflation raging at nearly 20% a year. In 1997-98, the Southeast Asian economies of Thailand, Indonesia, Malaysia, Singapore, Hong Kong all experienced different degrees of overheating with average annual GDP growth rates in the vicinity of 12%, and with enormous SAP bubbles in their stock markets, real estate prices, and IT and high-skilled labor sectors. In the UK, escalating real estate prices convinced the central bank in 2000-01 that a nasty SAP bubble, signaling dangerous overheating, was about to pop.

If, for some reason, the stimulative fiscal and monetary policies that caused the overheating are not decisively checked in time, the AD curve is pulled inexorably to the right **beyond Point 2** (at the intersection of AD_3 and the AS curve in Figure 7). Since no more increases in the growth of GDP are possible, given that we are indeed at Y_{max} at full employment and full capacity, the AS curve rises vertically beyond point 2 as shown in Figure 7.

The continuous and remorseless rightward shift in the AD—demand-pull inflation—rushes up the "vertical leg" of the AS. At this stage, very rapid increases in the rate of inflation are not accompanied by any further increases in employment or output growth that "maxes out" at Y_{max}. The economy staggers into the highly undesirable **Stage 3**, characterized by high and increasing rates of inflation, and no accompanying increase in GDP growth or employment, and closely followed by secondary effects such as inflation-induced collapses in consumer and investor confidence.

Clearly, the objective of prudent macropolicy would be to "slam on the brakes" and somehow arrest the rightward shift in the aggregate demand at the **very first hint of overheating** to prevent the catastrophic Stage 3 from occurring. This is the focus of case B, following the discussion on SAP Bubbles.

SAP BUBBLES

Examples of Speculative Asset Price (SAP) bubbles are the spectacular increases in stock prices, as in the NASDAQ in the US in the late 1990s. The "irrational exuberance" in the US stockmarket may have led to dangerous SAP bubbles in equities—primarily in the technology sector—and in real estate, contributing to an overheated US economy by 1999.[9]

Other examples of SAP bubbles are the equity markets of Southeast Asia in the early 1990s, and in Japan in the late 1980s. Housing prices in Singapore, Honk Kong, the US Northeast and West Coast, the UK and, of course, Ireland, at various times since the late 1990s are perfect examples. Yet other examples of SAP bubbles are the astronomical salaries and benefits that were necessary to attract highly skilled employees in sectors such as Information Technology (IT) and e-commerce, biotechnology, etc., in the US, Ireland and the UK.

Speculative asset price bubbles are considered to be "more dangerous" because while they may develop in a few specific sectors such as equities, real estate and high-skilled labor, the overall national rate of inflation as measured by conventional indexes <u>may not</u> be signaling any proportional escalation of inflation! In the US and Southeast Asia, as the stock prices, the IT salaries, and real estate prices were in the stratosphere in the mid to late 1990s, overall rates of national inflation remained deceptively benign.

Even if current inflation rates appear benign, and even if SAP bubbles are absent, inflation warnings could still be triggered by increases in expectations of impending (future) inflation. Long-term interest rates, for example, embody investor expectations, and are considered to be key indicators of future inflation. In the following chapter, we will discuss how and why long-term rates are invaluable forecasters of inflation "around the corner". Futures prices in commodities and precious metals, along with other leading indicators, are also other sources of "inflation warnings" to be discussed soon.

The exercise in Case B presented in **Figure 8** prescribes policies designed to move the economy from 2 to 3. Point 2 is now identified as an overheated economy, while Point 3 is clearly at some healthy sustainable growth (an "early stage 2") with inflation at $P_{moderate}$ and output growth at $Y_{moderate}$.

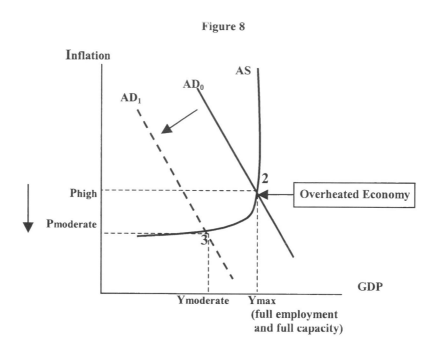

Figure 8

Exactly the opposite policies prescribed for Case A can be now implemented in Case B. Contractionary fiscal policies in the form of cutbacks in government outlays (spending) and increases in tax rates, or contractionary monetary policy, would take the economy from 2 to 3 in B. The first policy would generate a negative multiplier effect, the tax increases would decrease after-tax (disposable) income and decrease private consumption, and the central bank's monetary contraction would cause private capital investments to decrease by increasing interest rates. Borrowing costs would then escalate, slowing down interest-sensitive sectors such as construction. All three, or some combination thereof, would decrease aggregate demand (AD) causing the AD to shift left.

This scenario is the essence of **"engineering a soft landing"**. The term can be traced back to the US lunar landing program with references in astronautics journals traced back to the late 1950s. The lunar module had to be designed to "soft-land" on the moon's surface. The phrase was first used in a macroeconomic context in a 1973 <u>Newsweek</u> article. Typically, the tool used to engineer a soft landing is contractionary monetary policy given the relative autonomy and speed with which most central banks can change monetary growth and hence interest rates. Quick, decisive monetary contractions resulting in hikes in short-term interest rates allow central banks to slow down torrid and unsustainable rates of growth, gently deflate SAP bubbles, and bring inflation down by relieving wage pressure in labor markets where unemployment rates may often be lower than conventional definitions of "full employment". The central bank "cools down" the overheated economy in Case B by slowing the rate of GDP growth Y_{max} to $Y_{moderate}$, and the rate of inflation from P_{high} to $P_{moderate}$.

The US economy in 1994-95 and again in 1999-2000 provides a good example of soft landings. In the latter case, following six interest rate hikes totaling 1.75%, the SAP bubble in the technology sector (NASDAQ) was certainly deflated, the rate of growth of GDP fell from over 5% to a more sustainable 3% by early 2001, and then down to less than 1% by late 2001. First-time unemployment benefit claims again exceeded the benchmark 300,000 per week, implying a slowdown in labor demand pressure.

Other examples are the attempts by the Bank of England to deflate what it perceived to be a SAP bubble in housing and stocks in the UK in the late 1990s, and Zhu Rongji's attempt to cool an overheated China in the mid-1990s.[10]

Needless to say, a soft landing is virtually always a controversial policy move since the monetary brakes need to be applied well in advance of an observed increase in current inflation. Given the nature of this time-lapse between warnings of increases in future inflation and observed increases in prices, central banks sensing inflation in the future often find strong opposition from consumers and investors. These individuals may observe benign rates of contemporaneous inflation and may be lulled into a false sense of complacency. This often places them at odds with policy makers who may be detecting early warnings of upcoming inflation in long-term interest rates in the bond market (this will be discussed later), commodity futures, precious metal futures, wage pressure in skilled labor, and in early SAP bubbles.

If the monetary brakes are hit "too hard" or too long with severe and prolonged interest rate hikes, the soft landing—always a delicate process under the best of circumstances—can quickly becoming a **hard landing.** This would be characterized by recessions as the rate of GDP growth falls below $Y_{moderate}$, accompanied by general deflation, sharply increasing unemployment, and severely deflated asset prices, not to mention rock-bottom levels of consumer and investor confidence. Of course, different "grades" of soft and hard landings have been described by the business media, ranging from "hard soft-landings" to "soft hard-landings," and every possible combination in between.

One example of a "hard soft-landing" may be the US experience in 2001, or China's experience with growth falling to below expected levels, along with deflation in the wake of the sharp monetary contraction in the mid-1990s aimed at engineering a soft landing.[11]

The box on the following page briefly overviews the pitfalls of a common monetary policy such as that adopted by the Eurozone, against a backdrop of overheating and soft-landing discussed earlier.

Monetary Policy in the Eurozone: One Size Fits All?

In January 1999, eleven of the fifteen countries that made up the European Union (EU) agreed to relinquish domestic control over their respective monetary policies to the European Central Bank (ECB) based in Frankfurt. This extremely significant and emotionally charged event was described as the "grand experiment" by the original eleven countries in the Eurozone.

In the context of this chapter, one fundamental macroeconomic drawback of such a one-size-fits-all monetary policy for all 12 member countries (Greece qualified finally, and was accepted in 2000), was the fact that at any point in time, it was inconceivable for all of them to be in the same phase of their respective business cycles.

For example, the large economies of Germany, France, and Italy may be in a sluggish early Stage1, needing stimulus, but the "fringe" economies of Ireland, Spain, and Finland may be dangerously overheating, as was the case by the early 2000s. In this situation, the "fringe" economies would require the ECB to engineer a soft landing by decreasing monetary growth and raising interest rates while the big German, French, and Italian economies would perhaps require the opposite monetary policy—a cut in interest rates!

This conflict inherent in the concept of a "unified" monetary policy for all member countries, is seen by many economists to be a fundamental flaw in the "grand experiment" of European Monetary Union. Critics of a unified monetary policy claim that if "escape hatches" are not provided for countries to unilaterally engineer soft landings or to jump-start their economies independent of the ECB, the whole common monetary policy experiment may crumble.

Compounding this concern is the fact that the Eurozone countries are also bound by the Stability and Growth Pact which prohibits any unilateral increases in government spending and budget deficit creation beyond specified upper bounds. Violation of aforementioned upper limits could result in very significant national fines (up to 0.5% of GDP), loss of borrowing privileges, etc. (At the time of publication of this volume, policy makers in a

---

slowing-down Eurozone, were seriously considering a relaxation of the Stability Pact for exactly the reasons discussed here.)

Hence, the absence of monetary autonomy in conjunction with the severely curtailed ability of member governments to change (increase) government spending and to generate any multiplier effects leaves policy makers with only one tool to stabilize their domestic economies—changes in domestic tax rates. Given that this is probably the least nimble policy instrument requiring the most time to implement, a rapid unilateral policy response in blocks of nations locked into a monetary union becomes exceedingly difficult.

All skepticism aside, however, the monetary union has ploughed remorselessly forward. The gains from the total absence of exchange rate risk within the Eurozone, significantly lower transaction costs, lower long-term interest rates, greater price competition, trade and tourism, more merger activity than ever before, and greater monetary and fiscal discipline may make the Euro a truly global currency in the not too distant future.

In such matters, only time will tell. The first major test will come when one of the major economies (France, Germany, Italy) requires policy that runs counter to the ECB's prescription for the whole Eurozone.

5.6.2   COST-PUSH INFLATION

Demand-pull inflation is "driven" by stimulative fiscal and monetary policies. If an economy overheats because of a case of over-stimulation, then appropriate policy can be prescribed for a soft landing. In this sense, inflation can be "managed" by macroeconomic policy.

In **cost-push inflation**, however, the inflation is caused by exogenous non-policy factors such as oil crises and weather-related events. This inflation, also referred to as "commodity inflation", results in an overall decline in national output productivity, which translates to a leftward shift in the aggregate supply curve, as shown in **Figure 9**.

Here, at each and every price level, the output supplied decreases. This decrease is perhaps due to the fact that an oil crisis has forced a shift of production towards less efficient fuel sources, and hence towards lower productivity. The AS curve therefore shifts left.[13]

This is the kind of inflation that ravages economies during crises such as oil-shocks, or weather-related crises that ravage most of the agricultural output. Here inflation is found to be **countercyclical.** From Figure 9 we see that as inflation increases in cost-push inflation, GDP growth falls; Y_o falls to Y_{low}. It is the worst of both worlds; high inflation accompanies low GDP growth and the attendant higher unemployment. Since inflation and GDP growth move in opposite directions, cost-push inflation is considered countercyclical.

This is in sharp contrast to demand-pull inflation that is found to be **procyclical**. Earlier in this chapter, as the economy moved from stages 1 to 2 and into overheating, the rates of growth of inflation as well as GDP both increased. During soft landings, they both decreased. Since rates of change in inflation and output move in the "same" direction, demand-pull inflation is said to be procyclical.

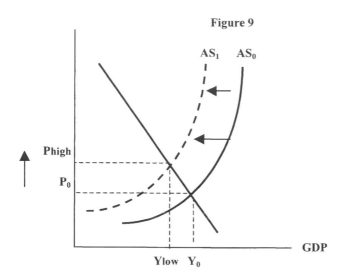

Figure 9

In the following chapter we will discuss the effect on inflation on long-term interest rates, followed by a description of the ultimate macroeconomic meltdown—**hyperinflation**. In the mean time, we explore additional inflation indicators in some detail. Accurate and reliable measures of inflation are imperative to determine if the economy is overheating, if a soft landing is under way, or if cost-push inflation has traumatized the AS curve. While conventional indicators such as the deflator and the CPI were covered earlier, the following additional and specialized measures of inflation are considered particularly important, especially in the context of this chapter.

5.6.3   THE INDEX OF LEADING ECONOMIC ACTIVITY, NAPM, AND SOME "NON-TRADITIONAL" INDICATORS

The US Index of Leading Economic Activity is probably the best-known index of impending economic activity in the United States. Developed and published by the United States Commerce Department until the end of 1995. The Conference Board, a private non-profit group based in New York, was given control of this index in 1996 by the Federal government. A few components were then dropped and others added. Perhaps, one of the more important additions was the addition of the interest rate spread.

Some studies have found that the spread between long- and short-term interest rates is a better predictor of the national business cycle and inflation than most other measures. This finding is, however, controversial, and this topic will be revisited when we discuss the yield curve in the next chapter.

Studies show that the current Conference Board index would have predicted all six U.S. recessions from 1958 to 1990, 3 to 15 months in advance. Emergence from those recessions would also have been predicted correctly from 2 to 8 months in advance.

Ten Components in the Current U.S. Leading Indicator Index
- Average weekly hours in manufacturing
- Initial claims for unemployment insurance
- New orders, consumer goods and materials
- Vendor performance, slower deliveries
- New orders, non-defense capital goods
- Building permits
- Stock prices, 500 common stocks
- Money supply, M2
- Index of consumer expectations
- Interest rate spread, 10-year T-bonds less the Federal Funds rate

The manufacturing sector in the United States is well represented by the monthly **Institute for Supply Chain Management (ISM)** index of manufacturing activity. (This was formerly, the National Association of Purchasing Management—NAPM—index). An overall reading below 50 implies a shrinking manufacturing sector, and vice versa. Most US recessions have "begun" with a contraction in manufacturing activity, and hence this is a closely watched index that may signal an impending slow-down in manufacturing, or an imminent recovery.

In contrast to the above indexes, the following are interesting examples of some non-traditional indicators used in addition to conventional ones.

Some "Non-Traditional" Indicators[12]

Dr. Clifford Sales, a physician specializing in treating varicose veins reports, "we use the level of 'pre-paid' (not covered by insurance) cosmetic surgery as a forward-looking indicator. The cost incurred in this treatment is not as prohibitive as other forms of cosmetic surgery ($400/session compared

95

to, say, facelifts at $7,000-15,000). The more expensive 'facelifts' are found to be price-inelastic and economy-neutral (the customers are wealthy), but the demand for varicose vein treatments goes into downturn at least 8-12 months before a full-fledged slowdown hits us". Dr. Sales also finds that the number of patient cancellations and no-shows increases months before an "official" recession hits the US. The indicator here would clearly be a leading indicator.

Dan Franzatti, a lawyer working for a leading insurer, states, "Most of the claims I handle are for workers' compensation. Whenever a plant closes or lays-off workers, many displaced workers file Occupational Disease compensation claims, usually through the same attorney. Occupational Disease has no specific date of loss, but instead the worker alleges that the time spent at work led to certain disabilities, usually of the repetitive stress type. During the recession of 1990-91, the NJ Division of Labor was absolutely inundated with these claims. With the huge layoffs and closings, the court system was clogged for years! More judges were appointed, and the new courthouse in Newark to process claims was swamped!" Dan also notes that often unemployment lags business cycles, and hence the indicator discussed here would be categorized as a lagging indicator.

Dr. Daphna Hawkin-Frenkel, a research scientist in biotechnology is employed by a flavor research company. "Flavor production is 'middle chain' in food production—all or almost all processed and prepared foods have added flavors. We get requests from virtually all the major food companies to develop a few key flavors. A soft landing or overheating is very hard to detect in our kind of research industry because at any point in time we are developing flavor requests made several months in the past—we are lagging indicators at best."

Dave Bishop, employed by a large food company, offers another interesting and related indicator. In the food sector, customers move away from private store labels (generics) and back to higher quality brand items when the near-term outlook looks good. Customers "demand more indulgence" in his company's product lines, with "expensive convenience packaging high on their wish lists" when the economy is humming along, and a slowdown is not in the cards. Capital spending, at least in this sector, is often on the rise in these scenarios. We label his industry's indicator as a short-term leading indicator.

Other "non-traditional" indicators include long-distance phone calls (the volume falls off months before a recession hits), film processing (tourists apparently cut back on the number of pictures they take), and the tourism industry in general (tourism suffers and those who do travel curtail their budgets). All these are leading and concurrent indicators. Before videos and DVD rentals came along, movie attendance was a great indicator—paradoxically, a countercyclical one. As recessions worsened, more individuals went to the movies to escape the reality of the times, as evidenced by the movie boom during the Great Depression!

5.7 DISCUSSION QUESTIONS

The following questions highlight some important topics covered here.

1. **In demand-pull inflation, growth and inflation go "hand in hand"; they are procyclical. But then how do we explain the fact that we have witnessed substantial and prolonged GDP growth with virtually <u>no</u> rise in inflation, as in the US expansion of the mid-late 1990s?**

There are several explanations. First and foremost, we assumed here that the AS curve was upward sloping (positively sloped) and basically stationary. This is an extremely vital assumption. In later chapters, we will find that supply-siders and New Economy theorists will insist that the curve is crucially affected by corporate tax cuts, productivity gains, and technological breakthroughs which will actually <u>shift</u> the AS to the right. Picture a rightward shift in AS when AD shifts to the right. You will find the intersection points result in an economy with increases in Y but not necessarily increases in P **(Figure 10)**. Growth without accompanying inflation is the result.

Second, lower global commodity (mainly oil) prices, coupled with a super-strong US dollar served to keep prices of imports low during the 1990s, thus keeping inflation in check.

Figure 10

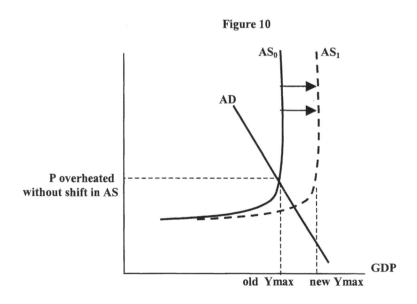

Third, with increasing amounts of global manufacturing, the additional capacity may result in a rightward shift in the effective Y_{max}. The "kink" may have shifted right (as presented in the following diagram), thus keeping conventional overheating at bay. In fact, one reason that Ireland in the late 1990s may have somewhat contained its overheating may be a similar rightward shift in the kink due to large numbers of Irish returning home to a booming Ireland from the UK and the US (see Figure 10).

2. **If the policy-making concepts of Stages 1-3 and soft-landing are really as intuitive as discussed in this chapter, why can't policymakers "manage" their economies to comfortably reside in a nice stage 2 on a permanent basis?**

Consistently managing or "fine-tuning" the economy is truly a delicate art, and is often unsuccessful. In fact, perfect soft landings are conspicuous by their limited examples. Monetary policy works with variable lags that can range from 6-18 months into the future. Furthermore, it would be naïve to assume that while the central bank is prescribing policy, all other variables remain essentially on well-known and predictable time-paths. The domestic economy could be buffeted by a host of factors in the meantime—exogenous shocks, the effects of fiscal polices enacted in the recent past, the state of the global economy, etc.

Furthermore, detecting early and contemporaneous signals of overheating or a soft landing is very difficult given the plethora of often-conflicting data.

Finally, and perhaps most damaging to the notion of "fine-tuning," is the claim by the rational expectationists/supply-siders that the AS is vertical, and by definition any attempt to stimulate the economy by fiscal and/or monetary policy is doomed to failure. Picture the AD shifting right in a diagram with a vertical AS curve. The only result would be an increase in inflation with no change in the rate of growth of GDP! This will be the subject of several later chapters when we finally demystify macroeconomic policy making in developed economies.

3. **How do exchange rates and current account balances come into the picture?**

It is generally believed that as the central bank increases monetary growth and lowers interest rates to spur growth, the domestic currency will weaken. The intuition is that domestic capital will flow out if foreign interest rates are now higher than the recently lowered domestic rates. This is a very short term and "knee-jerk" response at best. Exchange rates are determined not just by movements in short-term rates, but more importantly by the current and expected real growth rates of the economies in question as we
98

discussed earlier. If the domestic economy is strong, and real GDP is expected to continue growing (as in the US case of the 1990s), capital will continue to flood into the country to reap investment opportunities. This constant foreign demand for domestic currency will serve to appreciate the domestic currency. If, on the other hand, domestic growth is anemic and the fundamentals are weak, no amount of interest rate increase will attract any significant inflow.

Regarding current account balances, we find current account deficits to increase in periods of strong domestic growth as high domestic incomes result in a greater consumption of imports. On the other hand, current account deficits are typically found to decrease as the economy soft-lands or goes into recession. This is not due to an increase in exports but rather to a decrease in imports brought about by slowing domestic disposable incomes.

4.   Why do employment and real estate lag business cycles?

This is due to the fact that long-term contracts in employment and construction are often written while the economy is booming. Furthermore, employers are often reluctant to lay off workers at the first sign of slowdown, but instead, they will wait until the recession is incontrovertibly upon them. Along similar lines, they do not recall laid-off workers at the first hint of recovery, but wait until the economy is clearly back on track. Hence, these sectors are found to lag business cycles.

5.   Why aren't these alleged SAP bubbles captured by conventional indexes? And when SAP bubbles do exist, why can't individuals spot the warning signs before the bubble bursts? Why do we need the central bank to be the self-appointed guardian against such speculative crises?

SAP bubbles may not be fully captured by national inflation indexes such as the deflator and the CPI because speculative bubbles are often confined to very specific sectors, and often to very specific geographic parts of the economy. Witness the alleged SAP bubbles in real estate in California and the Northeast since the mid-1990s, in specific sectors in Singapore and Hong Kong in the late 1990s, or in housing and IT salaries in Ireland and the UK in the early 2000s.

Furthermore, with the G7 economies moving further away from conventional manufacturing, traditional inflation measures designed to capture increases in costs of raw materials, transportation costs, storage costs, and power consumption, etc., may not accurately reflect overheating in a predominantly service oriented economy. In fact, the only hint of overheating in such a service-based economy may be astronomical salaries (plus stock options, flexible hours, child care, etc.,) as employers compete for the dwindling pool of highly skilled workers.

The articles on the following pages place the major concepts discussed in this chapter in the context of macroeconomic news and information as encountered daily by investors and policy makers.

In the following simulated media "articles" please relate all the underlined portions to material presented in this and preceding chapters. Use diagrams liberally, wherever possible.

ARTICLE 5.1 THE EMERALD ECONOMY: PROGNOSIS

Maureen McGovern, Emerald Daily Times

The market for properties in Clover, the capital city of Liredan, is sizzling. In just the last year, some prices have actually doubled. John O'Grady, a 37-year old computer scientist, happily informs this reporter that **(a)** his house has appreciated almost as much as his company's shares!

And as shares have soared, **(b)** so has consumption. High-performance luxury cars are everywhere. BMWs clog the streets, and new dealerships dominate busy shopping malls. There is a 9-month wait list for Jaguars. Tourism is roaring. Gourmet dining is all the rage, and imported chefs serving tiny platters of healthy food command rock-star status. Nobody drinks plain old coffee anymore— gourmet coffee is the default option.

Growth in Liredan has been clocked at 8.86% a year, with unemployment at an **(c)** astoundingly low 4.1%. While the current account deficit just reached **(d)** a record high of 4.9% of GDP, the country has also logged a **(e)** budget surplus of 4% of GDP. Inflation, measured by the CPI, is higher at 4.8%, **(f)** up from 4.1% this time last year.

Irene Patterson of Infomacro, a business consulting institute, confides, "all this celebration and rejoicing notwithstanding, we are plain scared. The **(g)** past tax cuts, fiscal spending programs and restructurings which have led to this prosperity may now be cause for serious alarm."

"The current government plan of providing $1 billion in tax cuts, including tax relief on mortgages, is the exact opposite of what we need here now," laments Karl Brenner, economics professor at Cliffside University. "The new immigration law, **(h)** which allows in 250,000 highly skilled workers, primarily in the technology, R&D, engineering, financial analysis and medical

100

services, has helped put a lid on things." He adds, "But the pot will boil over if we stand by and do nothing."

All is not gloom, however. Dr. Kathy Shannon, a veterinarian at Clover Animal Emergency Clinic, is delighted. "We are actually seeing families coming back home. Distant aunts and uncles are not distant any more! Yes, we may be growing too fast and all that, but I believe that the **(i)** increase in national pride is a very good thing. This economy makes us all proud to be from Liredan."

Complicating matters, the metalworkers union and the dockworkers societies **(j)** are demanding yet another cost-of-living increase. If a desperate government caves in, this will be their third wage increase in 18 months. And this comes at a time when the economy, albeit growing at 8.86%, is tending to (k) "flatten out"—growth has been stuck at 8.84% for this current quarter.

Other concerns abound.

(l) Energy costs have soared along with growth and, just last week, first-time unemployment insurance claims hit their lowest weekly level in 8 years.

Prof. Brenner also warns about the current account deficit. "We remain dangerously reliant on foreigners' willingness to buy our assets. We have become addicted to **(m)** the inflows that finance our domestic shortfall, and this is perhaps the most dangerous aspect of this economy. We are supposed to be a lucky people—does this good luck extend to macroeconomics?"

Article 5.2   THE   SINGAPOREAN   CONUNDRUM   AND   THE CHINESE CHALLENGE

Wai Tze Kong, Far East Morning Post

Since the time of John Maynard Keynes, economists have long espoused the notion of "multipliers". According to this concept, policy stimuli such as lower interest rates, cuts in tax rates or increases in government spending have effects that ripple through the economy as the "money changes hands". Thanks to each successive individual transaction, the cumulative final outcome would be larger than, or a multiple of, the initial stimulus—hence the multiplier effect.

Singapore has befuddled policy makers. The National Policy Institute, a government-funded committee of empirical forecasters, has found that the multiplier effects generated in the Singaporean electronics and high-

101

technology sectors are on the order of 2.4 to 2.8, while those generated in the construction sectors are only 1.4!

This sharp difference has grabbed the national headlines and has focused national attention on the whole notion of such "multipliers". An impromptu national debate is now in progress, and this newspaper has taken the lead in monitoring the range of public opinion. Brief interviews were conducted by our roving team of reporters at Singapore's Changi airport and Orchard Street, and on Wang Fujing street in Beijing.

"You know, I always had a problem with this multiplier thing. You are, after all, borrowing from person A to spend on person B. **(a)** The net effect is therefore zero. Right? It all cancels out. So I've never really understood if this multiplier thing is real," says Isaac Goldy, a biotechnologist attending a conference in Singapore.

Thiam Joo Hiu, executive manager of the exclusive Orchard Star Hotel, took time out of her lunch break to tell us, "You know, multipliers are ok. I buy that. I studied all about it. **(b)** But what about the deficits that the fiscal stimuli create? And what about the fact that the interest rates are driven up by government borrowing? That, to me, is the real long-term challenge. I am not losing sleep over why the multiplier is bigger in one industry compared to another."

However, just recently, "the conundrum" of widely different multipliers in Singapore's construction and electronics sectors, may have been solved. Bill Chu and Ashok Govindrajan of Quantonics, a consulting group based in Singapore, find the solution to be "dreadfully trivial". They find that the composition of construction workers is mostly immigrant; Thai, Indonesian, and Malaysian workers on temporary work permits constitute a large part of the construction sector's labor force. These individuals remit most of their disposable income back to their families in their home countries. This simple fact accounts for the lack of any significant construction sector multiplier effect in Singapore relative to the electronics and hi-tech sectors that comprise mostly domestic (Singaporean) workers who "spend their money here at home". Conundrum solved!

And now, we address the Chinese challenge. Policy makers in China have been frustrated in their efforts to stabilize the economy. **(c)** Giant doses of infrastructure spending in conjunction with liberal growth in money creation have yielded sub-par growth. In spite of repeated successively larger doses of stimulation, the final multiplier effect is negligible at best.

We waited till Albert Chung, a computer hardware salesman, finished his Ginger Shrimp at the Great Wall Bistro in Beijing, to get his view. **(d)** "I am no economist, but I would bet that it goes right to the hugely different spending patterns of the two societies—Singaporean and Chinese. And don't forget, even within China, the spending and consumerism that you see in Shanghai and Beijing are not what you see in the western and central parts of rural China. Besides, the Chinese are now worrying about housing expenses, medical benefits, education costs for their kids, and so on."

He may have a point. China certainly has experienced the range of macroeconomic effects, from overheating to a soft hard landing and deflation, and back to growth painstakingly fostered by a combination of fiscal and monetary stimuli. The slogan of Bao Ba, **(e)** guaranteed 8% growth, still resonates with policy makers even though the government has officially shied away from publicly announced targets.

But as long as the multiplier effects are marginal at best, confounded policy makers and analysts will remain huddled over the table.

Article 5.3   ARE WE FINALLY IN A SOFT LANDING? SHOULD WE BE IN ONE?

Robert Anderson, Washington Financial Weekly

After seven interest rate hikes, it seems that the Fed may be finally **(a)** slowing the runaway train that is the US economy.

The numbers are just in—it took seven taps on the brakes to bring GDP growth down substantially from 5.1% last quarter to 3.4% in this one. And the stock market has lost over 40% in some sectors, **(b)** primarily in the high flying technology and internet companies.

Housing prices, however, still remain at their stratospheric levels. Even though **(c)** new housing permits fell for the first time in seven years, this month, the number of new houses going on the market **(d)** hit a staggering increase of 4.8% just last month.

"If you ask me, this was one big mistake on the part of the Fed," says Neil Villiers, a marriage counselor we interviewed on the train from New York to Maplewood, New Jersey. "They've slowed the economy down because they were worried about inflation. **(e)** I ask you, where is it! The CPI inflation rate is only 4.1%; it was 4% this time last year. And while growth has slowed, look at unemployment. **(f)** It is still at 3.9%, just slightly above the all-time low we had last year. So they've not slowed anything down but growth. I just wish they would leave well enough alone."

"I agree that inflation must be attacked at all costs," remarks Ruth Zeiss, a receptionist at Fargo Feed and Seed in Fargo, South Dakota. "We had **(g)** some bad recessions when inflation was near 20% back in the 1970s. But folks forget that nowadays. Anyway, I don't see what the fuss is about now—where is the inflation?"

At Fearless Discount Appliances in Claremont, California, owner Hank Fearless finishes showing a customer a new dishwasher before answering our questions. "It has been desolate here. Desolate for the last 8 months. **(h)** Ever since interest rates started crawling up, our phones stopped ringing. No body wants appliances! No washers, dryers, fridges, TVs. Nothing!" He leans over and whisper, "Hey, my name may be Fearless, but I gotta tell you—I'm scared!"

Separately, the Academy for Consumer Confidence once again reported that its confidence index took another tumble, with the index currently **(i)** at its lowest level in three years. Other news appears to be brighter. The nation's **(j)** current account deficit shrank to its lowest level in six years.

But gloom prevails. Alex Perone and Susan Fisher, two MBA students in Chicago, are concerned. "If the government spending cuts that were legislated into effect six months ago finally come on-line now, **(k)** we may stumble into a hard landing," worries Alex. "You know, soft landings are very hard to engineer—if you look back, there are very few successful examples." Susan adds that she sees, **(l)** "significant inventory building in progress. This implies an impending slowdown." And durable goods sales (not including capital goods for defense and aircraft) have fallen yet again for the third month in a row. Susan's wish is that "all this clears up before we enter the job market!"

"The auto market is shutting down," adds Alex. **(m)** "Already 35,000 jobs have been lost in the auto sector since last year. I mean, where does this end?"

As the controversial soft-landing unfolds, debate swirls and concerned citizens put their faith in their policy makers and hope that the economy enters a **(n)** sustainable growth phase with tolerable inflation soon.

SOME ANSWERS AND HINTS

Article 5.1   The Emerald Economy: Prognosis

(a) Sounds like SAP bubbles in the stock market and in real estate are well under way.

104

(b) Refer to the phenomenon by which consumption is stimulated by increases in stock and real estate prices.

(c)-(f) are examples of an economy that may be _____. Explain why the current account deficit is at a "record high" and why budget deficits tend to shrink when economies go from recessions to periods of recovery.

(g) These are policies contributing to the state of the economy described in questions (c)-(f).

(h) Using an AD-AS diagram, to show how the 'kink' may be shifted.

(i) Soft landings are very hard to engineer, and most unpopular. A booming economy restores pride, and consumer confidence. The general public abhors the idea of deliberately slowing down economic growth that has been so hard to come by.

(j) Wages and prices rise faster as costs increase and bottlenecks develop.

(k) Explain why growth "flattens out" at this stage?

(l) First time unemployment claims are good measures of labor market tightness. Remember the benchmark number for the US, below which the economy is very likely to overheat?

(m) Explain, using the NSI from chapter 2.

Article 5.2   The Singaporean Conundrum and the Chinese Challenge

(a) The comment ignores the subsequent injections of funds back into the "engine" of the economy, with each "injection" being determined by the MPC. This, after all, is the essence of the multiplier effect.

(b) Relate this to chapter 2. If the domestic economy is a safe haven and deficits are "sustainable", then the concern is misplaced. The second half of this quote refers to crowding-out. If government spending is cut back when multipliers are unleashed, the crowding-out effect would be mitigated.

(c) Massive road building, the Three Gorges project, power plants, railways, and the Olympics complex are just some examples.

(d) Compare MPC values for the two economies. Use the relationship between the MPC and the multiplier for China.

(e) Note how emerging economies can sustain higher "minimum speeds" relative to developed economies. An 8% growth rate would be dangerously incendiary growth for a developed economy.

Article 5.3   Are We in a Soft Landing?

(a) The Fed is in the process of engineering a soft landing. Use diagrams to show how this is being accomplished.

(b) This is a typical SAP bubble.

(c), **(d)** Housing lags business cycles as explained in the chapter. But ominously, new housing permits are falling.....

(e) Comment on the fact that inflation as measured by the CPI may not signal overheating.

(f) Note that unemployment lags business cycles. Explain why.

(g) What kind of inflation is Ruth referring to? Use diagram.

(h) Consumer durables are highly procyclical and may be leading indicators given their sensitivity to interest rates.

(i) Note that private consumption is 60-70% of GDP in most economies. With $\underline{C}$ falling, C is bound to drop.

(j) Explain why current account deficits typically shrink during slowdowns and recessions.

(k) Use a diagram to explain how this may happen.

(l), (m) Both these are symptomatic of a rapidly slowing economy. The auto sector is affected by a decrease in discretionary spending as individuals choose to continue to drive older cars. In addition, the higher interest rates adversely affects car loans. Note how Alex's $\underline{C}$ is influenced by news of job cuts.

(n) Sounds like stage two of demand-pull inflation. Explain, using diagrams.

Author's Note

Alex and Susan did fine. It took them a lot longer than anticipated, but eventually they both got great jobs. Susan is doing financial analysis for a large pharmaceutical company in New Jersey, and Alex is working in accounting information systems in Baltimore. They meet often.

Unfortunately, the bad news is that Ruth Zeiss lost her job at Fargo Feed and Seed when her company went "on-line" and found that they no longer needed a receptionist. The good news is that she retired and cashed in her pension just before the Fed deflated the SAP bubble.

Hank Fearless did not sell that particular dishwasher that was being demonstrated on the day we walked in to interview him. However, three days later, he managed to sell it to a couple remodeling their rental property. Despite that sale, Hank is still afraid.

Neil Villiers, the marriage counselor, reports that his business in Maplewood, New Jersey, is good. "As things slow down, the brokers and bankers are staying at home a lot more. So their spouses are now going crazy!" Consequently his marriage counseling business is booming. But we don't have a macroeconomic model for that. At least, not in this book.

---

[1] A change in government spending in actual "real world" macroeconomic policy typically implies a change in the real rate of growth of government spending. While macroeconomic variables are obtained from time-series data, in the static example

provided here, we resort to a one-step increase in government spending, purely for expository convenience.

[2] In later chapters, we will examine how this multiplier effect may have "vanished" since the early 1980s in most of the developed economies. But all that is in later chapters—for now, the multiplier effect is alive and well.

[3] The paradigm shift explanation of the Great Depression, including the liquidity crisis, will be covered in later chapters in detail.

[4] Examples of the US infrastructure spending during that period include the Civilian Conservation Corps and the Tennessee Valley Project.

[5] Contemporary deficits typically increase rapidly in recessions. The reduction in the national tax base as national income falls, coupled with the additional increase in government spending not just on infrastructure but on unemployment benefits, etc., causes deficits to increase rapidly in recessions. The opposite holds true as well; budget deficits shrink quickly in recoveries.

[6] The three methods by which money supply can be changed are (i) open market operations, briefly introduced in this chapter, (ii) discount rate policies, and (iii) changes in the reserve ratio. All three, along with policies and rules adopted by various major central banks ranging from the US Federal Reserve, the European Central bank, the Monetary Authority of Singapore (MAS) and the People's Bank of China (PBOC), will be discussed in detail in the chapter on central banking.

[7] Construction and real estate sectors, while cyclical, typically lag business cycles. Long-term construction contracts, building permits, labor contracts, supplies procurement, etc., are all in place well in advance of the actual construction process. Hence, even though the economy slips into recession, it takes a few months for the building contracts to run their course and for the "momentum" of the sector to wear off and reflect the new mood of the economy.

[8] As discussed earlier, private sector consumption C is the largest component of GDP—almost 70% of GDP in the US, and over 60% in Japan since the late 1990s.

[9] This, of course, is Chairman Greenspan's now-famous comment made in 1996.

[10] Premier Zhu Rongji was formerly the head of the People's Bank of China. He is primarily responsible for putting policies in place that cooled down a dangerously supercharged Chinese economy in 1994-95.

[11] The Chinese economy experienced a "hard" soft-landing when it was cooled down by Zhu Rongji's aforementioned policies from over 20% inflation and over 15% annual GDP growth in 1994 to deflation (or, at most, zero inflation) and just under 8% growth by 2000.

[13] In later chapters, the link between productivity shifts in AS curves will be covered. In fact, these shifts will relate to the supply-side model and the new economy paradigm.

[12] This box makes an exception to the anecdotal write-ups in the book. All the characters are real. These are actual names of students in the Rutgers University Executive MBA program in New Jersey, USA, who responded to a homework exercise in which they had to identify their own sector-specific "indicators". The author remains grateful for permission to quote.

6. LONG-TERM INTEREST RATES, THE YIELD CURVE AND HYPERINFLATION

This chapter introduces the role of intertemporal expectations into our analysis. Effects of current and expected inflation on long-term interest rates will be the focus of the first half of this chapter. This will be followed by a discussion of the ultimate macroeconomic meltdown—hyperinflation.[*]

6.1 EXPECTED INFLATION AND LONG-TERM INTEREST RATES: THE FISHER EFFECT[1]

Long-term interest rates are empirically linked to expectations of future inflation and, risk, and to the real rate of interest by the following expression, known as the Fisher Effect:

$$i_{LT} = r + \pi^E$$

where:

i_{LT} = nominal annual long-term interest rate which is the final interest rate that debtors pay to creditors for long-term loans.[2]

r = real interest rate. This is the real return on the loan to the lender and the real cost of the loan to the borrower. This is also the inflation-adjusted rate of return on the loan.

π^E = expected inflation over the duration of loan. We also subsume general expected risk (such as political risk) into this term.

Suppose company ABC needs to borrow $100,000 for 10 years from the general public for additional capital investment. Lenders are interested in undertaking this loan only if they can be better off, in real terms, by at least 10% at the end of the 10-year period when company ABC pays them back. Both the company as well as the lenders (individual investors, banks, etc.) do their respective macroeconomic analyses and find that inflation over the 10-year duration of the loan is expected to be 8%.[3]

Hence, lenders will lend to Company ABC for 10 years into the future at:

$$i_{LT} = 10\% + 8\% = 18\% = r + \pi^E$$

Lenders will charge ABC the sum of the real interest that they require ($r=10\%$) plus the expected inflation premium of 8%. This latter component is simply the amount that lenders need to add to compensate them for the loss in purchasing power of their principal amount due to the 8% inflation over the duration of the loan.

If this inflation (or general risk) premium were not factored in at the outset, lenders charging just $i_{LT} = 10\%$ would find a net real gain of only 2%

in year 10, with inflation having eroded 8% of the $100,000 loan. In other words, if expected inflation were not added in at the outset, the final real gain to the lender (and the real loss to Company ABC) would be:

$r = i_{LT} - \pi^E = 10\% - 8\% = 2\%$.

Hence, if inflation were indeed expected by investors to be 8% and if the real rate of return is 10%, then lenders will charge Company ABC the total of 18% for the 10-year loan. This would be the final i_{LT} demanded by lenders and paid by Company ABC.

The greater the uncertainty, the greater the expected inflation (risk) premium π^E, and hence, the larger the final lending/borrowing rate i_{LT}. It is precisely this expectations-driven feature of long-term interest rates that results in the bond market being a "forward looking" market.

In general—and particularly in the United States—bond markets are thought to be highly efficient in the speed with which all relevant information is processed effectively by both borrowers and lenders to arrive at an implicit risk premium π^E. An i_{LT} term that encapsulates forward-looking uncertainty is a direct product of this efficient information processing behavior on the part of borrowers and lenders. This is why the US bond market has its devoted fans who believe that "bonds know best" and who perceive the bond market to be an oracle—a macroeconomic radar, if you will—peering into the not-too-distant-future to accurately determine impending inflation and risk.

In fact, the dictum "bonds know best" is often a very good proxy for general business conditions "just around the corner", and not necessarily valid only in safe haven economies. Take, for example, long-term rates in Russia in the early 1990s following the dissolution of the Soviet Union. The long-term rates were of the order of 1200% (for medium-term debt), and an i_{LT} of this magnitude sent a very strong cautionary signal to the world community. Such a rate is very likely composed of a real rate of perhaps just 1% (as an example) and expected inflation/risk premium over the duration of the loan amounting to, perhaps, 1199%!

Here we have:

$1200\% = 1\% + 1199\% = r + \pi^E$

One typical scenario may be that the budget deficit in the above case has become unsustainable, and it cannot be financed by rolling over the debt and by issuing additional government bonds. Domestic and foreign lenders are not forthcoming. As budget deficits stagger into non-sustainability, long past the "safe" deficit/GDP ratio of 5%, a huge monetization becomes inevitable, and, in fact, may already be in progress. Inflation is expected to increase further and spin out of control in the very near future, thereby driving up expectations of inflation to dizzying heights in the current period. Few (if any) lenders would consider lending at long-term rates that primarily consist of huge expected inflation premia.

Long-term rates have "punished" US policy makers, too. In the waning days of the Bush administration in 1990, as the economy slowed into a mild recession, tax revenues shrank fast which in turn led to a rapid burgeoning of the budget deficit. This quickly led to an increase in the deficit/GDP ratio back to the 5% range, reminiscent of the non-sustainability of the mid-1980s. The "macroeconomic radar" implicit in the bond market quickly flashed its warning light. Nervous, efficient, forward-looking bond markets, sensing the increased probability of impending monetization, added an inflation premium that kept long-term rates stubbornly high. As we know, long-term real growth lives and dies by its long-term rates. Capital investment, real estate, and infrastructure are all vitally dependent on low i_{LT} rates. For the Bush administration in 1990, the high i_{LT} rates, spooked by inflation-wary investors, proved to be macroeconomically and politically fatal.

6.2 THE YIELD CURVE: A MACROECONOMIC PERSPECTIVE

Figure 1 presents the yield curve that is the time-plot of nominal interest rates on government bonds that range from short-term debt to long-term (30-year) government bonds. The typical yield curve has a positive slope, implying that longer-term lending horizons involve greater uncertainty and hence are associated with greater risk premia.

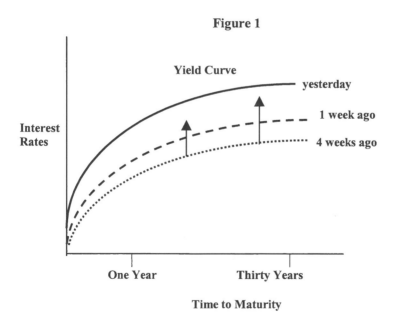

Figure 1

Figure 1 displays an economy where the yield curve has been drifting upward over the last 4 weeks. Here the bond market is signaling higher inflation and/or risk in the very near future as well as in the long run. Both, short- and long-term interest rates are being pushed higher as lenders demand greater compensation for the increased inflation/risk.

If the "long end" of the yield curve (long-term debt of at least five year maturity) rises relative to the "short" end, the bond market depicts an economy that is not experiencing inflation at the current time, but is expecting an increase in inflation in the medium to long term. The exact nature of this increase in inflation is determined by macroeconomic analysis. For example, it could be due to an economy on the verge of overheating, with expectations of increasing inflation derived from inventory depletion and early warnings of raw material and high skilled labor shortages. Or the inflation could be due to impending monetization as a result of budget deficit non-sustainability, or even could derive from some other macroeconomic scenario such as cost-push inflation due to an oil shock. The point here is that changes in expected inflation and risk are signaled by an efficient, forward-looking bond market. The underlying interpretations are up to macroeconomic analysis.

Interestingly, by early 2002 the George W. Bush administration encountered early signs of a possible recovery following the September 11, 2001 crisis, when the long end of the yield curve began to rise and to remain positively sloped. Future increases in inflation stemming from a healthy (and imminent) Stage 2 demand-pull recovery were presumably being signaled by the yield curve. Bond-watchers—"bond vigilantes"—were hopeful; the mood perceptively shifted from despondency to cautious optimism.

While yield curves typically slope "upwards" as in Figure 1, "inverted" or downward sloping yield curves are often experienced, with short-term rates higher than the long-term interest rates. Again, several macroeconomic scenarios can explain this.

One scenario examines the case of a central bank that has been tightening monetary growth and driving up interest rates to soft-land a previously overheated economy. As the soft-landing progresses and the rates of GDP growth and inflation are cooled down, expectations of inflation and risk fall, thereby driving down long-term rates. Hence, the drop in the "long end" of the inverted yield curve. This is why an inverted or "downward sloping" yield curve is often interpreted as a harbinger of macroeconomic slowdown or worse, a recession. The fear is that the attempted soft-landing will not only slow growth and bring down expectations of future inflation, but may go too far and, inadvertently, hard-land the economy into recession.

Another reason for inversion could be simply the fact that the demand for long-term borrowing may have gone down. A good example is the US experience in the early 2000s. As the budget deficit shrank to finally go into surplus, and as demand for loanable funds subsequently decreased, long-term rates also decreased, as in our discussion of the National Savings Identity in Chapter 2. In fact, the cutback in the demand for long-term borrowing led to the Treasury's decision in late 2001 to abolish long-term (30-year) Treasury Bonds.[4]

The following two boxes highlight the strong predictive nature of bond markets. The first box is an overview of the Asian experience following the currency crises of 1998, while the second pertains to the Maastricht Treaty of 1991 that established criteria for qualifying member countries to gain membership to the exclusive Eurozone.

The Missing Asian Bond Market

Soon after the currency crisis that ravaged Asian economies in 1997-98, Thailand's central bank governor reflected, "If I could turn back the clock and have a wish list, high in its ranking would be a well-functioning Thai-baht bond market."

Many analysts and policy makers cite the absence of bond markets as a vital ingredient in the meltdown in Asian currencies and the ensuing turmoil. With no bond markets, investors were going in "blind" with no forward-looking macroeconomic radar and were thereby deprived of vital macroeconomic information.

Bond yields of low-risk government securities serve as crucial benchmarks in a host of calculations. For example, in the market for corporate bonds, investors need a benchmark against which a company's risk of defaulting can be gauged. Yields of low-risk government bonds could be regarded as "hurdle rates" that firms should use when appraising investment objectives. Furthermore, government bond yields could serve as reference benchmarks in the derivatives markets also.

The currency crises traumatized savers, perhaps, worst of all. Without bonds, investors planning for retirement had to choose between high-risk equities or low-yielding bank deposits. With banks being shaky themselves, there was really no sensible instrument to plan for retirement. The absence of low-risk government bonds traded in an efficient bond market resulted in a bloated banking sector with banks focusing primarily on short-term lending (unlike bond-investors who may have longer investing horizons). The emphasis on short-term lending led some of Asia's big family owned business empires to favor projects with quicker returns, as opposed to more sensible long-term strategies.[5]

Some business tycoons simply bought their own banks. Lending and borrowing rates came to be determined in a highly inefficient and often corrupt manner. The rates were far from being driven endogenously by market-determined pressures in efficient forward-looking markets with both lenders and borrowers having access to full information. Instead, borrowing and lending rates were determined by expediency and required rates of return on very short-term projects. There was no "macroeconomic radar". There was no mechanism signaling market-determined expectations of impending risk. The warning lights could not start flashing because they were simply not there.

To rectify this situation, Singapore and Hong Kong moved with great alacrity soon after the meltdown. Singapore began to issue 10-year government bonds to extend the range of the ability of its bond market to "see further". **And this despite a budget surplus!** Hong Kong followed suit; both countries simply invested the proceeds of their long-term bond sales. China also embarked on a similar design and establishment of a sizable government bond market.

Thailand, Indonesia, South Korea and Malaysia began to issue bonds, too. However, these issuances were mainly in response to the budget deficits resulting from their respective currency crisis.

Moving further back in time, the following box highlights the role of long-term rates in qualifying for the monetary union in the countries that constitute the Eurozone. The European monetary union, wherein member countries sacrifice all monetary autonomy and their domestic currencies for a one-size-fits-all monetary policy and the Euro as currency, was labeled "The Grand Experiment". This box includes a brief overview of the "experiment" along with the primary focus on long-term rates.

Long-Term Interest Rates and the 1991 Maastricht Convergence Criteria.

The Maastricht Treaty, established in late 1991, was a milestone on the long road to European Economic and Monetary Union (EMU). "Maastricht" was the prelude to the adoption of one common currency, the euro, and one common monetary policy to be conducted by the European Central Bank (ECB) in Frankfurt.

Membership in this union of countries—the Eurozone—meant that all aspirant countries needed to get their key macroeconomic statistics "in sync", before they could abandon their currencies and adopt the euro. Countries were required to show strong evidence of fiscal and monetary discipline; one weak link of fiscal or monetary lassitude could jeopardize the integrity of the whole monetary union.

With this objective in mind, several benchmark targets for key macroeconomic statistics were prescribed by the accord. These were the "convergence criteria" that had to be attained by May 1998. At this point, the European Union countries that had successfully qualified for membership to the common currency would be announced. The "convergence criteria" are still valid today, as they apply to new aspirant countries as well:

(i) Budget deficits have to be under 3% of GDP. In other words, they have to be highly sustainable.
(ii) National debt has to be under 60% of GDP. Once again this criterion is aimed at ensuring fiscal rectitude.[6]
(iii) Inflation cannot exceed the average of the three countries with the lowest inflation by more than 1.5 percent.
(iv) Long-term interest rates cannot exceed the average of the three countries with the lowest long-term rates by more than 2%.

Low long-term rates imply macroeconomic radar that does not detect expected inflation risk in the future. Specifically, these oracles of inflation signal that fiscal discipline (sustainable deficits) has been attained and a highly inflationary monetization of runaway deficits is not forthcoming.

This last criterion was a particularly important convergence criterion given that some countries may have resorted to "creative" accounting measures and unique interpretations of "Maastricht" to attain criteria (i) and (ii). One-time sales of huge state owned assets, for example, could significantly reduce the deficit, conveniently bringing the deficit/GDP ratio under the qualifying 3%!

If the bond markets are indeed highly efficient in processing forward looking information, an endogenously determined (market determined) signal of "low future inflation," signaled by low long-term rates, may perhaps be a much more reliable indicator of fiscal discipline than published annual deficit figures.

6.3 HYPERINFLATIONS

Hyperinflations are easily the most traumatic of all macroeconomic disasters. The term "hyperinflation" refers not to just a very large increase in the price level, but to a rapid one as well. While there is no formal definition for the term, an economy is said to hyperinflate if inflation is greater than 50% a month. However, hyperinflations almost never stabilize with final inflation anywhere in that region but instead race uncontrollably past the 50% mark into stratospheric, inconceivable rates of inflation. For example, in less than two years beginning in 1922, the German average price level increased by a factor of 20 billion!

Generations who are unfortunate enough to be struck by the trauma of hyperinflations never forget them. The experience is indelibly seared into public memory. Hyperinflations change lives, policies, and entire generations, and almost inevitably result in a total overhaul of the incumbent government. In this section we will discuss the causes and eventual remedies of this macroeconomic disaster.

Usually, a hyperinflation is the result of an unsustainable budget deficit. As discussed earlier, and to be revisited again in a later chapter, once the deficit/GDP ratio exceeds an upper bound (around 5% for developed economies), further bond-financing becomes impossible. Domestic and foreign investors are reluctant to lend more funds to a regime that is perceived to be risky, or to one that has incurred extravagant and irresponsible spending. Such government spending could range from massive infrastructure projects gone awry, to ill-conceived and impulsive fiscal expansion or reckless military spending. The regime may be corrupt; large portions of the increase in spending may end up in their personal coffers or in overseas accounts. A prolonged conflict may be impending or even in progress.

In this situation, "rolling over" the debt that may have just matured, by issuing new bonds, suddenly becomes impossible. To make principal and interest payment on debt, the only option then is to induce or pressure the central bank to simply monetize the debt by "printing money." Typically, in these cases, the central bank does not have a high degree of autonomy. The money creating authority may be subservient to the deficit creating authority, thereby setting the stage for unmitigated money creation to finance giant runaway budget deficits. In fact, in the extreme case, fiscal spending and monetary creation may even be controlled by the same entity![7]

6.3.1 THE ANATOMY OF A MELTDOWN

(1) As severe monetization becomes necessary to finance the giant unsustainable deficits, inflation begins to rise. Consumers "buy now" to beat future price increases. This excess demand on consumption goods drives prices up further.

(2) With increases in inflation, workers demand higher wages to compensate them for rising expenses. These higher wages push up prices and a dangerous wage-price spiral begins to form with wages and prices mutually pushing each other upwards.

(3) As inflation gradually climbs higher, suppliers tend to hoard in anticipation of higher prices in the very near future. This artificially created shortage further exacerbates the excess demand pressure. Inflation now increases very rapidly.[8]

(4) Confidence is continuously plummeting all along. Wages continue to rise along with inflation.

(5) Typically, these countries have a large number of highly inefficient and unprofitable SOEs (State Owned Enterprises). Examples are steel, power, transportation, mining, and oil. Most owe their very existence to state

116

subsidies, tax credits, subsidized rent, power, transportation costs, and often, guaranteed prices for sub-standard globally uncompetitive output.[9] As inflation mounts, these SOEs now demand further subsidies, price supports, etc., or else they may threaten general (national) strikes that could cripple the whole country.[10]

(6) The government relents and caves in to this pressure from the sizable state-subsidized industry. Further price supports, subsidies, huge cost-of-living increases to match the rampant inflation, and subsidized housing (to name a few) are provided by the government and financed by yet more monetization! Given the magnitude of the SOEs, this is often a huge and fatal dose of money creation that becomes the proverbial last straw.

(7) Inflation is now completely out of control. Prices may be doubling or even quadrupling between breakfast and lunch time! The economy careens out of orbit, and investor and consumer confidence go into a total free-fall. And all along, as a sinister backdrop, inflation races inexorably upwards until the actual inflation rate becomes a meaningless statistic.

In the Hungarian hyperinflation following World War II, from July 1945 to August 1, 1946, the price level increased from 7964 to an inconceivable **$(24)(10^{28})$**. In the last two months of the hyperinflation, the rates of inflation were $(8.4)(10^5)$ percent and **a staggering $(41.9)(10^{15})$ percent.**

(8) All along, the hyperinflating economy experiences a massive flight of capital as individuals desperately convert domestic savings (and even daily paychecks) denominated in the ravaged domestic currency to some "hard currency" (US$, euros, even yen), or to precious metals (typically, gold). If a well-functioning bond market had existed, the warning signs would have long been flashing. Irrespective, individuals attempt to somehow preserve at least some modicum of real purchasing power from their life savings.

(9) Typically, the hyperinflating country attempts to stem this hemorrhage of domestic savings by instating capital controls. Often, this measure is of no avail; as savings and nest-eggs shrink rapidly, money floods out of the hyperinflating economy. Illegal secondary markets develop in hard currency and precious metals. The country continues to experience a massive capital exodus.

(10) As individuals convert savings in hyperinflated currency to hard currency or gold, the exchange rate collapses. The domestic currency is progressively worth less and less in terms of hard currency, until, like the inflation rate, the exact rate is irrelevant. Crucial imports such as food, medicine, and fuel, denominated in harder foreign currency, now become virtually unaffordable.

(11) Domestic currency becomes worthless. It loses all value, and its intrinsic paper value may even exceed its face value. Currency may now be used as kindling to light fires (as it was during the German Hyperinflation of 1919-23), or substituted for wallpaper (again, as in the German Hyperinflation).

(12) The economy deteriorates into a barter economy. Goods are traded in informal farmer's markets. The incumbent government is ousted from power. Chaos reigns.

Examples of inflation rates from some classic annualized hyperinflation rates are presented below:
1922 Germany, 5,500%
1985 Bolivia, exceeded 10,000%
1989 Argentina, 3,400%
1990 Peru, exceeded 7,000%
1993 Brazil, 2,400%
1993 Ukraine exceeded 5,200%

Author's Note:
The write-up in the following box illustrates the cruel reality and human cost of hyperinflation. This narrative, submitted by my former student Nadia Karalnik (from Russia), was part of a macroeconomics assignment, and is reprinted here in its original form. This is the only instance in this book where all the characters are real.

The Hyperinflation in Russia: The Words of Roza Beydman

By Nadia Karalnik, MBA Student, Rutgers University, New Jersey, USA
(At the time this was written, Roza Beydman was just about to become Nadia's mother-in-law.)

Roza immigrated to the United States in 1997. This is a personal story, in Roza's own words, of the events that took place in Russia in the early 1990s, when the country encountered a financial crisis and hyperinflation caused by the instability of the Russian economy.

"I worked very hard my whole life. My husband was an engineer and I was a teacher. Our modest salaries were enough to feed the children and to buy necessities. We always had to be careful with every ruble in order to make sure that every month we could put off (save) some money away. We never trusted that the government will support us once we retired, so we wanted to make sure that we had enough to support ourselves. We managed to collect (save) 15,000 rubles. Considering the fact that in 1990 an average engineer was making 150-200 rubles a month, this was a considerably large sum.

My husband and I both retired in 1986, when we turned 60 years old. Our pensions were 80 rubles a month each. We were very satisfied with our wise decision; the savings really gave us the comfort to be sure that there would be food on the tables today, tomorrow and in the future.

118

My husband passed away in 1989; he did not live to see the horrors of our falldown.

It was like a bad dream. At first, all food products and clothes disappeared from the stores, and the news about the possible price increases spread very fast around the city. Simple products like sugar and meat became great scarcities. For example, I had to stand in line for two hours to get sugar, and the limit was one kilogram per person. That was the period when money was not the problem. It was simply an issue of what was available for sale.

One day I went to the store and realized that the prices had suddenly increased. The loaf of bread that cost 30 kopeikas for years was now selling for 3 rubles! (100 kopeikas = 1 ruble). Everybody knew that something very bad was happening, but there was just nothing we could do to prevent it. My neighbors told me that the banks are offering high interest rates, so I decided to put half my savings into a savings account. It was only a matter of two weeks before my lifetime savings became worthless. I could now use this money to buy one pair of shoes.

The prices were growing every day and were so high that I couldn't even understand how much everything cost. It became pointless to have rubles; anybody who had a chance to convert rubles to dollars took advantage of it. The exchange rate went from 0.9 rubles per dollar to five thousand rubles per dollar. The dollar became the only valuable currency.

The situation got even worse when they stopped paying salaries and pensions. People who worked in factories were better off; they were paid in the products of the factory. For example, those who worked in the shoe industry were getting paid in shoes. They could then either sell their products or just exchange them for other products at the bazaar.

The elderly people took the hardest hit. Our minimal pension increases could not keep up with every day's inflation. If any of us saved any money, it lost any value and was long gone. We had to start selling personal belongings. Anything that had any value was for sale. The situation in the stores was very different now—the shelves were full of goods and there were no lines anymore. If you had the money, you could buy anything. I had relatives in the United States, and they would send me money every few months through private channels. I would not be able to survive if it wasn't for this assistance. Many old people were starving; they had no choice but to go out on the streets and beg for food and money.

This was a very difficult time in my life. All my life I was a loyal citizen of my country. Even when all my relatives left to go to the United States at the end of the 1980s, I refused to go because I wanted to grow old and die in my mother country.

Unfortunately, this patriotism was gone as soon as the food was gone from my table. The country that cannot provide its citizens with bare minimum necessities is not worth my love and faithfulness. This is the reason why I took the first chance I got to emigrate. Everything that I have just told you seems like a bad dream now; but it was a horrible reality just a few years ago."

Reprinted with the kind permission of Nadia Karalnik.

The story in the box illustrates the ruthless power of macroeconomic policies gone awry. Even if individuals "do the right thing" and work hard, save wisely and invest prudently, errant macropolicy can, unfortunately, eradicate all their accumulated wealth in a matter of weeks. Such is the destructive power of irresponsible macroeconomics.

Our next task is to examine whether hyperinflations can indeed be tamed. If so, how? How can they be prevented? And how challenging is the implementation of such macroeconomic policies?

6.3.2   HYPERINFLATIONS: REMEDIES

Given that unsustainable deficits necessitating tremendous monetizations are typically the underlying causes of hyperinflations, the remedy would then have to address (i) the deficit non-sustainablity as well as its consequence, and (ii) huge amounts of newly created money in circulation.

First and foremost, the deficit has to be brought back to within its sustainable range by large, difficult spending cuts; item (i) has to be resolved. Government spending cuts could involve significant cuts in salaries of government employees, cuts in pension programs, sharp reductions in subsidies and tax breaks to large state-owned enterprises, and perhaps, most important—privatization of formerly inefficient unprofitable SOEs.

This last item is, perhaps, the most influential in bringing deficits down, as SOEs often consume very significant portions of national tax revenues.[11] Privatization of even a few giant SOEs may result in sharp reductions in national budget deficits, thereby bringing them back into the sustainable range. This policy is, however, beset with challenges. Large-scale privatization would indeed increase national unemployment, as SOEs tend to be characterized by overemployment anyway. As the inefficient companies with outmoded capital stock and globally uncompetitive output are shut down—some for good—unemployment is only exacerbated. Coming in the wake of hyperinflation and macroeconomic collapse, this increase in unemployment is an exceedingly difficult policy to implement.[12]

Often, "austerity measures" required by the IMF as conditions for present and future debt assistance in the form of emergency credit lines, include strong privatization as well as spending-reduction clauses. These ensure that fiscal reform, no matter how unpleasant, is indeed tied to the IMF's short-term financial assistance.

The other side of the equation that needs to be addressed is to somehow roll back the enormous sums of money that are currently in circulation. Compared to the privatization policy just discussed, this, paradoxically, may be the easier policy to implement.

One method to shrink the huge amount of money in circulation is to introduce "new" money. Here the government introduces a new set of notes, with, for example, one million units of the "old" hyperinflated currency now equivalent to one unit of the new currency.[13] Sometimes, the currency is redesigned with the zeros lopped off the old denominations. These conversions only apply to some specified upper limit of accumulated depreciated currency. Not all the depreciated funds can be converted, just a fraction can, and the nation as a whole experiences net welfare loss.

It should be noted here that while the above policy of shrinking the money in circulation is a necessary condition to remedying hyperinflations, it is by no means a sufficient measure by itself. Without fiscal reform in the form of difficult privatization of SOEs, deregulation, and spending cuts that bring budget deficits back into the sustainable range, money supply contraction by itself will be at best a very short-term check on inflation.

To ensure that hyperinflations can never recur, in addition to strong fiscal discipline (which is imperative), monetary autonomy—independence—is vitally important. Institutionally, the central bank needs to be independent of fiscal pressure. Central bankers must be free from pressure by the fiscal authority to monetize away runaway deficits caused by the irresponsible fiscal misadventures of the past. The central bankers' job tenures, as well as the operating budget of the central bank, should not be a function of their degree of cooperation with the government. In other words, the central bank must be secure in its independence to be able to reject pressure from a fiscally irresponsible government to print money and finance away unsustainable deficits.

A large body of empirical macroeconomic research finds enough evidence to substantiate that strong monetary discipline does indeed breed strong fiscal discipline.[14] Strong monetary autonomy is positively correlated with smaller budget deficits since any moral hazard stemming from an implicit monetary "escape hatch" for fiscal profligacy is now removed. Here, governments (the fiscal authority) realize that there is no "friendly" central bank to bail them out of the latest fiscal fiasco by printing more money, and hence greater fiscal restraint is exercised. Consequently, strong monetary autonomy also results in lower levels of inflation and lower long-term interest rates, as fears of expected future monetizations correspondingly subside.

In addition to institutional autonomy, another method is a constitutional and legislative directive ensuring monetary and fiscal discipline. Such a measure may include a constitutionally specified upper limit on inflation and budget deficits with serious penalties for failure. For instance, the Bank of New Zealand Act of 1989 included a clause whereby the Governor of its central bank would be fired if inflation broke through its upper bound of 2 percent!

6.4 MONETARY DISCIPLINE: THE HAZARDS OF PEGGING

Institutional autonomy may not always be possible. At the other polar end of monetary autonomy, the central bank may simply be an extension of the fiscal arm of the government; the central bank may have been nationalized at some point in the past. Or central bankers may be subservient to the government for renewal of short-term tenures or operating budgets, or may even be subject to "approval" (explicit or implicit) from the fiscal authority before any significant monetary policy can be passed.

In these and other related cases when institutional/constitutional monetary independence does not exist, central bankers often resort to pegging or locking their currencies to those of other countries with strong monetary discipline. In this system, a pegged rate implies either a fixed exchange rate or a narrow range within which the domestic currency is allowed to fluctuate with a "hard" currency of an economy characterized by high monetary and fiscal discipline.

The mechanism by which monetary discipline is attained is as follows.[15] Let the country that seeks to gain macroeconomic discipline be a type A country. The one with the hard currency stemming from a long history of fiscal and monetary credibility will be the type B country (the US, for example).

Initially, A pegs its currency to B's at the rate of, say, 4:1. A's central bank ensures that, by daily purchases and sales of the two currencies, the ratio 4:1 is attained.[16] At some time in the future, once again, a familiar dangerous pattern emerges in country A. Its central bankers come under intense pressure from the government of A to increase money growth and to monetize the sizable deficit that is virtually impossible to finance by issuing any more debt.

This time around, however, with the peg in place, if monetization were to be allowed and more units of A's currency were to be printed, the domestic currency would weaken and be less valuable in terms of the harder currency of country B. In other words, the exchange rate may slip from 4:1 to 6:1 if the huge monetization were allowed to take effect. To safeguard the integrity of its well-announced and globally recognized peg, the monetary authority would thus be in a position to legitimately refuse pressure to monetize. (We revisit this topic in Chapter 11 in more detail.)

Examples of exchange rate pegging abound. The East Asian currencies were pegged to the US dollar in varying degrees for most of the 1990s, till the pegs blew apart in 1997-98. Hong Kong, and Singapore have had fairly tight pegs to the US dollar for decades, and the cases of Argentina and Brazil pegging to the US dollar in the1990s are now legendary. So is the precursor to the Euro, known as the ECU (European Currency Unit), which was part of the ill-fated ERM (Exchange Rate Mechanism) established in the European Union by 12 member countries in 1979.

For attaining monetary autonomy (and indirectly fiscal discipline), pegging is a short-term measure at best. It works well <u>as long as the economies of the type-A country and the type-B county are both in the same phase of their respective business cycles.</u> If, for some reason, B's economy were to overheat, B would be attempting to engineer a soft landing by contracting monetary growth and, hence, by raising its interest rates. This would imply that A would also have to match B's raising of interest rates to keep the exchange rates at 4:1 (to continue the earlier example). This would be fine as long as A also needed to engineer its own soft landing to slow its own overheated economy.

But if A were not overheating but instead slowing down or already in recession, this policy of driving up its own interest rates to ensure that the peg with B remained intact would only exacerbate A's recession! Instead of being jump-started with lower rates, the economy would go into shock as rates now perversely increase!

Policy options at this stage are to either persist with the peg and contract growth in A, or to allow the peg to snap, and to enact the exact opposite monetary policy and revive A's economy by a stimulating dose of lower interest rates.

This was the basic scenario prior to the collapse of the European Exchange Rate Mechanism (ERM) in 1992. The German increases in interest rates following dangerously large unification expenses came at a time when Italy, the UK, and Spain needed the exact opposite monetary policy prescription. These economies were slowing rapidly and they needed a dose of monetary stimulus in the form of lower, not higher, interest rates.

Similarly, in the Asian case in the later 1990s, dangerous SAP bubbles developed, and as the US economy progressively powered up while growth began to slow in East Asia, the overvalued pegs could not be maintained. We will discuss these cases further in later chapters.

Brazil: A Real Plan

After averaging between 15% and 50% from 1940 to 1980, annual inflation in Brazil exploded into triple digits during the 1980s; from 1980 to 1984, inflation averaged 127%, and then rose to 475% from 1985 to 1989.

In the period 1990-1994, inflation went from an annual inflation rate of 2775% to 2309%. The growth in process was temporarily checked at times

123

by the repeated introduction of new currencies to "soak up" the vast amount of past monetization—at one stage four new currencies were introduced within six years. But these measures were not accompanied by difficult fiscal reform (privatization, etc.) and hence became temporary and cosmetic measures at best.

Then in 1994, Brazil, following the lead of other Latin American countries suffering the same plight, instated the Real Plan to stabilize its economy. Success was immediate; inflation fell to 73% in 1995 and then to 2% by 1998!

The success of the Real Plan can be attributed to the fact that it was a well-announced and adhered-to plan, and, most important, it was accompanied by absolutely necessary fiscal reform. "Announcement" aspects of macropolicy are extremely important. Policymakers must undertake an extensive public education campaign to explain exactly what the planned measures hope to achieve and exactly how key macroeconomic statistics—inflation, employment—will improve, thanks to the bitter medicine. It must be made clear to the general public that the tough measures are a necessary first step to future growth. Further, any and all safety nets (unemployment insurance, job training, etc.) that may be available to displaced workers must be described fully and readily available.

In Brazil, the specific procedures for attaining fiscal and monetary discipline were clearly and repeatedly explained. Monetary discipline was signaled by locking the value of the real to a pre-determined consumption bundle, and then pegging the real to the US dollar. In addition, the much harder fiscal reform aimed at privatization and liquidation of large inefficient state-owned sectors, was begun in earnest. Eighteen banks were liquidated during this time. In addition to financial reform, massive deregulation was pursued in industries such as telecommunications, transportation, utilities, and petroleum.

This vital combination of fiscal discipline in conjunction with monetary discipline signaled a determination on the part of Brazil to become serious about macroeconomic reform. This in turn resulted in, perhaps, the most tangible validation of its macroeconomic reform from the global investment community—Brazil began to attract large global capital inflows, the vital ingredient for long-term capital growth.

6.5 DISCUSSION QUESTIONS

The following question/answer format serves to highlight some key issues.

(1) **So it is by no means clear that a 5-year government bond paying 25% interest annually is better for attracting global capital than one that pays 8%?**
Real rates of return drive global capital flows. The country paying 25% may have current and expected inflation at 24%, which results in an inflation-adjusted (real) return of just 1%. The other country may have inflation at only 2%, thereby yielding a higher real rate of 6%.

(2) **Why are tax increases not an option in financing unsustainable deficits? Why must the only options be monetization or debt default?**
Remember, that the deficit is *exposte* tax revenues for the year. There was a certain tax rate t_1 in effect in the economy in year 1. At the end of year 1, after all the tax revenues are collected, the economy in question finds that it has incurred an unsustainable deficit. This is the issue that needs to be addressed. An increase in tax rates to t_2 will only influence the deficit in year 2; it will do nothing to solve the problem in year 1.

(3) **It seems that the same countries continue to experience hyperinflations or high inflations. Is real macroeconomic reform never possible?**
While we do see the "same countries" struggling with hyperinflations over long periods of time, dramatic reform is indeed possible. One example is Germany. Following the trauma of the hyperinflation during the Weimar Republic (1918-22), Germany eventually became Europe's bulwark against inflation. The "legacy" of the hyperinflation was an inflation-phobic central bank in Germany, obsessed with monetary discipline. In fact, the Bundesbank came to be the repository of severe monetary discipline for the whole continent from the 1960s onwards. The French adopted the Franc Fort policy in 1982 by virtually pegging to the D-mark, and saw inflation become a non-problem by the late 1980s. The ERM discussed earlier, and later the Euro, were strongly influenced by this comforting backdrop of German monetary discipline.

Another example of a country that had reformed its unsustainable ways—albeit briefly—was South Africa in the early 2000s under the leadership of Tito Mboweni, its reformist South African central banker, as discussed below.

Please explain/critique the underlined sentences/phrases in the following "articles" using material from this and preceding chapters. Use diagrams liberally.

ARTICLE 6.1   TITO MBOWENI AND THE SOUTH AFRICAN RAND

Uluthu Mbeki, <u>Nairobi Business Journal</u>, (early 2000).

Tito Mboweni, governor of the Reserve Bank of South Africa, may be considered the savior of the rand. Charismatic, effervescent, and fond of pink ties, he explains the bank's workings in the local languages of Sesotho and Zulu.

Unlike his predecessors, he does not believe that the Reserve Bank **(a)** <u>should intervene and artificially support the value of the rand</u>. In a speech to college students last week, he announced that he would let the markets decide the value of South Africa's currency instead of wasting a fortune trying to shore up its value artificially.

Upon hearing this, the markets approved, the people were thrilled, and it is hardly surprising that by the year 2000, South African banknotes are known as "Titos".

Mboweni understood that global investors would inject capital into South Africa only if they were truly **(b)** <u>convinced that serious macroeconomic reform was under way.</u> But changing investor perceptions was a daunting task—most African central banks did not have good records.

Angola's "reforms" included simply lopping off six zeroes from its currency. The head of Congo's central bank was actually arrested for sedition after espousing a tight money policy that included no monetization. And Sani Abacha, the dictator of Nigeria in the late 1990s, had given his central bank a standing order to transfer about $15 million to his Swiss bank account every day.

Against this backdrop, Tito somehow managed a miracle. He pushed through a tight monetary policy and was part of a government plan to advocate smaller wage hikes to the unions, **(c)** to <u>launch major privatization programs, to negotiate free-trade pacts, and to refuse public servants' pay demands</u>.

The markets responded.

(d) <u>Long-term rates fell from almost 14% to under 10 percent within six months of his taking office.</u>

"It is all about credibility now", said Tijjan Malabar, a staff economist at the Reserve Bank. "There are no fixed exchange rates, no fixed value of gold—it all has to do with the reputation and credibility of a country's fiscal and monetary policies."

But credibility comes slowly; it often takes years to build. We hope Tito has time on his side.

Postscript: *All to no avail. By 2002, the rand had begun to collapse. Capital flooded out of South Africa. Unfortunately, in spite of Tito's earlier example and leadership, the macroeconomic reforms could not combat entrenched interests and did not take hold.*

ARTICLE 6.2   YUGOSLAVIAN DISASTER: A MACROECONOMIC CRIME

Lubka Martancik, Central European Journal

When the government of Slobodan Milosovic was caught ordering the Serbian National Bank to issue $1.4 billion in credits to friends of Mr. Milosovic, the writing was on the wall.[17] This shocking illegal plunder equaled more than half of all new money creation in Yugolslavia in 1991, and proved to be just the tip of the iceberg.

The stage was set for a series of mismanaged and corrupt policies to lead to hyperinflation lasting 24 months, **(a)** the second-highest and second-longest in history. It peaked in January 1994, when the monthly inflation rate was 313 million percent!

Per capita real income fell by around 60% by the time the hyperinflation was over. Food was impossible to afford. Starvation was common. For city dwellers, relatives living in the country with access to farms were often the only source of good.

(b) For weeks on end, all gas stations in Belgrade were closed. Huge piles of domestic currency (dinars) were exchanged for a single German Mark or US dollar; there was an epidemic of capital flight.

By December 1993, 94% of all government expenditures were being financed with newly printed currency, with deficits long unsustainable. Since 1991, the dinar was officially devalued 18 times; 22 zeros were dropped off over time. Just in 1992, there were 5 devaluations, with monthly devaluations often over 99%.

The mint cranked out 900,000 notes a month, but they became worthless just hours after being printed. At one point, a 500 billion dinar note was worth a little over 4 German marks when printed. The currency collapsed on January 6, 1994, and the government officially declared the German mark as legal tender.

In an attempt at reform, the (c) central bank introduced a "superdinar" pegged to the Deutsche mark at 1 to 1. In a little over three weeks, an amazing 15 zeros were dropped from the dinar! Inflation did fall from 312 million percent in January 1995 to a negative 6.2% in March, 1995. But without any serious fiscal reform, this proved to be an empty gesture, and by 1998, more than 70 percent of the superdinar's value was gone.

This scenario was a text-book case of a macroeconomic meltdown and a poignant example of great and grave macroeconomic irresponsibility. The economy was already destroyed long before the war began, and an entire generation had been robbed of its hard-earned savings by its own government.

ANSWERS AND HINTS

ARTICLE 6.1   TITO MBOWENI AND THE SOUTH AFRICAN RAND

(a) Central banks can artificially strengthen their currencies by actively purchasing domestic currency and selling foreign currency. (Alternatively, they can deliberately devalue their currencies by doing the opposite.) Such attempts to intervene in foreign exchange markets and to artificially change the value of the domestic currency are very short-term measures at best. Market pressures usually prove to be far more powerful than limited (and costly) central bank interventions.

(b) High real, or inflation adjusted, rates are crucial for attracting capital inflows. This fact implies low expectations of future inflation and risk. Expectations of future inflation can be lowered only if domestic and foreign individuals truly believe that deficits will remain sustainable and monetary policy will be tight and disciplined.

(c) Tito has tackled the most difficult elements. He has said "No" to government workers and officials. He is willing to risk unrest in the streets that will undeniably follow the privatizations and the resulting lay-offs. In short, difficult and unpopular fiscal reform is a reality under this regime.

(d) Bonds know best, and the bond market has rewarded Mr. Mboweni with lower long-term rates. By the Fisher effect (equation presented in the chapter) expectations of future inflation have fallen, given the government's grim determination to undertake serious fiscal and monetary reform. So while short-term rates may have risen due to the tight money policy, long-term rates have actually fallen thanks to lower expectations of future inflation!

ARTICLE 6.2   YUGOSLAVIAN DISASTER: A MACROECONOMIC CRIME

(a)   Just a comment here: the largest example of hyperinflation was the Hungarian Hyperinflation in 1945, discussed in the chapter.

(b)   With capital flight, domestic currency is sold in exchange for units of foreign (hard) currency. This downward pressure on the domestic currency results in a massive depreciation of the currency and its eventual collapse. All along, imports get progressively more expensive (and, eventually, prohibitive) for domestic residents as the domestic currency drops in value.

(c)   This is the relatively "easy" part. Introducing new currency or pegging to strong currency is relatively painless to initiate. The fiscal reform resulting in even greater unemployment is the bitter medicine.

---

[*] While high and rising long-term rates are usually manifested in hyperinflations, the main reason for including hyperinflation in this chapter along with long-term interest rates is to partition the discussion of inflation into two manageable chapters (5 and 6) instead of one very large and unwieldy chapter.

[1] Named after Irving Fisher who did seminal research in monetary theory in the early 1920s.

[2] Long-term debt ranges from 5 to 30 years in this chapter. A well-articulated and rich body of theoretical and empirical research exists in the finance and macroeconomics literature in the area of long-term rates and expectations. Our focus here, however, will be primarily on macroeconomic intuition as it pertains to expected inflation and risk. To this end, several simplifying assumptions have been made to highlight the macroeconomic policy-making aspects of this subject without sacrificing the theoretical integrity of the intertemporal models.

[3] For purely pedagogic reasons, we assume just a simple one-shot "interest rate" for the loan duration. In addition, the notion of rational expectations where all investors arrive at similar distributions of expected values given a common information set will be discussed later in Chapter 10.

[4] Once again, the discussion here is predominantly "macroesque". A finance text may have an entirely different focus. One must also note that several other scenarios, in addition to the two cited here, can explain an inverted yield curve.

[5] In fact, if these tycoons sought long-term finance from outside their giant conglomerates, they would have to do so in dollar- or yen-denominated bonds.

[6] In criteria (i) and (ii), if the deficit/GDP ratio fell uniformly towards 3% and if the debt/GDP ratio approached 60% "at a satisfactory rate," the country was eligible for EMU qualification.

[7] Article 6.2, at the end of this chapter, is a shocking and true account of the hyperinflation in Yugoslavia in the 1990s, under Slobodan Milosovic.

[8] In fact, the severe hyperinflation that ravaged Russia following the dissolution of the Soviet Union was such a serious and crippling problem that hoarders, if caught, would receive the death penalty.

[9] The author hastens to add that not all SOEs are uncompetitive and need to depend on State handouts. Snow Lotus Cashmere, Tsing Tao beer, Magic Panda cellular phones, etc., are high quality world players who also happen to be Chinese SOEs. These enterprises have successfully re-invented themselves to become competitive. Such exemplary SOEs, however, be they in China, the rest of Asia, Europe, or in the Americas, are unfortunately in the distinct minority. According to the Chinese government, its greatest challenge lies in reforming these SOEs and minimizing their drag on the economy without causing a resultant increase in unemployment to destabilize the country.

[10] A "general strike", designed to bring the country to a standstill, is illegal in the United States due to legislation passed by President Truman.

[11] During the early 1990s, when the Ukraine was ravaged by hyperinflation, the national mining sector (SOE) was consuming a shocking 50% of national tax revenues in price supports, subsidies, etc.

[12] China has been nowhere near a hyperinflation since the market liberalization of the 1980s, but nevertheless, the gradual privatization and overhaul of SOEs that happen to be inefficient remain among the government's top priorities. The policy has been to proceed gradually, unlike the Czech Republic and the former Soviet Union in the early 1990s when they performed large-scale national privatizations in just months. The Chinese government plans to merge efficient SOEs with ones that are failing. In this way, the morale, work ethic, and productivity of the "good" SOEs may be transferred to the less successful ones.

[13] Witness four new currencies in Brazil in six years in the 1980s.

[14] See Budget Deficits and Economic Performance, Chapter 7, Richard C.K. Burdekin and F.K. Langdana, 1992.

[15] This is an extremely intuitive and general explanation at this stage. More detail is reserved for later, after construction of the ISLM model.

[16] Instead of a fixed target rate, this could also be a range. For example, the central bank could ensure that B's currency fluctuates by only +/- 2% with that of A's.

[17] Please see the excellent article, "Yugoslavia Destroyed its own Economy," Steve Hanke, Wall Street Journal, 4/28/99, for more details.

7. ISLM: THE ENGINE ROOM

The preceding chapters have included definitions and analyses of discrete components and aspects of the macroeconomy. We discussed the goods market and the multiplier effect in some detail, before exploring overheating and soft and hard landings using AD-AS analysis. The previous chapter included a fairly detailed study of calamitous hyperinflations, and ended with a discussion of the intertemporal and expectational influences underlying long-term interest rates.

In all the previous chapters, almost as a recurring theme, the ISLM model has been referenced and anticipated. This chapter finally introduces "the engine room" and brings us to a stage where we can synthesize and simultaneously analyze all the components of the macroeconomy that have been treated as discrete elements up to this point.

For example, when we increased government spending to generate multiplier effects, *a la* Keynes, one of the effects was an increase in interest rates stemming from an increase in the demand for loanable funds due to additional government borrowing. The resulting negative effect on capital investment was, however, conspicuously absent in the goods-market-multiplier-effect story. The whole channel of influence was simply missing! In another example, while monetary expansion designed to jump-start an economy by decreasing interest rates and increasing capital investment was discussed, the effect of the resulting increase in national income on money demand, feeding back on interest rates, was also missing from our discrete money-market story. Not to mention the absence of the confidence terms, the tax rate, the effects of inflation on real money supply, and the influence of the global economy from the various analyses in preceding chapters.

The ISLM model—the mainstay of macroeconomic policy analysis—remedies the above shortcomings and provides us with a well-articulated and sophisticated model that incorporates all the missing "feedback" channels into the analysis of macroeconomic policy.

The following sections first derive and then explore the IS and LM curves. We will soon see that the IS and LM curves are simply the goods and money markets placed in (i,Y) space. The derivation will be followed by several full-scale macropolicy exercises introducing and utilizing the whole ISLM model.

7.1 THE IS CURVE

By definition, the IS curve is simply a plot in (i,y) space (with interest rates and GDP growth on the two axes) comprising points where the goods market is in equilibrium.

Ignoring the trade sector, the condition for equilibrium in the goods market is[1]:

$$Y = C + I + G \qquad (1)$$

Substituting the expressions discussed earlier for consumption, $C = \underline{C} + bY$ and capital investment, $I = \underline{I} - fi$, we obtain:

$$Y = (\underline{C} + bY) + (\underline{I} - fi) + G \qquad (2)$$

Simplifying, and solving for i, we get the IS curve[2]:

$$i = \underline{A}/f - Y(1-b)/f \qquad (3)$$

where $\underline{A}$ is simply a term for notational convenience comprising consumer confidence $\underline{C}$, investor confidence $\underline{I}$, and government spending, **G**.

On close examination we find equation (3) to be a straight line presented in slope-intercept form in **Figure 1** with intercept $(\underline{A}/f)$ and slope $(1-b)/f$.

Figure 1

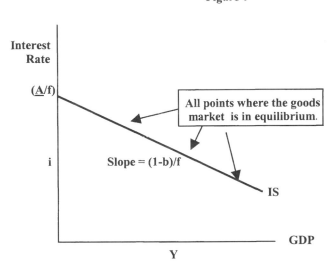

7.1.1   SOME IS EXERCISES

Now that we have derived the IS curve, some IS exercises are in order.

1. How will the IS curve respond to a collapse in investor confidence?
Very simply, as $\underline{I}$ falls, the intercept term $(\underline{A}/f)$ will fall. With no change in the slope (b and f are held constant), the IS undergoes a parallel drop from IS_0

132

to IS_1, as depicted in Figure 2. The opposite holds true: a surge in investor confidence (perhaps due to news of an impending tax cut, or some such uplifting announcement or expectation) will cause the IS to shift up from IS_0 to IS_2, again, without any change in slope.

2. How would the IS shift with a collapse in consumer confidence, C?
We get the same result. The intercept term falls, dropping the IS curve from IS_0 to IS_1 with no change in slope, since b and f are constant. Similarly, a surge in consumer confidence results in the IS shifting up from IS_0 to IS_2 with no change in slope.

3. How will changes in government spending affect the IS curve?
Increases in government spending G will also increase the intercept term (A/f), thereby shifting the IS up from IS_0 to IS_2. Cutbacks in government spending outlays will cause the IS to shift down from IS_0 to IS_1 as G drops, decreasing the intercept component. Once again, neither of these shifts will cause the slope of the IS to vary.

As summarized in **Figure 2**, any combinations of changes in consumer confidence, investor confidence, or government spending will result in a parallel shift in the IS curve.

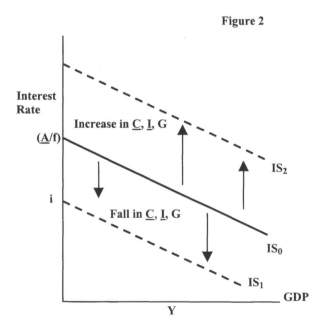

Figure 2

7.1.2   INTRODUCING TAXES INTO THE IS CURVE

Let **t** be some average tax rate prevailing in the economy under consideration.

We now define C_T as the after-tax consumption function given by:

$$C_T = \underline{C} + bY_D \tag{4}$$

Where Y_D is the disposable (after-tax) income defined as:

$$Y_D = Y(1 - t) \tag{4a}$$

Substituting this expression for after-tax income into (4), we obtain the consumption function incorporating a tax rate **t:**

$$C_T = \underline{C} + bY(1 - t) \tag{5}$$

Using the equilibrium condition for the goods market and the after-tax consumption function, we obtain the expression for the IS curve with taxes.

$$i = \underline{A}/f - [1 - b(1 - t)]Y/f \tag{6}$$

We can see that the intercept term $\underline{A}/f$ is exactly the same as with the IS_0 curve presented earlier in expression (3). But the slope in expression (6), $[1 - b(1 - t)]/f$, now includes the tax rate **t**. As displayed in **Figure 3**, the slope is now larger with the incorporation of the tax rate in IS_t.[3]

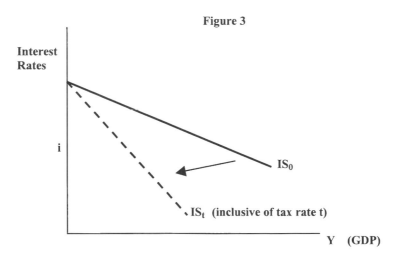

Figure 3

4. If the tax rate were to be increased from some $t_0=35\%$, to a higher rate $t_1=43\%$, how would the IS be affected?

An increase in the tax rate with all other variables held constant would increase the absolute value of the slope, making the IS steeper from $IS(t_0)$ to $IS(t_1)$. The intercept term, however, does not specifically incorporate the tax rate t, so in the absence of any additional macroeconomic changes, the intercept will remain the same. The final result here will be a clockwise pivot in the IS around the same intercept point as displayed in **Figure 4**.

A tax cut from t_0 to some lower rate t_2 (30%, perhaps) would decrease the absolute value of the slope term causing the IS to be flatter without changing the intercept term. In this case, the IS pivots counter-clockwise from $IS(t_0)$ to $IS(t_2)$ with the cut in taxes.

Figure 4

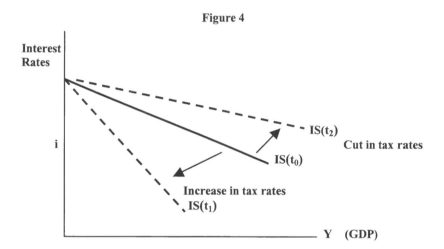

5. How would the IS react to increases in tax rates in an economy struggling to recover from a prolonged recession? Or how would an economy, nervously eyeing an approaching slowdown, react to tax increases?

This extremely important IS exercise will later help explain part of the problem faced by the Japanese economy in the early 2000s. After struggling to recover from years of stagnation and collapsed equity prices, the Japanese economy was showing a glimmer of recovery in the mid-1990s when the government, despite strong advice from policy makers world wide, increased tax rates in 1996 in a desperate attempt to increase tax revenues. Consumer and investor confidence, just about to stage a comeback, promptly went into free-fall!

A similar and certainly more traumatic case was experienced by the doubling of tax rates during the Great Depression in the United States (to be covered in a following chapter). More recently, in 1990-91, when state taxes in the US were driven up to boost tax revenues, a similar combination of tax increases related to confidence collapses was experienced. In 1990, the state tax increase in the US, in conjunction with several other factors, resulted in the largest 3-month drop in consumer confidence on record.

The IS curve in all these instances experiences a "double whammy" caused by increasing taxes at a time when the economy is exceedingly vulnerable to adverse macroeconomic policy. The intercept term falls as fragile consumer and investor confidence plunges, and the slope gets steeper due to the increase in the tax rate as shown in **Figure 5**, with IS shifting from IS_0 to IS_1.

The opposite may also hold true. The euphoria generated by a perfectly timed tax cut may cause the confidence terms to soar, lifting up the intercept, and causing the IS to flatten.

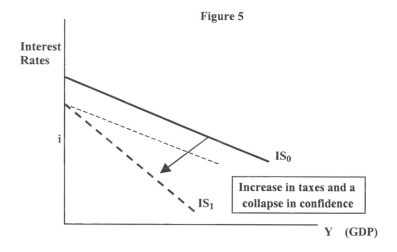

Figure 5

7.2 THE LM CURVE

The LM curve, by definition, is simply a curve in (i,y) space comprising all points where the money market is in equilibrium. The condition for equilibrium in the money market is simply given by:

Money supply = Money demand

Here money supply is defined as the real money supply in units of goods (as described earlier), and denoted M/P, where M is the nominal money stock denominated in local currency ($), and P is the price of a representative market basket denominated in $/good.

The central bank can indeed control the growth of the nominal money stock M, but the general price level P is endogenously determined within the economy.

Money demand for transactions is now defined as some positive function of national income and a negative function of interest rates:

Money demand = kY – hi (6)

where **k** is the sensitivity (elasticity) of money demand to a unit change in national income **Y**, and **h** is the sensitivity of money demand to a unit change in the interest rate **i**. Both **k** and **h** will be held constant here.

The greater the national income, **Y**, the greater the demand for transactions and hence for money, and the greater the interest rate **i**, the smaller the optimum cash balance demanded. The intuition here is that the transactions demand for money increases with greater national income **Y**, while the opportunity cost of carrying money in the form of non-interest bearing cash is the interest forgone by not investing it in some interest-bearing account, hence the negative sign before the interest term.

Equating real money supply with money demand, we obtain the equilibrium condition in the money market as:

M/P = kY - hi

Simplifying and solving for i, we obtain the **LM curve:**

i = (k/h)Y – (1/h)M/P (7)

Once again, this is an equation of a straight line with slope **(k/h)**, and negative intercept **– (1/h)M/P,** as presented in **Figure 6**.

Figure 6

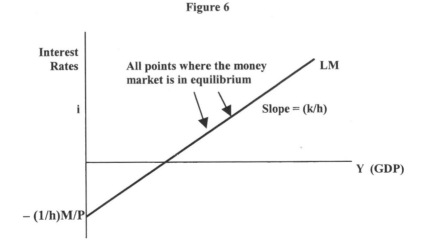

137

All points on this line represent points in (i,Y) space where the money market is in equilibrium. The slope is positive, and will be held fixed here since k and h are constants. The negative intercept is an algebraic construct, devoid of macroeconomic meaning *per se* but vitally important in determining how the LM shifts when the nominal money stock or prices change.

7.2.1   FACTORS THAT SHIFT THE LM

What will be the effect on the LM curve of an increase in the nominal money stock, M?

The change in M by the central bank will affect the intercept term. Since this is a negative term, the increase in M would lead the intercept to become a larger negative number (for example, from – 40 to –48), thereby decreasing the intercept. With no change in the slope (there is no M in the slope term), the result of an increase in M is a parallel downward, or rightward, shift in LM from LM_0 to LM_1.

A decrease in money growth (decrease in M) results in an upward (leftward) shift in LM and, once again, will not affect the slope as shown in Figure 7.

What will be the effect in the LM curve of an increase in the price level P (an increase in inflation)?[4]

An increase in the price level will cause the ratio M/P to fall, and given the minus sign that precedes the intercept term, we now find the intercept to be 'less negative' (increasing from say, –40 to –30). Again, with no change in the slope, an increase in P results in an upward, or leftward, shift in LM from LM_0 to LM_2.

A decrease in P would cause the LM to incur a parallel shift down (right) as the intercept term decreases in **Figure 7**.

Important "Rules" for Shifting LM

(1) **If the ratio (M/P) decreases due to either a decrease in M and/or an increase in P, the LM shifts up (to the left).**

(2) **If the ratio (M/P) increases due to an increase in M and/or a decrease in P, the LM shifts down (to the right).**
    Basically, if the real money supply (M/P), increases, the LM shifts right, and vice versa.

(3) **The slope does not change in either case.**

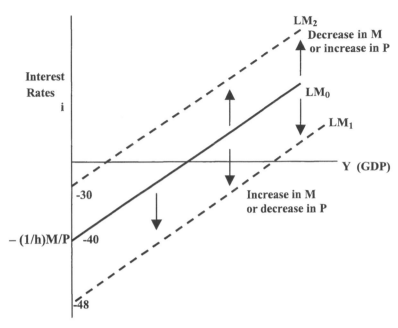

Figure 7

The stage is set for finally superimposing IS onto LM. The intersection point, E_0 at (i_0, Y_0), in **Figure 8** is defined as a point where both goods and money markets are simultaneously in equilibrium by virtue of the fact that (i_0, Y_0) lies on IS as well as LM. (Note that the LM axes have been normalized to only focus on non-negative interest rates.)

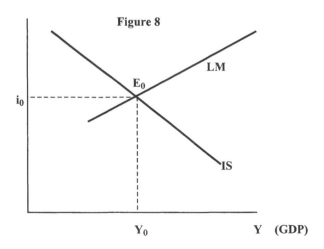

Figure 8

In an earlier chapter we synthesized both the goods and money markets to derive the aggregate demand (AD) in (P,Y) space. In terms of our ISLM framework, this simply translates to point (i_0, Y_0) in (i,Y) space transposing to the (P_0, Y_0) point on the aggregate demand (AD) in (P,Y) space as depicted in **Figure 9**.

Alternatively stated, every point on the aggregate demand curve has a corresponding point in (i,Y) space where both goods and money markets are simultaneously in equilibrium. Hence, the point (P_0, Y_0) corresponding to goods and money market equilibrium, (i_0, Y_0), "drops down" from the IS and LM intersection point.[5]

Figure 9

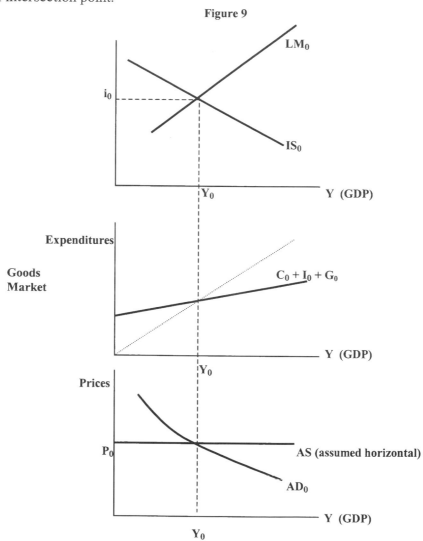

The goods market is presented below the (i,Y) space, and it feeds into the IS curve. The IS is, after all, nothing more that the goods market transposed into (i,Y) space.

The aggregate supply (AS) in (P,Y) space is at present assumed to be a horizontal line. This unrealistic horizontal AS is used in this early ISLM chapter purely to facilitate discussion. As we will see next, this clever construction suppresses any inflationary changes stemming from policy changes. This convenient horizontal AS curve will prove immensely beneficial to our early ISLM policy runs by allowing us to deftly abstract from any changes in P whatsoever. (In the next chapter, however, we shed the horizontal AS and incorporate the real thing. The ISLM will then be at its maximum potential for the closed economy case.)

7.3 ISLM-ADAS POLICY EXERCISES

The stage is finally set for large-scale macroeconomic policy simulations using the ISLM-ADAS model. The following sequence of steps will significantly simplify the analysis.

Survival Guide to ISLM-ADAS Policy Analysis

1. Make all moves in (i, Y) space first. Here any and all shifts/pivots in IS and shifts in LM are to be made. (A summary of all ISLM shifts is presented near the end of this chapter).
2. "Drop down" to (P,Y) space and adjust AD accordingly to conform to the Y just obtained in (i,Y) space. At this stage, we obtain the final values for the rate of inflation (P) and output growth (Y) in the economy in this particular exercise.
3. Ask the question, "Has P (rate of inflation) changed?"
    If the answer is **Yes**, then go back to (i,Y) space and adjust LM till the Y values "line up".
    If **No**, then deftly skip Step 3 and go to Step 4.
4. Close the goods market and the labor market (to be incorporated in the next chapter). Determine how the final values of consumption (C) and private capital investment (I) compare with the original values.
5. Present all your results boldly, step back from the diagrams, and analyze the implications of your results.

In "real time", steps 1 to 4 would all be taking place simultaneously and could span a period ranging from days to months depending on the policies in question, the stage of the economy in its business cycle, and consumer and investor expectations.

Armed with the Survival Guide, we are finally set to perform our first ISLM-ADAS policy exercise.

7.3.1   ISLM-ADAS POLICY EXPERIMENT I

The purpose is to determine the effect of an increase in government spending on GDP, inflation, private consumption, private capital investment, and interest rates. Once again, we assume a horizontal AS curve in Figure 10.

The economy is initially at some low GDP growth rate Y_0, presumably in need of macroeconomic stimulation from an increase in government spending from G_0 to G_1 in the form of infrastructure building, defense outlays, etc.

Initially, the interest rate is i_0, inflation is P_0, and the rates of private consumption and capital investment are C_0 and I_0.

Following the Survival Guide, **Step 1** occurs in (i,Y) space. As G increases, the IS shifts to the right (up) as the intercept term increases (as in the IS practice exercise). This shift is depicted in **Figure 10**.

Moving to **Step 2**, we now "drop down" to (P,Y) space so that the AD laterally shifts from AD_0 to AD_1. Remember, the AD is the representation of the intersection of IS and LM transposed to (P,Y) space.

With the completion of Step 2, we now obtain the final rates of inflation (P) and GDP growth (Y) in this exercise. Output growth has now increased from Y_0 to Y_1, but inflation is still unchanged at P_0![6] This result is due solely to the fact that the AS curve is assumed to be horizontal, with the specific purpose of artificially suppressing any changes in the rate of inflation. In **Step 3**, the answer to the question "Has P Changed?" is "No," and this allows us to skip to step 4.[7]

We now "mop up" in the goods market in **Step 4** by ensuring that the equilibrium in the goods market lines up with the final growth rate Y_1 in (i,Y) and (P,Y) spaces. Once again, the expenditure line, the IS curve, and the AD curve are all different representations that include the same goods market with different axes, and hence they must all "line up" at the same Y value.

Continuing with Step 4 in the goods market, we now determine if C_1 is greater than or less than C_0. We simply plug in the initial and final national income values, Y_0 and Y_1, into the consumption function.
The initial rate of private consumption is:
$C_0 = \underline{C} + bY_0$
And the final rate:
$C_1 = \underline{C} + bY_1$

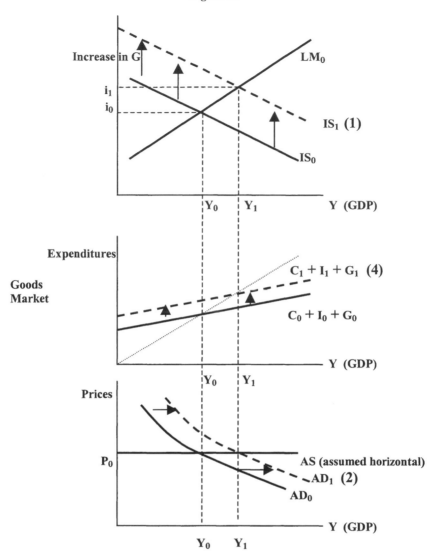

Figure 10

Since Y_1 is greater than Y_0 as seen in Figure 10, C_1 must therefore be greater than C_0. In other words, since private consumption is a function of national income, and given that we observe an increase in national income arising from the increase in government spending, private consumption must therefore increase.

143

What will be the effect on private capital investment I?

In this case, we examine the investment function to explore the change in capital investments due to changes in the interest rates that have gone up from i_0 to i_1.

Initially, capital investments are:

$I_0 = \underline{I} - fi_0$

Finally, after interest rates have been driven up by increased government borrowing, from i_0 to i_1, we obtain the level of capital investments as:

$I_1 = \underline{I} - fi_1$

Since interest rate i_1 is greater than i_0, and since this increase exerts a negative effect on capital investments, we conclude that capital investments fall from I_0 to I_1.

The **results** are presented in **Step 5**. The increase in government spending from G_0 to G_1 results in an increase in the rate of growth of output (Y). This result should actually be quite familiar as it has been discussed in detail in an earlier chapter—this is the **multiplier effect**, due to an increase in government spending. The increase in consumption from C_o to C_1 is, of course, the mechanism driving this multiplier. The decrease in private capital investment was also discussed in an earlier chapter, and is the **crowding out** due to an increase in bond-financed government spending. Here, government spending jump-started the economy by stimulating consumption, but the increase in G adversely affected private capital investment. The rate of inflation is still P_0, by construction of the horizontal AS.

7.3.2   ISLM-ADAS POLICY EXPERIMENT II

The central bank, under pressure to "do something" to spur growth, increases monetary growth and lowers interest rates. Show the effect on all key variables. Assume a horizontal AS curve.
Step 1:
LM shifts out in **Figure 11** as M_0 now increases to M_1 because the central bank increases monetary growth.[8] (The IS remains stationary since there is no change in G or in consumer or investor confidence in this example.)
Step 2:
We "drop down" to (P,Y) space and adjust AD until the Y_1 obtained in (i,Y) space lines up with the Y in (P,Y) space. We get the final GDP and price at this stage. Y_0 has increased to Y_1, and once again, thanks to the construction of the horizontal AS, there is no change in inflation; the rate is still P_0.
Step 3:
Has P changed? No. So we skip to Step 4.

Figure 11

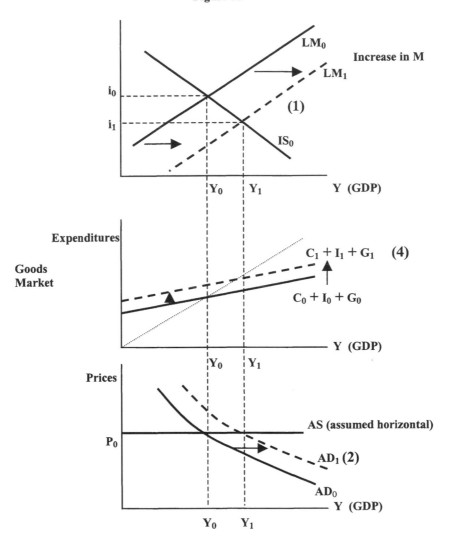

Step 4:
We adjust the goods market by shifting the expenditure line to the right so that the value of Y lines up to be consistent with Y_1.
Is $C_1 > C_0$?
Yes. Since $Y_1 > Y_0$, and since $C = \underline{C} + BY$, consumption will indeed increase as Y increases.
Is $I_1 > I_0$?
Yes. Since interest rates in this policy exercise fall from i_0 to i_1, capital investment given by $I = \underline{I} - fi$ will increase.

145

Results:

The increase in money supply and the resulting decrease in interest rates result in boosting GDP growth from Y_0 to Y_1, increasing consumption from C_0 to C_1, and increasing private capital investment from I_0 to I_1. Inflation is deliberately held constant here at P_0 by construction of the AS.

Policy Challenge in China

After successfully cooling down an overheated economy in the mid-1990s, policy makers in China were faced with a more daunting problem—to prevent the soft landing from going "hard". With GDP growth "officially" hovering at 8 percent, barely in accordance with the "bao ba" ("guaranteed" 8 %) growth policy by the early 2000s, policy makers were desperately searching for ways to re-ignite growth.

However, repeated infusions of mammoth amounts of government spending on infrastructure in the early to mid-2000s did not yield the much-anticipated and hoped-for multiplier effects. In fact, the multiplier effect was negligible at best. How then does one explain this Chinese conundrum?

The explanation lies in the value of the low Chinese MPC. China is essentially a country with two marginal propensities of consumption. The Eastern seaboard with the high-growth zones of development and including the big cities of Beijing and Shanghai, boasts higher MPCs than the rest of the country where the MPC is very low.

In fact, the extreme Western provinces perhaps have a third and lowest tier of MPC. This is hardly surprising given the marked difference between disposable incomes and employment and basic living standards between rural Western and Central China, relative to the dynamic and more prosperous urban Eastern Seaboard.

Lower MPCs imply lower multiplier effects from the expression:

Multiplier = 1/(1-MPC) = 1/(1-b) where b is the MPC.

This explains why an MPC of, say, 0.1, will have a multiplier effect of only 1.1. An increase in government spending equal to 1 million units of currency will result in overall GDP increasing only to $1.1 million units, for example. This makes Keynesian jump-starting extremely challenging. Until the consumers/citizens in Central and Western China truly believe that better times are ahead, stop hoarding any increase in incomes into their savings, and spend more on consumption, multipliers will remain low.

Diagrammatically (Figure 12) this translates to Chinese IS curves (for the Western and Central regions) being relatively steeper relative to, say, the US type IS curve, since the slope of the IS is 1/b, with b being the MPC. The same vertical increase in the intercept due to the same increase in G will result in a far larger change in Y for a flatter US type IS curve relative to that for the steeper Chinese IS. In Figure 12, the multiplier effect for the US is denoted $\Delta Y(USA)$, while that for the Chinese IS curve is $\Delta Y(China)$.

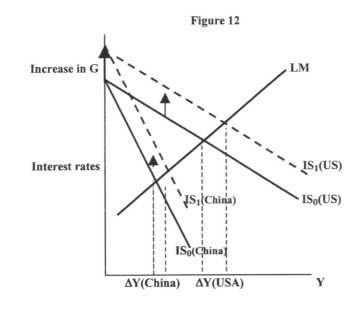

Figure 12

7.3.3   ISLM-ADAS POLICY EXERCISE III: AN INCREASE IN TAX RATES

Policy makers in Country K are very concerned. The budget deficit has reached unprecedented proportions. There is a general sense that something "has to be done" to remedy this. Country K has been in the throes of a long recession and is just about to announce its first mildly positive GDP growth.[9] Against this backdrop, policy makers decide that it is time to drastically increase tax rates to generate higher tax revenues, and bring the budget deficit down. (Assume a horizontal AS curve.)

Show the effects on all key macro variables and, in particular, focus on the possible final effect on the budget deficit. Hint: Tax revenues, T, are given by:

$T = tY$

where t is the average national tax rate and Y is the level of national income.

The analysis is presented in **Figure 13**.

Step 1:

Here IS pivots clockwise with the increase in tax rates. In addition, a significant tax increase coming on the heels of an economy just struggling to

147

crawl out of recession will, in all likelihood, traumatize consumer and investor confidence. Both confidence terms, $\underline{C}$ and $\underline{I}$, will fall. The final result on the IS curve is a clockwise pivot due to the tax increase as well as a shift down (to the left) due to the decline in the intercept caused by the fall in confidence triggered by increasing taxes at such an inappropriate time.

Figure 13

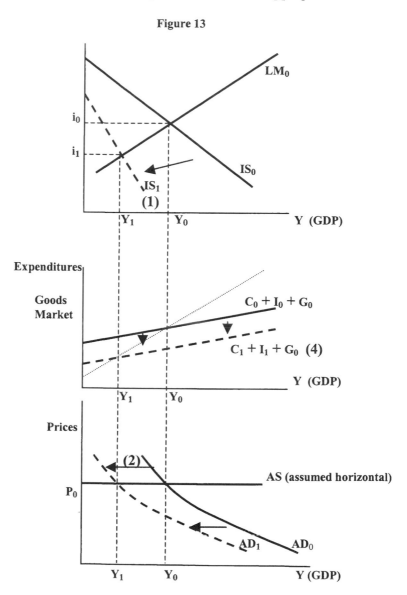

The LM will not budge since there is no change in M (or P). The ISLM equilibrium is at Y_1, and i_1.

Step 2:
We drop down to (P,Y) space and adjust AD to the left until the Y values are consistent at Y_1. The final GDP growth here has now fallen to a lower Y_1, with prices artificially held constant at P_0.

Step 3:
Has inflation changed? No. So we skip to step 4.

Step 4:
Adjust the expenditure line in the goods market so that its equilibrium is at Y_1, consistent with the other two diagrams.

Is $C_1 > C_0$?

No. Since $Y_1 < Y_0$, $C_1 < C_0$ too, by plugging into the consumption function. In addition, consumption falls further because consumer confidence, $\underline{C}$, has also collapsed due to the tax increases. Consumption here is hit by a "double whammy" of lower disposable income (Y_1) and collapsing confidence.

Is $I_1 > I_0$?

It may appear that capital investments should increase since interest rates fell to i_1, but on closer examination this result is unclear since investor confidence, $\underline{I}$, has also collapsed due to the tax increases. In fact, investor confidence, $\underline{I}$, is even more sensitive to current and expected tax increases than $\underline{C}$!

The decline in interest rates in isolation would increase I, but in conjunction with the collapsing confidence the result is now ambiguous—technically it depends on which influence on I is larger. Empirically, however, the influence of $\underline{I}$ tends to "win out". If the macroeconomic outlook looks dismal and further tax increases are imminent, no amount of interest rate lowering will induce investors to borrow for additional capital investment. This situation is known as a **"liquidity trap"** in which no amount of monetary creation and lowering of interest rates—even down to zero—may induce an increase in capital investment if investor confidence has collapsed. Examples abound, from the Great Depression in the US to Japan and Argentina in the early 2000s.

Results: GDP, interest rates, consumption and capital investments fall, and there is no change in inflation by construction of the AS.

7.3.4   ISLM-ADAS POLICY EXERCISE IV: SIMULTANEOUS INCREASES IN GOVERNMENT SPENDING AND MONETARY GROWTH ("FINE-TUNING")

Country K increases government spending to spur growth, but it wants to avoid "crowding out" private capital investment. Hence, it also increases M to lower rates to offset the interest rate effects of the increase

in G. Show the effect on all key macrovariables. Once again, assume a horizontal AS curve.

Figure 14

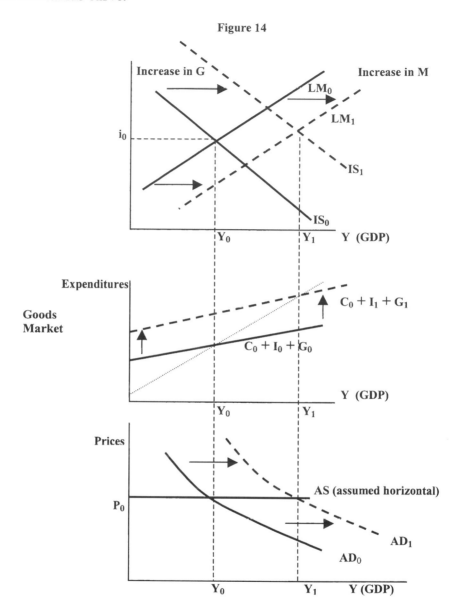

Step 1:
As G increases, IS shifts up (to the right) as depicted in **Figure 14**. And as M is increased, LM also shifts to the right. Here the shifts are coordinated to leave the interest rate unchanged. Note that just the IS shift without an
150

accompanying LM shift would have caused interest rates to rise (as in exercise I) and to crowd out capital investment.

Step 2:
Drop down to (P,Y) space and align the Y1 values by shifting AD. GDP growth has now increased to Y1 and inflation is still artificially held at P0.
Step 3:
Skip since no change in inflation, and go to Step 4.
Step 4:
Adjust the expenditure line in the goods market to be consistent with GDP Y1.

Is C1>C0?

Yes, since $Y_1>Y_0$. By plugging this into the consumption function, we can conclude that $C_1>C_0$.

Is $I_1>I_0$?

No change in capital investments here since interest rates are deliberately left unchanged by the joint fiscal-monetary policy mix adopted here. We assume no change in confidence.
Note:
Depending on the relative rightward shifts in IS and LM, we technically have an ambiguous effect on interest rates and, hence, on capital investment. The final interest rates could be higher or lower than i_0, depending on the magnitude of the IS shift to the right, relative to that of the LM. In all cases where G and M simultaneously increase, however, Y will increase.
Results:
GDP growth increases from Y_0 to Y_1, consumption increases from C_0 to C_1. There was no change in interest rates and, hence, no crowding out of capital investment by policy design in this particular example. Finally, we found no change in inflation by construction of the horizontal aggregate supply curve (AS).

While the primary reason for incorporating the horizontal AS in this chapter has been the deliberate suppression of changes in P, the actual shape of the AS is not completely without "real world" merit. Recalling the discussion on demand-pull inflation from an earlier chapter, Stage 1 inflation was that experienced in the early stages of a macroeconomic recovery. The economy was finally beginning to turn around, presumably after some effective demand-side stimulus, and was characterized by substantial excess labor supply (hence, no wage pressure), excess plant capacity, and raw materials in abundance.

This Stage 1 was characterized by rapidly growing GDP (Y_0 to Y_1) and no significant increase in the rate of inflation (still P_0), and these results are consistent with the AS curve used in this chapter.

7.4 SUMMARIZING IS AND LM SHIFTS

The **Table 7.1** describes the shifts in IS and LM due to changes in each of the factors in the left-hand column <u>individually</u>, with all others held unchanged.

Table 7.1

Summarizing IS-LM Shifts		
	IS	LM
Increase in G	Shifts Right (up)	No Change
Decrease in G	Shifts Left (down)	No Change
Increase in Tax Rate	Pivots Clockwise	No Change
Cut in Tax Rates	Pivots Cntr-clockwise	No Change
Increase in Confidence	Shifts Right (up)	No Change
Decrease in Confidence	Shifts Left (down)	No Change
Increase in Money Growth	No Change	Shifts Right
Decrease in Money Growth	No Change	Shifts Left
Increase in Inflation (P)	No Change	Shifts Left
Decrease in Inflation (P)	No Change	Shifts Right

7.5 THE GLOBAL IS
In the following chapters, the IS curve will abstract from the trade sector. However, smaller economies with greater trade sectors relative to their domestic GDPs (Singapore's trade sector including re-exports is well over 100% of GDP) would certainly need to implement an IS that includes exports and imports. A "global IS" is therefore briefly overviewed below.

7.5.1 Global IS: A Brief Overview

Including the [Export-Import] term in the expression for equilibrium in the goods market, we obtain:

Y = C + I + G + (Exports – Imports)   **(1a)**

Proceeding with the IS derivation, the **global IS curve**, incorporating the trade sector, is:

$$i = [\underline{A}/f + (\textbf{Exports-Imports})] - Y(1\text{-}b)/f \qquad (3a)$$

In economies such as Singapore, Thailand, and Taiwan, for example, where their trade sectors are significant portions of their respective GDPs, the IS curve must indeed incorporate exports and imports to allow any meaningful macroeconomic policy analysis.

In this case, the net exports term, (Exports-Imports), is now also a component of the intercept term. As depicted in the global IS in **Figure 15**; the intercept is now [**A**/f + (**Exports-Imports**)].

Figure 15

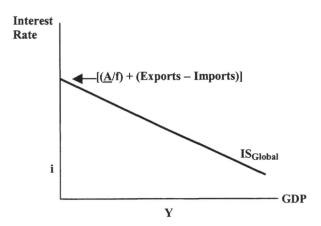

An increase in exports, stemming from strongly growing foreign economies with healthy national incomes, would increase foreign demand for domestic exports and cause the IS_{Global} to shift up. In Figure 16, the domestic income of the trade-dependent country (Singapore again, and to some extent, even China) is denoted as Y. The income of its big trading partner (the US, for example) is denoted as Y*. Most of Singapore's electronics and IT exports (89%) go to the US. As the US economy soars—as Y* increases—Singapore's exports will increase, since exports are a positive function of foreign national income.[10] This translates to a rightward shift in IS_{Global} to $IS_{Global1}$.

A recession in a large foreign economy, on the other hand, would cause foreign national income to fall, thus resulting in a decrease in foreign demand for the domestic country's exports. In this case, as displayed in **Figure 16**,

153

exports would fall, thereby decreasing the intercept term and causing IS_{Global} to shift down to $IS_{Global2}$.

Hence, recessions as well as booms can, to some extent, be transmitted globally via the linkages of exports and imports to national incomes.

Figure 16

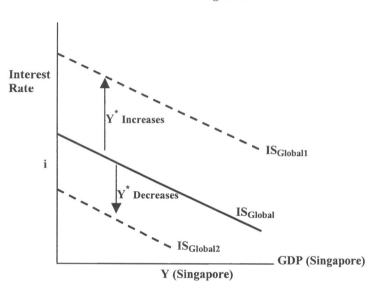

Of course, another factor causing shifts in the global IS is the exchange rate. A depreciation, or devaluation of the exchange rate, may make exports "cheaper" in the near term.[11] This is typically accomplished by an increase in domestic monetary growth that weakens the currency by increasing its supply and thus makes it "cheaper" in the global foreign exchange markets. Domestic residents now find their exports to be "cheaper", and their imports now become more "expensive". An appreciation (strengthening) of the domestic currency serves to make exports "more expensive" to foreigners but imports "cheaper" to domestic residents.

A currency devaluation is depicted in **Figure 17** by simultaneous shifts in the global IS and the LM. The IS shifts to the right as exports increase, and the LM also shifts to the right as, after all, it is the monetary expansion that results in the weakening of the currency (the devaluation) in the first place. The result presented below is a <u>short-term effect</u> at best, given the eventual increase in inflation, not included in Figure 17. Unfortunately, the short-term results, an increase in national GDP from Y_0 to Y_1 accompanied by an increase in national exports can be dangerously misleading.

Governments facing re-election may be tempted to pressure central banks to devalue the currency and spur the economy. Unfortunately for citizens, the eventual and inevitable increases in inflation will occur with a lag—after the election. In Europe, after many cycles of devaluations followed by increases in inflation that negated any temporary increases in GDP and exports, the European economies finally decided to peg their currencies to the German currency (and, hence, to German monetary discipline) to preclude any pressure from European governments on their respective central banks to devaluate. The first such attempt was the Exchange Rate Mechanism (the ERM) begun in 1979, where the member countries' currencies were pegged to the D-Mark, followed by the current Eurozone, wherein they relinquish control of their domestic monetary growth to one common European central Bank (ECB) and one common currency, the euro, thereby making devaluations impossible. The ERM and the euro will be revisited in greater detail in Chapter 11.

Figure 17

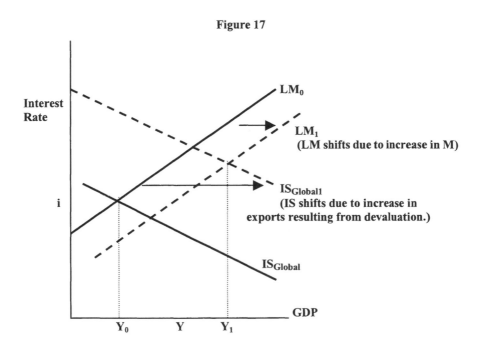

Summarizing factors that shift the global IS[12]:

Changes in domestic **government spending, confidence and tax rates** affect the global IS in much the same way as the closed-economy IS. In addition, increases in **foreign national income (Y*)** shift the global IS to the right, and vice versa. **Devaluations**, or deliberate weakening of the domestic exchange rates, shift the global IS to the right (along with the LM), and revaluations shift both global IS and LM to the left.

The next chapter incorporates our first "real" AS curve; inflation enters the ISLM-ADAS analysis. But first, the following question-answer format followed by simulated articles should, once again, assist in reviewing the chapter material and clearing up any lingering questions pertaining to the introduction of the "engine room".

7.6 DISCUSSION QUESTIONS

1. **When we increase government spending, G, why do we make the first move in (i,y) space instead of shifting the expenditure line in the goods market, which incorporates G so explicitly?**

Once again, the sequence recommended by the Survival Guide is purely for convenience. In actuality, all the changes from solid to dashed lines are taking place simultaneously in all the diagrams over a period of time. Furthermore, the IS curve really <u>is</u> the goods market. It is, after all, one and the same thing—the IS line is the goods market represented with different axes, namely, the **i** and **Y** axes.

2. **In the example done earlier, when confidence fell following a tax hike, we had to incorporate this into the analysis. In other words, we had to "know" that confidence would fall. Shouldn't the model be giving us that as a result?**

A more mathematical model would indeed incorporate confidence as an endogenous variable, explicitly dependent on future tax rates, etc. (See Burdekin and Langdana, 1999). In this volume, however, we focus on the ready applicability of our analyses and hold confidence exogenous. In other words, we specify if confidence is headed up or down as in ISLM Exercise 3, and then let the model yield the final effects on Y, interest rates, C, I, etc.

3. **Could the analysis all be done mathematically? And, if so, how would this affect the results which are ambiguous and depend on the relative magnitudes of two (or more) shifts?**

Yes, all the equations could be solved simultaneously, preferably using matrix algebra and Cramer's Rule. The ambiguous terms would remain so; we would have results with algebraic terms whose signs are dependent on relative combinations of elasticities.

156

4. The ISLM-ADAS seems well defined and straightforward. Then why are there so many conflicting analyses and policy prescriptions?

Unfortunately, the AS curve is not nearly as conveniently "well-behaved" as in this chapter. In the following chapters we will encounter two "real world" AS curves with fundamentally different policy prescriptions and implications. In fact, in some economies, both will be found to be consistent! And this will be shown to be primarily the source of most of the macroeconomic confusion.

Please critique/explain the underlined sentences and phrases in the following simulated articles using an ISLM-ADAS framework incorporating a horizontal AS curve.

ARTICLE 7.1   A MONETARY PUZZLE IN NIPPONICA

Ishihara Kawanomoto, Far East Economica

Policy makers in the Republic of Nipponica are confounded. Since last year, **(a)** monetary policy has been eased substantially, with interest rates virtually at zero percent. And yet, there is no sign of growth within sight. A sense of **(b)** defeatism and gloom pervades the country, particularly in the headquarters of the ruling party headed by Fujimoto Agaji.

The sense of despondency isn't just confined to Nipponica but afflicts the whole region. The **(c)** neighboring countries of DeSarawa, Kwanton, and Uwaji Baru are all in various states of recession or slowdown as their exports sectors have basically shut down due to the sharp decline in Nipponica's economy and in its citizens' desire for imports.

The government seems to be at a loss, and analysts around the globe aren't faring any better. "This is most confusing," says Brian Perry of Hong Kong Global Consulting, "The monetary stimulus isn't jump-starting Nipponica's output at all. **(d)** We should be seeing at least a Stage 1 recovery—but instead, we see more recession!"

Shreedhar Venkatesh of KD-South Asia finds that, "The fact that the real estate sector and the stock markets of Nipponica have both been 'corrected' by over 40 percent during the last year has to figure in the equation."

When this reporter interviewed commuters at Wanfuji Station in Wanju, the capital of Nipponica, he heard several possible explanations.

Janet Hara, Director of Marketing for a medical electronics firm explained, "my company **(e)** just laid off 250 workers last week. Every family has at least one family member who has lost his or her job.

"If Akaji doesn't fix this economy, he is out!" Kim Willys, owner of Willys Custom Landscaping in Wanju said. "So what if interest rates are zero? I don't know of **(f)** anyone who would buy a house in this climate. What's the point? My business is dead."

As the gloom deepens in Nipponica and its neighboring countries, so does the puzzle. **(g)** Why are the lower rates not jump-starting the "engine" of the economy?

ARTICLE 7.2   DISCIPLINE OR DISASTER?

Rebecca Barclay, New Orleans Weekly News

Senator Jenkins' campaign has now "gone national". Two weeks ago, he was Senator Who? And now, as the nation gets infected with Jenkins Fever, both major parties have hustled to form Action Committees to deal with this new challenge from "Contender Jenkins" and his grassroots movement that threatens to sweep over them like a veritable prairie fire.

"No, of course we aren't scared," said Todd Gakk, the President's chief political aide, "but we aren't going to ignore what's going on."

'What's going on' is that Senator Jenkins and his rallying cry of Discipline! Discipline! Discipline! has resonated in the country as none other over the last several elections. Last night in Bridgewater, New Jersey, an expected audience of 3,000 turned into a crowd of over 6,000! Over the weekend in Blacksburg, Virginia, a planned rally for 2,500 drew over 10,000, with people driving five hours from Washington, DC!

Here is the Jenkins' Message:
1. "We need government discipline. A severe reduction in government spending is long overdue".
2. "We need fiscal discipline. Let's raise taxes until all this deficit and all this debt is paid for in the next two years". (Deafening roar of approval).
3. "We need monetary discipline. Greed must be stamped out. Our greed and our excesses in the stock market and in real estate have caused immense overvaluation. The central bank must burst this bubble by tightening money and raising rates....."

4. "Discipline is the key!" (Thunderous applause).

However, all aren't on board. At the National MBA Conference in Denver, Colorado, Juan Pereira found Jenkins' policies to be "Puzzling. I see them causing recession! Could my analysis be wrong or is Jenkins' policy agenda totally faulty?" he wonders. Lori Graham, an MBA student from a huge Midwestern university, feels the same way. "I see the Discipline agenda to be strongly contractionary—no doubt in my mind!" Ricard Hu, an Executive MBA from a US program based in Singapore, is even stronger in his denunciation. "These policies remind me of the erroneous policies recommended by the IMF to the Asian countries soon after the 1997-98 crises—totally contractionary and totally wrong!"

So, is Jenkins recommending Discipline or Disaster? Hopefully, as the analysis continues, the hard macroeconomic truth will emerge. In the meantime, the disciples flock by the thousands to the man of the hour.

Use ISLM-ADAS to analyze Senator Jenkins' policies. Remember that the results here are contingent on the horizontal AS curve.

ANSWERS AND HINTS

ARTICLE 7.1   A MONETARY PUZZLE IN NIPPONICA

(a) Show the LM shifting to the right with an increase in M and a resultant decrease in equilibrium interest rates in ISLM space.

(b) Sounds like the confidence terms, $\underline{C}$ and $\underline{I}$, are falling. IS should be shifting left. Clearly, the net effect has been a final drop in equilibrium GDP—Y has been falling. Interest rates are very low due to the combination of a shift in LM to the right and a shift in IS to the left. The AD has shifted significantly to the left to "line-up" with the lower Y in (I,Y) space.

(c) Using a separate ISLM-ADAS framework for the combined neighboring countries, incorporate a global IS, and show how and why Nipponica's falling national income (Y*) affects the economies of its neighbors. That is, this time the "domestic" economies (Y) in the ISLM analysis are Nipponica's neighbors.

(d) Mr. Perry is neglecting the effect of the leftward shift in IS due to the falling confidence in Nipponica. The huge drop in the stock market, referred to by Mr. Venkatesh, has undoubtedly traumatized the confidence terms.

(e) Increasing signs of unemployment are disastrous for consumer and investor confidence.

(f) Capital investments increase with lower interest rates, but fall with a collapse in investor confidence, I. In fact, the influence of investor confidence—especially when it is falling—is usually the dominant effect on capital investment. It seems that Nipponica may be in the throes of a "liquidity trap". Low interest rates, even close to zero, may not help spur capital investment if confidence has hit rock bottom.

(g) Show how a leftward shift in IS due to a collapse in confidence is negating the effects of the rightward shift in LM caused by the monetary expansion.

---

[1] IS and LM get their names from Keynes' early notation. "IS" stands for investment=savings and "LM" is adopted from his notation for money supply (M) and money demand (L).

[2] The terms **b** and **f** are held constant. As a quick review, from previous chapters we know that **b** is the marginal propensity to consume, while **f** is the sensitivity (elasticity) of capital investment to changes in interest rates.

[3] The absolute value of the slope is taken here. By plugging in some value for t (say, 0.40 for a 40% tax rate), the comparison between slopes can easily be made.

[4] At this stage, we use 'change in price level' interchangeably with 'change in inflation'. When the entire ISLM is put together later in the chapter, we will revisit exactly in what form the data pertaining to P, Y, M, etc., are presented and analyzed.

[5] This somewhat non-academic description of the link between the point on the AD and its equivalent point at the intersection of IS and LM will prove immensely useful when ISLM policy exercises are conducted.

[6] Please note that changes in endogenous variables, as in Y_0 to Y_1, are changes in rates of growth. Y_0 could be 3% GDP growth, while Y_1 could be 3.9%, for example. When P_0 stays "the same", this means that the rate of inflation remains unchanged. If P_0 is 2%, then this means that prices are still growing at an average rate of 2% at the end of the policy exercise.

[7] The rate of inflation is endogenous and will indeed change in the following chapter when the horizontal AS curve is abandoned for a more realistic one.

[8] The precise mechanisms by which central banks actually increase money supply and, hence, lower interest rates will be discussed in Chapter 11.

[9] Recall from a previous chapter that recessions, by themselves, exacerbate budget deficits (G-T). The tax base (T) shrinks as national income falls, and government spending (G), in the form of transfer payments (unemployment insurance, welfare, etc.), increases as jobs dwindle.

[10] Along similar lines, Singapore's imports will be a positive function of its own national income, Y.

[11] This is most definitely a very short-term perspective. Devaluations are inevitably inflationary; the increase in monetary growth will finally increase inflation, thereby negating any short-term increases in exports. In fact, it was this vicious cycle of devaluations followed by bouts of rising inflation and wages that prompted most of the countries in the European Union to form the Eurozone by adopting one common highly disciplined monetary policy. This topic will be revisited in Chapter 11.

[12] This discussion of "factors that shift the global IS" in addition to the ones that shift the closed-economy IS cites only two key determinants of shifting, namely, changes in foreign income and devaluation. Other factors also shift the global IS, such as tastes and preferences for imports and exports, etc. These are not included here at this time.

8. THE CLASSICAL MODEL

In this chapter, changes in the rate of inflation are finally incorporated into the ISLM-ADAS analysis. This raises the overall level of sophistication of our analysis from Chapter 7 by incorporating a "real world" aggregate supply curve into the ISLM analysis. The stage is also set for an explanation of paradigm shifts between Keynesian and supply-sider models.

We begin by deriving our first fully articulated AS curve: the aggregate supply curve adopted by the classical economists. This AS was the centerpiece of macroeconomic policy in the United States through the Great Depression and into the early 1930s.

The following table presents a time chart tracing the major changes in models—paradigm shifts—that have occurred in the US economy (and generally in developed economies) since the early part of the last century. Each of the models chosen to "characterize" a period of US macroeconomic history indicates a clear and strong consensus on the part of policy makers (the incumbent government) and researchers regarding "the" operative macroeconomic model in question. In cases where there is no clear consensus model, either from the national policy or research perspective, both models are listed as in the third column of **Table 1**.

Each of these models will be described and analyzed in the following chapters chronologically, beginning with the classical model. In periods in which both models simultaneously exist and vie for center stage, both models will be analyzed. Later, (in Chapter 10) after discussing how two models can indeed legitimately coexist, the reader will have to choose the paradigm that, in his/her opinion, best describes the economy in question.

Table 1

Till Early 1930s	Late 1930s to Late 1970s	Late 1970s to present
Classical Model	Keynesian Model	**Developed Economies** Supply-side (rational expectationist) leading to the New Economy since the mid-1990s **Or** New Keynesian **Emerging Economies** New Keynesian

8.1 CLASSICAL AGGREGATE SUPPLY: DERIVATION

Before the Classical AS curve can be diagrammatically derived, two additional concepts must be introduced, namely (i) the production function and (ii) the labor market.

The economy's production function is given:

$$Y = f(k,n) \qquad\qquad (8.1)$$

where output Y is some function of capital k and employment n. We hold the economy's capital stock k constant at $\underline{K}$.

This makes output supply simply a function of its only variable, employment, given by:

$$Y = f(n) \qquad\qquad (8.2)$$

The production function, a plot of the output produced in (Y, n) space is presented in **Figure 1**.

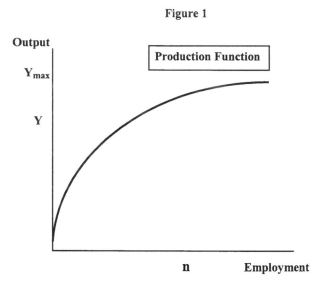

Figure 1

The convex shape of the production function in Figure 1 is attributed to the Law of Diminishing Marginal Returns. With capital held fixed, as employment increases, output increases too. After a point, however, additional increases in employment result in increasingly smaller increments in output. In other words, the production function begins to flatten out, resulting in its characteristic convex shape.

After all, with capital stock (the number of machines, for example) held fixed, simply increasing workers will increase output only up to some finite upper limit (Y_{max} in Figure 1), at which point all the capital stock is being maximized (the machines are all being used at maximum capacity).

Dovetailing the production function is the labor market, presented in Figure 2. Labor demand and supply are functions of the **real wage** defined as W/P, where W is the nominal wage (in units of currency, $), and P is the price of a representative market basket, denominated in $/good. The real wage W/P, the ratio of the two, is therefore denominated in units of goods. In other words, the real wage is the real purchasing power of the nominal paycheck W.

This formalizes the increase in the real purchasing power of one's paycheck upon being transferred (by one's parent company) at the same salary (W) to another part of the country where the cost of living (P)—real estate and insurance, for example—is significantly lower. In this example, the real wage W/P, would increase, and vice versa.

Labor demand intuitively increases as real wages fall (the demand for labor slopes "down"), while labor supply increases as the real wage increases (slopes "up") as in **Figure 2**.[1] Here the labor market is in equilibrium at a rate of employment n_0 and real wage W_0/P_0.

Figure 2

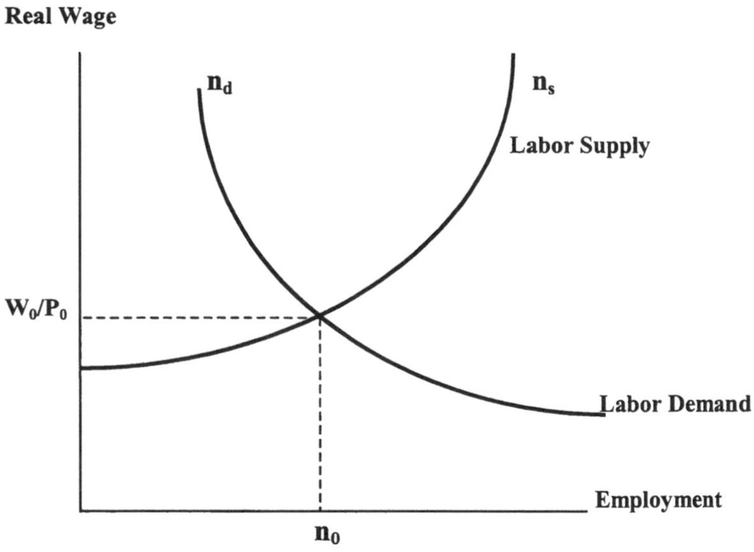

The crucial assumption made by the classical economists is that nominal wages (W) and prices (P) are fully flexible. That is, if inflation were to increase by say, 3 %, nominal wages, by this definition, would also rise by the same amount (3%). This would in turn leave the ratio, the real wage W/P, unchanged. The same holds true for drops in inflation. Here, by the classical assumption of full wage-price flexibility, nominal wage growth would <u>also</u> <u>fall</u> by the same percentage, thereby leaving the ratio unchanged.

This crucially important assumption will "drive" the derivation and slope of the classical AS curve and will be fundamentally responsible for the implications of fiscal and monetary policy in the classical world. Later, the sudden collapse of this assumption will bring us to our first major (and calamitous) paradigm shift. But first, we derive the classical AS below in **Figure 3**.

Figure 3

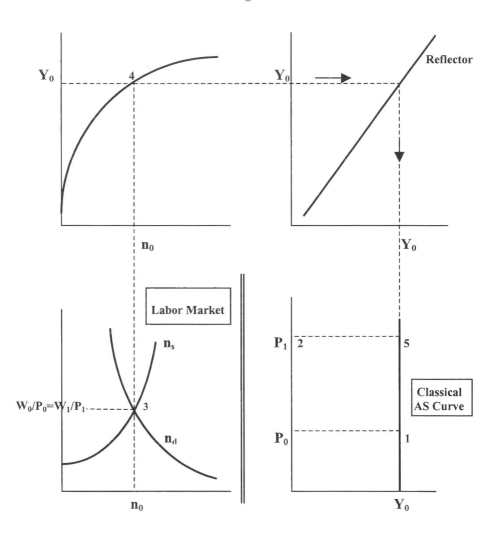

Examining Figure 3, the two figures on the left are the production function on the top and the labor market below. Equilibrium employment in the labor market at n_0 is consistent with employment n_0 in the production function since the rates of employment in these two diagrams must "line up". The initial GDP is Y_0. The figure in the top right corner with the Y-Y axes is simply a "reflector" designed to "reflect" values of Y emanating from the production function down by 90 degrees into (P,Y) space in the bottom right of Figure 3, in which the Classical AS is about to be derived.

Derivation Sequence
(the numbers in Figure 3 match the following steps):
1. The first step in the classical AS derivation is to plot the initial "given" point. Initially, GDP is at Y_0 and the price level is at P_0, and this point (P_0, Y_0) is plotted in (P,Y) space.[2]
2. We now allow P_0 to increase to P_1. To keep the derivation simple, let P_0 increase by, say, 50 percent to P_1 By the classical assumption, since nominal wages W are fully flexible, W_0 must also increase by 50 percent to W_1. The real wage is consequently unchanged with $W_1/P_1 = W_0/P_0$.
3. Since the real wage is unchanged, equilibrium employment (in the labor market) is still at n_0.
4. With employment unchanged, we see that n_0 employment still corresponds to GDP Y_0 in the production function. So, even when P_0 increased to P_1 in Step 2, GDP remained unchanged at Y_0.
5. We plot the new higher price P_1 and the unchanged GDP, Y_0, into (P,Y) space and join this point to the initial point (P_0, Y_0) in order to diagrammatically obtain the classical AS curve in Figure 3

The existence of the double-lined "firewall" between the lower two plots is included to emphasize that the vertical axis in the labor market is different from that in the diagram in the bottom right corner in which the AS has been derived. The "firewall" ensures that lateral transposition of macroeconomic variables does not erroneously take place between these two diagrams.

Also, as in earlier diagrams, all variables are expressed implicitly as rates of growth. For example, Y_0 is the initial rate of growth of GDP, while n_0 is the rate of growth of employment, and so on.

Putting all the markets together for the first time in **Figure 4**, the ISLM (i,y) space, the goods market diagram, and the AD curve are identical to those from Chapter 7. The new additions are the production function, the labor market, and, most important, the new, vertical, classical aggregate supply curve. The horizontal AS curve from the previous chapter, introduced for pedagogical reasons, is now replaced by the vertical Classical AS curve.

The crucial assumption driving this economy is the full flexibility of nominal wages and prices. As discussed earlier, the IS and LM curves represent goods and money market equilibria in (i,Y) space, and the AD is simply the representation of simultaneous goods and money market equilibria in (P,Y) space.

Figure 4

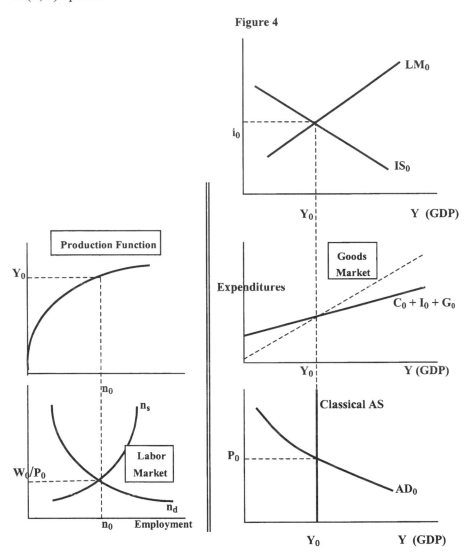

8.2 POLICY EXERCISE I: INCREASE IN G

Incorporating the classical AS curve into our earlier ISLM-ADAS framework, we now explore the effect of increased government spending on the key macroeconomic variables.

Once again, we use the survival guide of Chapter 7. The numbered steps below match the corresponding numbers in **Figure 5**.

1. As G increases, so does the intercept term in the IS, and consequently, as discussed in the previous chapter, IS_0 shifts up (to the right) to IS_1.
2. We "drop down" to (P,Y) space. The aggregate demand, AD_0, shifts laterally by the same lateral shift in IS. This time, though, with the vertical classical AS curve, the new equilibrium—the point where the latest AD curve (AD_1) intersects the AS—is at a <u>higher rate of inflation</u>, P_1, and the <u>same</u> rate of growth of GDP, Y_0.
3. Has P changed? Yes, inflation has changed. Instead of deftly skipping Step 3 and going to Step 4, as we did in the previous chapter, we go back to (i,Y) space and adjust the LM.
4. The increase in price from P_0 to P_1 reduces the ratio (M/P), thereby shifting the LM to the left, as in our discussion in Chapter 7.[3] Equilibrium in (i,Y) space must be consistent with equilibrium in (P,Y) space, and hence the LM shifts left until equilibrium in ISLM space is at Y_0, consistent with the Y_0 in (P,Y) space—the Y_0 must "line up". Final interest rates are now at i_{final}.
5. We close the goods market. Since the equilibrium here must be consistent with Y_0, the expenditure line will not shift.
   Is there any change in private consumption C?
   No. Since there was no final change in Y (still at Y_0) and since
   $C = \underline{C} + bY$, there will be no change in C.
   Will there be any change in private capital investment, I?
   Yes. Since interest rates have increased to i_1, and since $I = \underline{I}$-fi, capital investments will fall; $I_1 < I_0$.
   And, finally, government spending has increased from G_0 to G_1, by policy. Therefore, since the expenditure line does not shift and since the final goods market equilibrium is still at Y_0, we can conclude that the increase in G must exactly equal the decrease in I, in order for the total, C+I+G, to be unchanged.
   The increase in G has directly resulted in an equal and offsetting decrease in I: this economy suffers 100 percent crowding out.
6. **Results:**
   An increase in government spending does not increase Y here. GDP growth stays unchanged at Y_0. <u>Here there is no multiplier effect stemming from an increase in G in an economy with a classical AS</u>. There is no change in private consumption. Interest rates are driven up to i_1 by the increase in government spending. Capital investment suffers 100 percent crowding out. Inflation now increases to a higher rate P_1. And in the labor market, nominal wages increase; W_0 increases to W_1 in

the same proportion as the percentage increase in prices from P_0 to P_1. Equilibrium employment stays at n_0 in this economy.

Figure 5

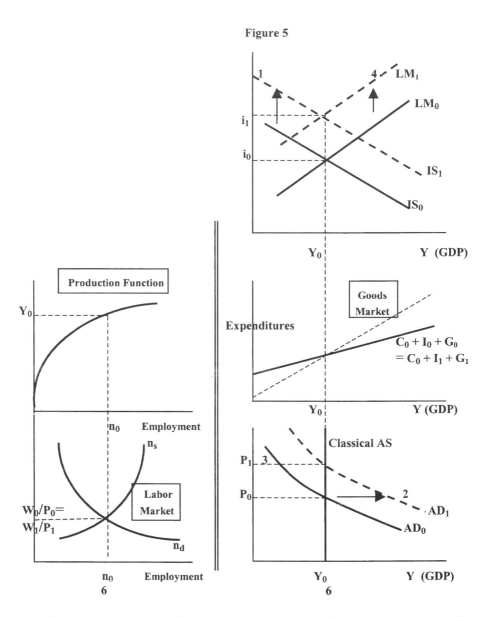

In summary, the results are sobering—especially after contrasting them with those for the same policy exercise from the previous chapter. Fiscal expansion does not yield any increase in GDP or employment growth; the only results are higher inflation, higher interest rates, and severe crowding out.[4]

While this discussion could be thought of as a predominantly historical exercise, since the classical model existed before the 1930s, the relevancy of this exercise cannot not be overstated. We will soon see that the modern-day supply-siders as well as new economy adherents in the US and Europe <u>also</u> <u>subscribe to a vertical AS curve</u>. In fact, it is commonly referred to as the New Classical AS curve! While this modern vertical AS curve is obtained from a somewhat different set of conditions, the ISLM exercises in this chapter will indeed apply to these modern curves too.[5]

8.3 ISLM-ADAS POLICY EXERCISE II: INCREASE IN M

Current GDP growth is at Y_0, given to be a sluggish rate. The central bank is under pressure to increase M and reduce interest rates and to "do something" to increase GDP growth. Using an ISLM-ADAS with a classical AS curve, analyze the effects of this monetary expansion.

(The numbers in **Figure 6** once again correspond to the following sequence from the ISLM survival guide.)

1. LM_0 shifts to the right as the central bank increases monetary growth from M_0 to M_1. At this stage, the real money supply increases from M_0/P_0 to M_1/P_0, and this causes the rightward shift in LM_0 to LM_1. (Since there is no change in government spending G, or in tax rates, foreign income, exchange rates, or in confidence, IS will be unchanged in this exercise.)
2. Dropping down to (P,Y) space, the AD_0 shifts out laterally to AD_1 by the amount of the lateral shift in LM. However, equilibrium in AD/AS space is still at Y_0, given the vertical Classical AS, and inflation has increased from P_0 to P_1.
3. With the change in P, we cannot skip Step 3. LM must now be adjusted until equilibrium in (i,Y) space is consistent with that in (P,Y) space. In other words, the Y_0 in the AD/AS diagram must "line up" with the same value, Y_0, in the final ISLM diagram.
    Since P_0 increased to P_1, the real money supply now falls from M_1/P_0 to M_1/P_1, and this causes the LM to snap back to LM_0 from LM_1.
4. We now close the goods market. Since equilibrium is still Y_0, the expenditure line will not shift. With no change in final Y, private consumption C will not change. And with no change in final interest rates, capital investment I will also not change. There is no change in G, by policy. In the labor market, by the classical assumption, nominal wages will increase in proportion to the increase in the rate of growth of

171

prices; W_1/P_1 will again be equal to W_0/P_0, thereby leaving the real wages unchanged. Equilibrium employment will still be at the rate n_0.

Figure 6

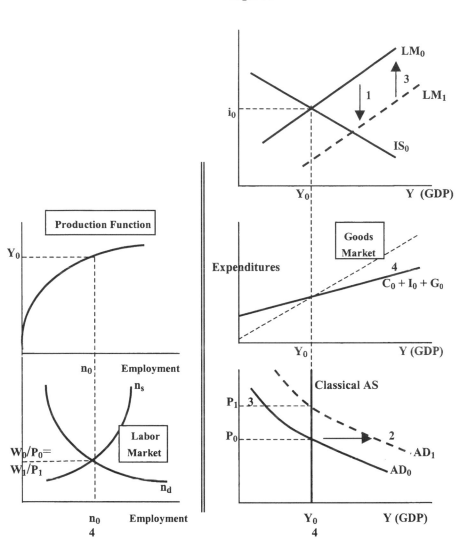

In conclusion, the effect of a monetary expansion, again in stark contrast to the result obtained in the previous chapter, will only be to exacerbate the rate of inflation. Prices and wages will be driven up. There will be no change in GDP growth—no multiplier effect—and no effect on private capital investment. Interest rates may be temporarily lowered, but as the inflation kicks in and P_0 increases to P_1, the LM snaps back until interest rates are back to i_0.

In fact, as inflation increases, long-term interest rates (not shown in the ISLM analysis) would typically increase, thanks to the Fisher effect discussed in an earlier chapter.[6] And higher long-term interest rates against a backdrop of expected increases in inflation would negatively impact long-term capital growth.

Once again, this result, which may appear chronologically obsolete, has huge contemporary policy implications. In later chapters we will find that the European Central Bank adopted a similarly vertical AS curve in the late 1990s—the New Classical version—as the centerpiece of the theory underlying its monetary policy objectives for the countries constituting the Eurozone.

8.4 THE "NATURAL" RATES OF GDP AND EMPLOYMENT GROWTH

Both the ISLM-ADAS exercises involving expansionary fiscal and monetary policies and incorporating the Classical AS curve only increased the rate of growth of domestic inflation **(Figure 7)**. There was no effect on GDP growth or on the rate of employment. This neutrality of demand-side stabilization on GDP and employment resulted in the output and employment growth rates being labeled "natural" rates of growth by the classical economists.[7]

Figure 7

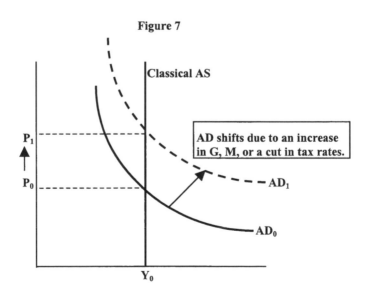

According to the Classicists, attempting discretionary demand-side stabilization by changing G, M or tax rates would only change the rate of inflation, P. The "natural" rate of growth in output, Y_0, would remain unaffected by fiscal and monetary policies. As nominal wages increase in proportion to prices, employment again stays at the "natural" rate, n_0.

There is no role for fiscal and monetary stabilization in an economy characterized by a vertical AS curve—shifting the AD by changing G or t or M only affected nominal variables such as P and W.

This notion of "natural" rates that could not be changed by macroeconomic intervention was indeed justified in an economy dominated by a vertical classical AS. However, this notion of non-intervention was to prove macroeconomically fatal when, during the Great Depression, the model changed—the paradigm shifted—and, unbeknown to policymakers, the Classical AS swung into the Keynesian model where fiscal and monetary stabilization are indeed effective.

The next two chapters describe the causes and effects of the shift from the Classical to the Keynesian model, followed by a description of the macroeconomic calamity known as the Great Depression

As per our usual format, the following questions and cases will underscore, clarify, and review the salient points made in this chapter.

8.5 DISCUSSSION QUESTIONS

1. **It is clear that "full flexibility" is the vital assumption responsible for the classical AS being vertical. Why did the Classicists make this assumption? How could they justify it?**

Going back to the introduction of this book, we have seen that macroeconomic models—unlike models in physics or engineering, for example—must reflect the contemporaneous real-world environment in which they are based. Prior to the 1930s, policy makers and researchers witnessed a long period where prices increased gradually and steadily and nominal wages did indeed increase in proportion.[8] Employment grew at some steady growth rate, n_0. The notion of involuntary unemployment was absent in the Classical world. They simply did not "see" huge involuntary unemployment because it was not a major feature of their observed macroeconomic "world".

The assumptions of full nominal wage and price flexibility reflected observed macroeconomic reality, and these assumptions were crucial to the model and the model worked—until the assumption of full flexibility of wages and prices came crashing down in the 1930s.

2. If Y_0 could not be changed, how would recessions be cured?

Once again, there was no role for fiscal and monetary policy in either jump-starting or soft-landing an economy in the classical paradigm. Shifting the AD would affect only inflation. In Chapter 10, when we revisit the vertical AS in the New Classical model of the supply-siders, we will explore how the thrust of macroeconomic policy shifted from changing G and M to focusing on factors such as deregulation, technology, productivity enhancement, and business and personal tax cuts. The objective changed from shifting AD to shifting AS.

3. In the "real world", typically how long does it take to go from Steps 1 to 4 in the Survival Guide?

The real-time duration of each exercise depends on the history—the distribution—of consumer and investor expectations, and the location of the economy on its phase of the business cycle. For example, following a monetary expansion, inflation may take longer to increase in Economy A where there is no history of monetary irresponsibility. However, in Economy B, notorious for its monetary looseness, even the vaguest suggestion of a planned increase in M will send inflationary expectations through the ceiling. In this example, Economy B would race from Steps 1 to 4 at a much faster rate than Economy A.

4. In the exercise in this chapter where M was increased, does the LM actually shift out to the right for a while and then "snap back" as P increases?

Yes. Inflation follows monetary expansion with a lag. We may actually experience a period with lower interest rates soon after an increase in M as the LM shifts to the right. Inflation will, however, inevitably increase from P_0 to P_1, thereby causing the LM to finally "snap back" to its original position. Once again, the timing of the change in inflation following a change in monetary policy depends on the economy and the macroeconomic situation in question. We will revisit this lag when we discuss Milton Friedman and the role of monetary policy in Chapter 11.

Please explain/critique the underlined sentences/phrases in the following simulated articles using material from this and preceding chapters. Use diagrams liberally including ISLM/ADAS analyses incorporating a Classical AS.

Article 8.1   TAX HIKE PLANNED IN CLASSICO!

Peter Cordeiro, <u>California Financial Gazette</u>

Late last week, investors at home and abroad were busy digesting the big news from the republic of Classico that its tax rates would be almost doubled in an attempt to "eradicate" the country's fiscal imbalance.

Government officials were out in force yesterday explaining to the public and to Classico's biggest trading partners (such as the US and China) that this policy was indeed necessary and that Classico's **(a)** <u>economy would not be affected by such a sharp tax hike</u>.

"We have always done the responsible thing in fiscal policy," intoned Antonio Hadrian, Classico's senior Finance Minister at a press reception on the palace grounds. "Our fiscal excesses last year were due to massive spending on dams and waterworks to prevent a recurrence of the flooding that took place two years ago. But these huge fiscal outlays **(b)** <u>came at the expense of business spending</u>."

He added that the nation had just emerged from an incredible infrastructure building campaign before the floods hit, and this had caused national budget deficits to be **(c)** "<u>larger than we think prudent.</u>"

The President himself weighed in with some appropriate comments at the ball to honor a visiting delegation of academics, businesspersons, and MBA students from the US. "I can assure everyone that the **(d)** <u>planned tax increases will raise tax revenues</u> without slowing down our economy. We have the assurance of the Classical Bureau of Economists," and with that everyone visibly relaxed, and the ball featuring the famous Classico Symphony was a huge, rowdy success.

However, not all were nearly that sanguine. Media consultant Monica Swanson worried that, "From the macro I know, **(e)** <u>this policy will be deflationary</u>. This is not good for my business…I am worried."

The following day, Valerie Ericsson, CFO of Classico Pharmaceuticals, was kind enough to talk to us. She agrees with Monica's analysis. "Yes, we can expect prices to fall and confidence, too. Our growth shouldn't falter—but expect housing, stock prices, and **(f)** <u>also wages to be heading down</u>."

Upon relating this analysis, Daniel Ladd, a nutritionist accompanying the visiting MBA delegation, commented, "Well, **(g)** <u>if prices fall and wages fall, then we are at the same place....right?</u>

Article 8.2   WHEN BUMPER STICKERS SAY IT ALL

Joanna Penman, <u>Midwest Financial Times</u>

"Look, I'm no rocket scientist," says Prof. Claus Elderberry to the crowd of reporters gathered outside his university office, "but I know that **(a)** <u>if our central bank lowers interest rates, we will be able to borrow more to build more houses and factories,</u> and to hire more workers. The economy will finally be able to drag itself out of this two year recession."

He then ends his presentation by passing out bumper stickers that say Lower Rates NOW! and by disseminating the central bank's email address. "Be interest rate activists," he attempts to shout, his hoarse voice now barely audible. "You have a right to a central bank that puts jobs first—email the bankers to lower rates."

Claus hardly looks the activist—just another typical professor in a rumpled tweed jacket. Professor Elderberry is also not an economist. "They're too cautious—I don't care for them," is his summary dismissal of that profession. He is, instead, a marine biologist with a "passionate hobby for economics and finance".

And he is not alone. Several prominent business leaders, large numbers of students, and several prominent politicians have climbed aboard his bandwagon. Business students throughout the country, however, have been very reluctant to climb on.

"His policy just won't work," explains Rob Foley, an MBA student getting a joint MBA-MD degree at the St. Martin School of Management in Milwaukee. **(b)** <u>"(His policies) will only get us more inflation—and who needs that?"</u> Rob adds, "Besides, the <u>rates will surely go back up again in say 6-8 months.</u>"

His classmate Tina Cassandra resonates, "You see, if you are in a Classical economy, you will have higher wages too—this Claus guy just doesn't understand that!" Tina works at Zinard.Com, a media-consulting agency franchise, and **(c)** she also is worried that long-term interest rates would rise if the professor's policies are put into effect.

Last night at the Lampatt Business School in St. Louis, Dr. Erica Glassberg, Chairperson of the National Finance and Accounting Consortium, included the following comments in her address at the banquet honoring the graduating class. **(d)** "I am not convinced that interest rates would head back up following a cut by the central bank. It is a little more complicated. If consumer confidence falls, we could conceivably be in an economy where the central bank lowers rates that are stuck in the 'low position' due to a further deterioration of confidence in this country." She adds ominously, "growth will not increase. This is the dreaded 'liquidity trap' situation that plagued Japan in the early 2000s when its rates were virtually at zero percent and there was no growth. In fact, the US wrestled with a similar concern in the wake of September 11, 2001."

Asked to comment after the conference, Vice Chairperson Jim Ziakus' enigmatic explanation to this reporter was, "It is tough to explain—**(e)** she shifted two curves, Elderberry only shifted one."

Confused? You're not alone! Stay tuned for more macro reports in this column!

ANSWERS AND HINTS

Article 8.1   Tax Hike Planned in Classico

(a) Show the effects of a tax increase using an ISLM-ADAS framework. Use a Classical AS curve (hence, the thinly veiled name of the country). A fall in Classico's national income would translate to fewer imports from the US and China. With no change in final Y in Classico due to the results of the ISLM analysis with the Classical AS, Classico can claim that its imports from the US and China would not be affected.

(b) The increase in G resulted in 100 percent crowding out in Classico. Businesses could not afford to borrow and spend because past increases in government borrowing (to finance the increase in G) had presumably driven up domestic interest rates in Classico.

(c) The deficits sound dangerously close to non-sustainability. Refer to earlier discussions on this subject.

(d) In this case, with Y unchanged, an increase in the tax rate will lead to higher tax revenues.

(e) As AD drops left, P will fall.

(f) The crucial assumption here is that nominal wages and prices are indeed fully flexible.

178

(g) Yes, real wages remain unchanged.

Article 8.2   When Bumper Stickers Say it All

(a) Prof. Elderberry is referring to just the investment function in isolation. Incorporate his advocated policy in an ISLM-ADAS framework with a Classical AS to demonstrate the fallacy of Elderberry's comments. His comments illustrate the danger of looking at just one component and not at the whole picture (not at ISLM in its entirety).

(b) Show the LM "snap back" in the above ISLM-ADAS exercise. The increase in P and the consequent shift back in the LM occurs with a lag following the initial monetary expansion.

(c) The Fisher effect again (from Chapter 6).

(d) If $\underline{C}$ and $\underline{I}$ fall, the IS drops to the left, too. In this case, the LM may not need to "snap back". Interest rates remain very "low". The combined effect is a much lower final interest rate with no change in GDP growth, and a decrease in P. Determine the effect on capital investment and consumption.

After the terrorist attacks in September 11, 2001, confidence indexes in the US plunged. As the Fed aggressively increased M to lower rates, the final rates fell significantly due to simultaneous shifts in IS and LM, in this framework.

It was a similar story for Japan, with the difference being that the confidence terms plunged with the collapse of its financial sector beginning in the mid to late-1990s.

In the next chapter we will discuss these scenarios from the Keynesian perspective.

(e) She "shifted" both IS and LM. Prof. Elderberry just shifted the LM.

---

[1] This is a simplified version of the labor market. Later, in Chapter 10, labor supply and demand will be functions of expected and current tax rates in the supply-sider paradigm.

[2] The Y_0 coincides with Y_0 in the production function reflected down into (P,Y) space. The P_0 is not anchored by any lateral location.

[3] In this case, the ratio M/P_0 fell to M/P_1. There is no change in monetary policy in this example; M stays unchanged.

[4] Contrast this with the result from Chapter 7 incorporating a flat AS. An increase in G resulted in a strong multiplier effect as Y increased along with private consumption C. Conveniently, in Chapter 7, inflation was conspicuously absent by construction of the horizontal AS.

[5] The New Classical AS is also known as the Rational Expectations AS curve. This curve is the "engine-room" of the supply-sider paradigm and will be the subject of Chapters 10 and 11.

[6] The interest rates in the ISLM space are short-term (typically one-year) interest rates.

[7] This comment anticipates the neutrality propositions proposed by the later rational expectationists (Robert E. Lucas, Robert Barro) in an era of New Classical macroeconomics that began in the late 1970s-early 1980s.

[8] Note that the classicists had no serious experience with <u>falling</u> prices. It was assumed that nominal wages would also fall in proportion to prices. They were wrong.

9. THE KEYNESIAN MODEL

John Maynard Keynes and the General Theory

In Cambridge, England, as you walk up King's Parade keeping that late-medieval architectural gem, King's College Chapel, to your right, you will come to a fairly nondescript lane known as King's Lane.[1] It is not prominently marked; one could easily miss it. Leave the crowds behind by taking a right and turn down King's Lane, keeping King's College to the right. The lane ends in a sharp left to form an elbow where Queen's Lane begins. At this elbow in the lane, look up to your right at the row of windows located directly above a (usually locked) gateway into King's College. These windows belong to the room where macroeconomic history was made— Keynes' office at King's College in Cambridge University.[2]

One version of the story has John Maynard Keynes "looking out" of these famous windows to realize that the paradigm then in existence (the Classical model), was hopelessly defunct. He "saw" global depression, and, more importantly, in the long lines of unemployed workers he witnessed involuntary unemployment, a concept conspicuously missing from the Classical model.

Clearly, unemployment and growth rates were not at some fixed "natural" rates n_0 and Y_0, as specified by the Classicists. Something was dreadfully wrong. A paradigm shift had occurred and he, John Maynard Keynes, had discovered the new model.

At about this time (January 1935), he wrote a memorable letter to his father's friend, George Bernard Shaw, informing him in characteristic fashion, "...I believe myself to be writing a book on economic theory which will largely rationalize (not, I suppose, at once, but in the next few years), the way the world thinks about economic problems...." He had concluded earlier that his theories would "revolutionize the way the world thinks about economic problems".

His seminal work, The General Theory of Employment, Interest and Money, set against the backdrop of the Great Depression, was published in 1936, and is considered by many to be one of the most influential books of the 20th century.

Nobel laureate Paul Samuelson had this to say about The General Theory:*

It is a badly written book, poorly organized...it is arrogant, bad-tempered, polemical....it abounds in mare's nests and confusions....flashes of insight and intuition intersperse tedious algebra. An awkward definition suddenly gives way to unforgettable cadenza. When it is mastered we might find its analysis to be obvious and at the same time, new. In short, it is a work of genius.

Keynes' new paradigm, which would later bear his name, flew in the face of the Classical model. It did acknowledge and explain involuntary unemployment and recession and it did provide specific macroeconomic policies to alleviate them. And Keynes was right in his letter to George Bernard Shaw— it did revolutionize the way the world made macroeconomic policy.

* ___Introducing Keynes___, *Peter Pugh and Chris Garratt,*
Totem Books, Cambridge, England 1994.

We now turn to a diagrammatic derivation of the Keynesian AS curve followed by the usual sequence of policy experiments and simulated articles.

9.1 KEYNESIAN AGGREGATE SUPPLY: DIAGRAMMATIC DERIVATION

The <u>crucial assumption</u> underlying the Keynesian AS curve is:
If labor demand (n_d) is greater than labor supply (n_s), nominal wages (W) adjust in proportion to the change in prices (P). But if n_d is less than n_s, nominal wages (W) do not adjust to changes in the price level and are said to be "sticky downwards".

The derivation is presented in the four diagrams in Figure 1. The two diagrams on the left (from top to bottom) are the production function and the labor market with employment at n_0, real wages at W_0/P_0, and GDP growth (from the production function) corresponding to employment n_0 to be Y_0.

The two diagrams on the right (top to bottom) are the Y-Y reflector designed to reflect values of Y from the production function by 90 degrees down to the lower diagram which is the (P,Y) space in which the Keynesian AS is to be derived.

9.1.1 DERIVATION SEQUENCE

The following steps match the corresponding numbers in **Figure 1**.

(1) Plot the initial given point (P_0, Y_0) into (P,Y) space. The value of Y_0 is reflected over from the production function. The initial value of P_0 can be plotted anywhere; our objective is to determine how subsequent changes in price affect the P and Y values.

(2) Increase P_0 to P_1. Assumption: Price changes first and nominal wages W adjust after a lag, if $n_d > n_s$. If $n_d < n_s$ then, by Keynes' assumption, nominal wages W simply will not adjust. Since we now have W_0/P_1 as the current real wage, we find that $n_d > n_s$ along this real wage line in the labor market diagram.

By Keynes' assumption, W_0 will adjust fully in this situation and increase to W_1 in the same proportion as the increase in prices from P_0 to P_1.

(3) This leaves the real wage unchanged: W_1/P_1 now equals W_0/P_0. We are back to where we started. Employment is still n_0 and GDP is still Y_0. So far, this is reminiscent of the derivation of the Classical AS curve. We plot (P_1,Y_0) and join to (P_0,y_0).

(4) We now <u>decrease</u> P_0 to P_2. Note that prices had indeed decreased (collapsed by as much as 25-30 percent) during the Great Depression when this AS curve was being formulated.
The real wage in the very short run is W_0/P_2. We find that this gives rise to a situation where $n_d < n_s$, by examining the labor market. By Keynes' assumption, in this case, W_0 stays unchanged.

Figure 1

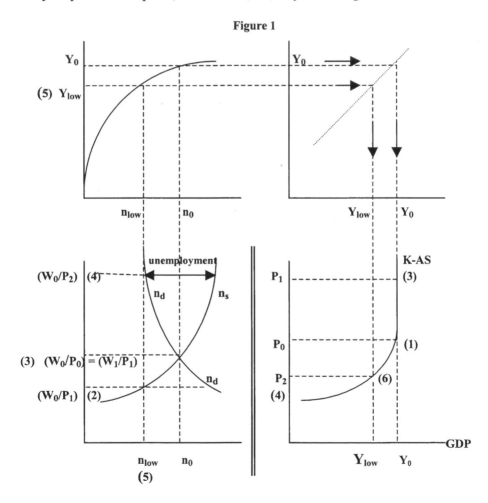

183

This was not a wholly preposterous assumption. Typically, as supply exceeds demand, nominal wages should fall or their rates of growth should decrease. But, as we shall see very soon, in the Great Depression a wage floor prevented this downward mobility in W, thereby rendering nominal wages "sticky downwards".

Employment n_0 now decreases to n_{low} as the number of workers employed will be determined by the labor demand at the higher real wage W_0/P_2. The number of workers seeking employment at W_0/P_2 will be determined by the labor supply curve. The difference between the number actually seeking work at W_0/P_2 and the number employed will be the amount of "involuntary unemployment" which was conspicuously missing in the theoretical framework of the Classical model.

(5) From the production function, output falls to y_{low} corresponding to n_{low} in the labor market.

(6) We reflect this lower output value over to the bottom right diagram and plot (P_2, Y_{low}) and join to (P_0, Y_0) to get the Keynesian AS curve.

The AS curve derived here should look familiar. This was the AS encountered in Chapter 5, where concepts such as demand-pull inflation, overheating and soft landing were discussed. The same phenomena will be re-visited in an ISLM-ADAS framework in this chapter. This time, we will use a labor market to illustrate the explicit effect on employment and real wages, and the production function will be linked to output.

The following Survival Guide will assist us in analyzing macroeconomic policy in an ISLM framework involving the Keynesian AS curve.

9.2 SURVIVAL GUIDE FOR ISLM WITH KEYNESIAN AS (K-AS)

1.   Make all moves in (i,Y) space. Make all shifts to IS and LM here.
2.   "Drop down" the final Y value into (P,Y) space. The AD shifts accordingly to ensure that the Y values in (i,Y) and (P,Y) spaces are consistent—the Y values must "line up". At this stage, one obtains the "final" P and Y values of the policy exercise.
3.   Simply adjust the expenditure line to ensure that goods market equilibrium is consistent with the final value of Y.[3] Once again, determine if consumption and capital investment (I) have changed relative to C_0 and I_0, using the consumption and investment functions.

Examine the labor market. If final real wages are such that labor supply exceeds labor demand, then nominal wages will not change with the change in prices. A change in unemployment will occur. If final wages are such that labor supply is less than labor demand, nominal wages will adjust in proportion to the change in prices. The final level of employment must match that of the final output in the production function. (The employment rates in both the labor market and the production function must again "line up".)

4. Present your results boldly.

Armed with the survival guide, we proceed to the following policy exercises incorporating the Keynesian AS curve.

9.2.1   POLICY EXERCISE I: INCREASE IN G

The government launches a massive infrastructure spending campaign to jump-start the economy and put people back to work. Huge power plants, thousands of miles of roads and railways, a new port, an extension of the subways for the nation's largest cities, and several new airports are planned. Using an ISLM-ADAS in a Keynesian paradigm, analyze the effects of this policy on all the key macro variables.

The steps below are represented by corresponding numbers in **Figure 2**.

Note that the starting point $(W_0/P_0, n_0)$ in the labor market in Figure 2 lies on the labor demand curve. At this initial point we have initial unemployment denoted un_0, depicted as the difference between the available labor supply at the initial real wage and the existing labor demand. As long as the initial point in (P,Y) space lies on the positively sloped portion of the AS curve, we always start at this point in the labor market. The intuition is that initially, at (P_0, Y_0), the economy is still far from attaining Y_{max} at full employment and maximum capacity. There is still room to grow the economy from Y_0 to Y_{max}. This initial level of slack in the economy therefore implies some initial level of involuntary unemployment un_0 which will steadily shrink as we approach the kink in the AS curve at Y_{max}.

Proceeding with the exercise, as G increases on infrastructure outlays:

(1) The IS_0 curve shifts to the right to IS_1. Interest rates increase to i_1, GDP growth increases to Y_1.

(2) We drop down into (P,Y) space. The Y value in (P,Y) space must match the Y_1 in (i,Y) space. The AD_0 shifts out to AD_1. Inflation now increases to P_1, and GDP increases to Y_1.

(3) The expenditure line shifts to the right to be consistent with Y_1—after all, the IS and the expenditure line both represent the same (goods) market in different spaces. The goods market is now at a higher equilibrium consistent with equilibrium in ISLM space. Once again, we abstract from the trade sector.

How does C_1 compare to C_0? Since $C = \underline{C} + bY$, as Y_0 increases to Y_1, C_1 will therefore be larger than C_0. Private consumption has increased. Is $I_1 > I_0$? Since $I = I - fi$, and since interest rates increase from i_0 to i_1, capital

185

investments will decrease to I_1. That is, $I_1 < I_0$. Private capital investment has been crowded out.

Figure 2

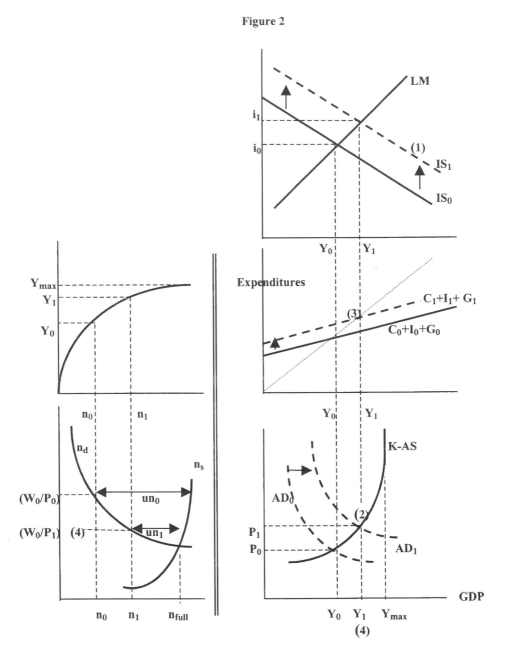

(4) In the labor market, as P_0 increases to P_1, nominal wages will not adjust since labor supply exceeds labor demand at both W_0/P_0 and W_0/P_1. So

the real wage drops as the denominator increases (to P_1) while the numerator (W_0) stays unchanged.

With this fall in real wages we see (in the labor market) that unemployment shrinks to un_1. Here labor demand increases as real wages fall while labor supply falls.

Employment increases to n_1, determined by the labor demand at the new lower real wage, and this coincides with GDP of Y_1 in the production function. Note the "firewall" between the labor market and (P,Y) space designed as a reminder that the two diagrams have different vertical axes.

The values Y_{max} in the production function and n_{full} in the labor market are included in Figure 2 for completeness, at this stage. In the following section, their presence will be justified as we revisit overheating in the context of ISLM-ADAS.

The final results are radically different from the neutrality results obtained in the previous chapter. An increase in government spending in an economy characterized by a Keynesian AS curve result in:

- The famous Keynesian multiplier effect. GDP growth increases from Y_0 to Y_1.
- Interest rates increase to i_1 as a result of the demand for loanable funds necessary to finance the bond-financed deficits.
- Private consumption increases to C_1. After all, this increase in consumption drives the multiplier effect.
- The rise in interest rates adversely affects—crowds out—private capital investment, which falls from I_0 to I_1.
- Inflation increases from P_0 to P_1.
- The rise in inflation erodes real wages. They fall to W_0/P_1. Nominal wages do not change.
- Unemployment decreases to un_1—employment increases to n_1.

Here, an increase in G jump-starts the economy. Both GDP growth and employment rates increase, and we obtain the Keynesian output-inflation tradeoff. In stark contrast to the laissez faire role for government in the Classical world, activist discretionary government spending does indeed make a difference as multipliers are unleashed. Unlike in the Classical world, in the Keynesian world there is a role for government in stabilizing the economy.

Large infrastructure spending by China (and Japan) through the early 2000s has attempted to generate such effects and to revive growth.[4] Following the Great Depression, the US had its own version of early infrastructure spending in the form of the TVA (Tennessee Valley Authority), a construction project that included a vast complex of dams, power stations, canals, and roads. Another post-depression example is the CCC (Civilian Conservation Corps) that hired involuntarily unemployed workers to undertake the reforestation of many major national parks, as well as road construction, flood control and public works. In fact, it was finally the massive increase in G due to the defense buildup before and during WW2 that enabled the nation to finally emerge from the Great Depression.

The early version of the stimulus package in the wake of the September 11, 2001, terrorist attacks was a textbook Keynesian policy recommendation. A bond-financed $100 billion increase in G included spending on reconstruction in New York and Washington D.C. The package helped to finance security enhancement at airports, bridges, tunnels and power-plants, an across-the-board increase in the size and capability of US intelligence and defense agencies and personnel, and large increases in government-funded research to ensure against biological and chemical terrorism. These measures were taken in the hope that large injections of spending would not only serve to shore-up collapsing consumer and investor confidence (the latter was already low long before 9/11/01) but would also prevent the economy from slumping into a full fledged recession by aggressively shifting the AD towards the right by increasing G.

9.2.2 POLICY EXERCISE II: INCREASE IN MONETARY GROWTH

Under pressure from the government the central bank increases M and lowers interest rates to attempt to revive economic growth and employment.

1. Following the guide and using the same initial points as the previous exercise, we see in **Figure 3** that initially, as M_0 increases to M_1, LM_0 shifts to the right.[5] Interest rates drop to i_1 and GDP growth is at Y_1. Note that when central banks "lower interest rates," this usually implies an initial increase in monetary growth.
2. We "drop down" to (P,Y) space, and adjust AD so that AD_1 is consistent with Y_1 in (i,Y) space. Inflation has increased to P_1.
3. Closing the goods market, the expenditure line shifts to the right. C_1 is greater than C_0, since Y_0 has increased to Y_1. I_1 is greater than I_0, since interest rates fell. There is no change in G_0, by policy. In the labor market, as price increases the real wage dips to W_0/P_1, resulting in higher employment at n_1 and lower unemployment, un_1. (Note that since labor supply is greater than labor demand, nominal wages W_0 do not change).
4. A monetary expansion has jump-started this economy. GDP growth has increased to Y_1, interest rates have fallen to i_1, private consumption and investment have both increased, and employment has also increased to n_1.

The ease and speed with which monetary policy can be enacted usually makes it the first choice of policymakers attempting to revive their sluggish economies with demand-side stabilization.[6]

Figure 3

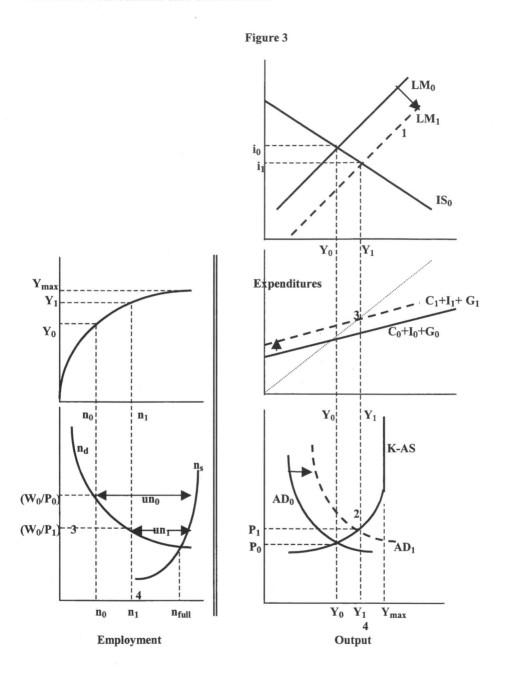

Employment   Output

From Stage 2 to Overheating

If monetary stimulus continues to be applied, the LM will shift further to the right, driving down interest rates as presented in **Figure 4**. The value of Y also increases as AD mimics the most recent LM and shifts further to the right. As the AD pushes the economy towards the kink and the point of maximum sustainable growth, the economy begins to overheat.[7]

Figure 4

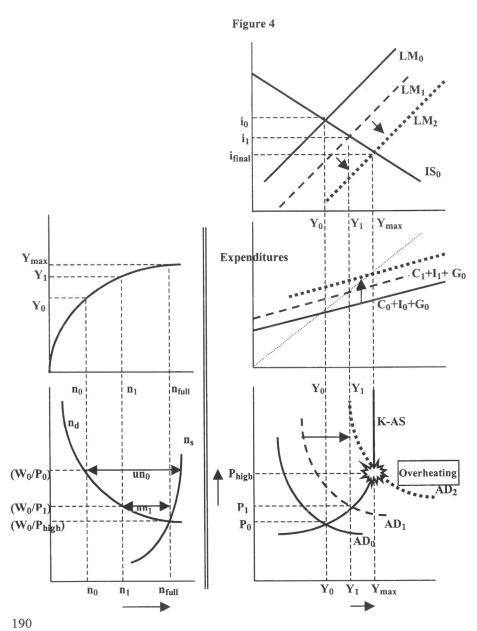

As prices increase, real wages keep falling from W_0/P_0 to W_0/P_1, and so on. Employment consequently increases while unemployment progressively decreases (the horizontal gaps between labor supply and labor demand keep shrinking).

Eventually output growth hits Y_{max} at full employment as the AD reaches the Keynesian kink amidst full fledged overheating. Interest rates have fallen to i_{final}.[8] Here, the real wage Wo/P_{high} is at the intersection of labor supply and demand. There is no involuntary unemployment. The labor market is at full employment, n_{full}, which also corresponds to Y_{max} in the production function.

The economy has transitioned from a nice Stage II recovery at Y_1, where there was still room for the economy to grow (see Figure 3), to an overheated economy as a result of "too much" demand-side stimulus. Output growth is raging out of control, inflation is rising rapidly, skilled labor is virtually impossible to find, and commodities and futures prices are probably climbing. In all likelihood, dangerous SAP bubbles may be developing in the equities and real estate markets, as well as in wages and benefits of certain kinds of high-skilled labor as discussed earlier in Chapter 5.

9.2.3   POLICY EXERCISE III: ENGINEERING A SOFT LANDING

The next logical exercise is to cool down this overheated economy by engineering a soft landing using ISLM-ADAS. The result of the exercise just completed in Figure 4 is now taken <u>as the starting point</u> at which the central bank "taps the brakes" and increases interest rates by contracting monetary growth.

1. **In Figure 5**, LM_2 shifts to the left to LM_1 as the central bank contracts monetary growth and "drives up" interest rates from i_{final} to i_{higher}. GDP growth falls from Y_{max} to $Y_{moderate}$. This process can take from six months to two years—monetary policy acts with "long and variable lags" as Milton Friedman said.
2. AD shifts left to line up with $Y_{moderate}$ in (i, Y) space. Inflation now falls to $P_{moderate}$ from P_{high}.
3. The expenditure line drops left. Consumption decreases as Y falls. Capital investment decreases as the higher interest rates slow down interest-sensitive sectors. Government spending is unchanged here.
    In the labor market as the rate of inflation (P) falls, the real wage rises. The level of employment now falls to n_{lower} and unemployment actually increases. The red-hot labor market has been cooled down. If the economy can indeed be finally stabilized at $Y_{moderate}$, $P_{moderate}$ and n_{lower}, then a soft landing has been successfully engineered.

Figure 5

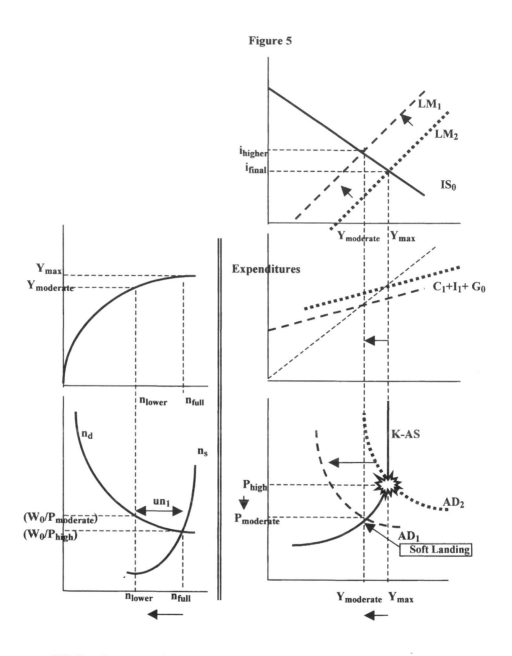

While decreases in government outlays and tax increases can also eventually slow growth, they involve long-term decision making and implementation lags. Contractionary monetary policy, however, can be enacted at very short notice by an autonomous and responsible central bank at

192

the first whiff of overheating. Hence, monetary contraction remains the policy of choice for engineering soft landings.

Examples of perfect soft landings are few. Such deliberately planned slowdowns are fraught with macroeconomic risk. Often, it is impossible to separate deliberate increases in unemployment (and expected unemployment) from large accompanying declines in consumer and investor confidence. These falling confidence levels cause the AD to be driven <u>further</u> leftward due to the confidence-induced leftward shift in IS, thereby turning an intended soft landing into a hard landing.

9.2.4   POLICY EXERCISE IV: WHEN LOW INTEREST RATES DON'T WORK—INCREASING M AGAINST A BACKDROP OF COLLAPSED CONFIDENCE

We are given that confidence has crashed in this economy. It may be due to a bursting SAP bubble, resulting in sharply deflated stock prices, plunging real estate values, and a weakened banking sector. The central bank is now under pressure to jump-start the economy by increasing M and lowering interest rates. But despite this, confidence remains unmoved. Expectations are at rock-bottom since the near-term future, for whatever reason, continues to look bleak.[9]

The following steps match those in **Figure 6**.

1. IS_0 falls left to IS_1 as confidence (consumer and investor) falls. Interest rates fall and GDP drops.

2. Against this "given" backdrop of falling confidence, the central bank increases M and lowers rates further to revive growth. Interest rates are now very low at i_{final} and growth is increased, to some degree, to Y_{final}.[10] Note that the final location of Y_{final} depends on the magnitude of the IS shift to the left, relative to the LM shift to the right. In this case, Y_{final} happens to be lower than Y_0. The economy is still in recession compared to the initial rate of growth, Y_0.

3. We drop into (P,Y) space and AD_0 shifts left to AD_{final}. Inflation is lower at P_{final} and growth has fallen to Y_{final}. For diagrammatic clarity, only the initial and final AD curves have been shown in (P,Y) space in Figure 6; the AD shift stemming from the initial drop in IS to the left is not presented.

4. The expenditure line in the goods market shifts left to be consistent with Y_{final}. C_{final} is significantly less than C_0 since both Y and $\underline{C}$ have fallen. Capital Investments I_{final} are also lower than I_0. Technically, the effect on final capital investments is ambiguous since we have falling interest rates which tend to <u>increase</u> I, as well as falling investor confidence ($\underline{I}$) which tends to <u>decrease</u> I. Generally, in an economy characterized by

plunging confidence, the effect of falling $\underline{I}$ on capital investments is found to dominate that of falling interest rates. Hence, while the algebraic effect on investments is ambiguous, in all probability I_{final} will be less than I_0.

Figure 6

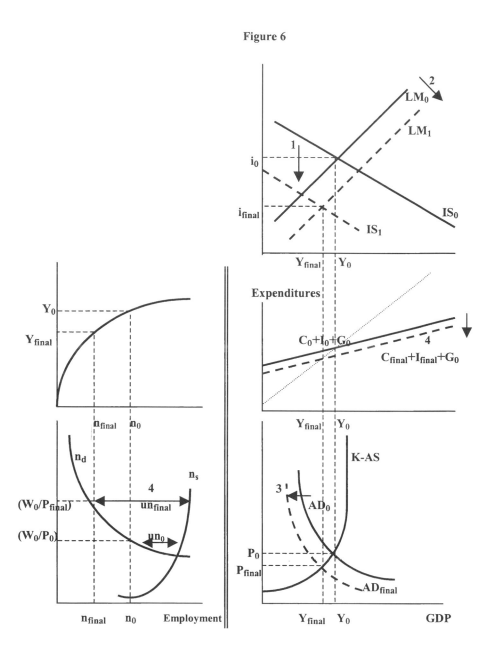

As prices fall, we may see an increase in the real wage and a decline in employment from n_0 to n_{final} (and a rise in unemployment to the higher rate un_{final}).

While the increase in M provides some macroeconomic relief by nudging the economy "back towards the right" after the severe contraction caused by the drop in IS, any additional fall in confidence could snap the IS further back to the left, thereby negating any positive effects of the monetary intervention.

9.3 THE PHILLIPS CURVE

If we were to plot the changes in the rate of inflation against changes in the unemployment rate in Exercises I and II in Figures 2 and 3, we would find that as P (rate of inflation) increases from P_0 to P_1, the unemployment rate—the laterally measured "gap" between labor supplied and labor demanded—decreases from un_0 to un_1. This, of course, is accompanied by the increase in the employment rate (n) and output growth (Y).

A.W.H. Phillips, a New Zealander, plotted and studied British inflation and unemployment data in order to plot the above relationships in a curve which today bears his name. As presented in **Figure 7**, the Phillips Curve illustrates an inverse relationship between the rates of inflation and unemployment, with increases in inflation accompanied by decreases in the unemployment rate (and, presumably, increases in output) and vice versa. This was the quintessence of the Keynesian model, depicted now as an exploitable relationship between inflation and unemployment, and known as the famous (and later controversial), output-inflation tradeoff.

Figure 7

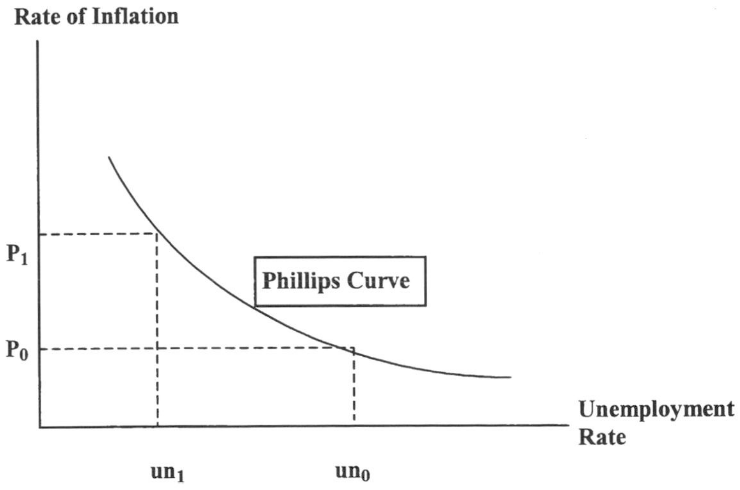

195

In this Keynesian paradigm, if the unemployment rate is considered to be "high", increases in demand-pull inflation caused by shifting the AD to the right by appropriate fiscal and/or monetary stimuli would be the remedy. On the other hand, if unemployment is "too low" and overheating is imminent, contractionary demand-side policies would lower the inflation rate, increase unemployment, and soft-land the economy. All this is validated by the empirically observed relationships embedded in the Phillips curve.

Emerging Economies and the Keynesian Paradigm

Most emerging and newly industrialized economies (NICs) display strong Keynesian characteristics. Typically, their labor markets are individually characterized by excess labor supplies at existing real wages. These economies have endemic rates of high "initial" unemployment. One could make a strong case for the starting points in labor markets to resemble point n_0 in ISLM exercises I and II of this chapter.

Usually, in these economies, an x percent increase in the inflation rate may not necessarily induce the same x percent increase in nominal wages. For instance, if inflation were to go from 3% to 5% in China, it is unlikely that average nominal wages (W) for the whole economy would leap by 5% in the near-term.

The significant excess supply of labor, the absence of sophisticated bond markets, the resulting lack of accurate information pertaining to current and expected inflation, and the inability to manage real wages by collective bargaining or negotiation allow for a degree of nominal wage stickiness in these economies.

This accounts for the fact that emerging and newly industrialized economies are usually Keynesian in nature, even though specific wage floors of the kind used in the Great Depression may be conspicuously absent.

9.4 THE YIELD CURVE AND THE KEYNESIAN PARADIGM

The shape of the yield curve ranges from the "normal" upward sloping curve discussed in Chapter 6 and replicated in **Figure 8** to the "inverted" yield curve presented in Figure 9.

The **upward-sloping yield curve,** with long-term interest rates higher than the short-term ones, is often thought to be indicative of an economy in the early stages of a sustained recovery. As discussed earlier, the interest rates in the (i,Y) space in the ISLM-ADAS analyses are <u>short-term rates,</u> corresponding to the left end of the yield curve. If the economy were initially in some late-Stage I or early-Stage II recovery, the rate of inflation would

196

eventually increase as the AD is shifted right presumably by some combination of fiscal and monetary stimulus. Demand-pull inflation is, after all, procyclical; the rate of inflation increases along with GDP growth. As expectations of an economy growing into Stage II increase, so do expectations of future accompanying increases in inflation.

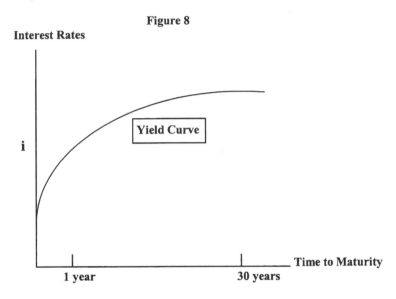

Figure 8

In the current time period, the efficient bond market incorporates these expectations of future macroeconomic growth, thereby adding on these increases in expected inflation premiums to long-term loans. As explained by the Fisher effect (see Chapter 6), bonds do "know best" and lenders will indeed incorporate expectations of future inflation rates while making long-term loans in the current period. This forward-looking feature results in final long-term nominal interest rates being higher than short-term ones, giving the yield curve its "healthy" upward slope, indicative of vibrant Stage 2 growth expected in the not too distant future.

On the other hand, an **inverted yield curve** is often thought to be indicative of an impending recession or, at the least, an expected slowdown .in the near-term.

ISLM-ADAS Exercise III, where an overheated economy was soft-landed using monetary policy, helps explain this sentiment. Using the overheated economy as our starting point, as in the exercise, we have the central bank engineering a soft-landing by contracting monetary growth and driving up interest rates.

Since these are short-term rates, the "short" (left) end of the yield curve rises up sharply in **Figure 9** as the central bank "steps on the brakes" to slow the economy down fast (China in 1995, US in 1999-2000). This action causes

197

GDP growth to slow from Y_{max} to Y_1, and the overheated inflation rate to fall from a dangerous P_{high} to a manageable P_1, as depicted earlier in Figure 5.

Figure 9

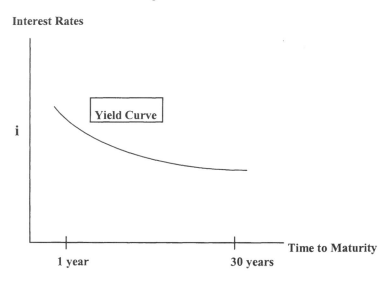

Once again, in the current period, the bond market sees all this activity in its forward-looking macroeconomic "radar". Individuals know that the central bank is driving up short-term rates—the only rates that central banks can influence directly—and this, in turn, will eventually decrease inflation in the future to P_1 as the economy slows to some Y_1.

Lenders in the current period expect less inflation in the future. According to the Fisher effect and a competitive market for loans, this expectation results in their charging lower long-term nominal interest rates for long-term loans made in the current period, thereby resulting in a fall in the "long" end of the yield curve. In the current period, with the short end rising due to current central bank's contractionary monetary policy, and the long-end falling due to falling long-term expectations of inflation as investors expect a recession (or at the least, a slowdown), the yield curve adopts the inverted shape.

Both the cases discussed here linking the shape of the yield curve to expected macroeconomic performance are, at best, "most likely" scenarios. By no means is an inverted yield curve always a harbinger of an impending recession or slowdown. By the same token, a positively sloping yield curve is not necessarily always synonymous with expected strong growth.

For example, in the case of a "healthy" upward-sloping yield curve, other factors besides policy-induced demand-pull inflation could be driving up future inflation. The culprit may be cost-push inflation due to an expected oil

198

crisis (Chapter 5). This would drive-up expectations of future increases in inflation, thereby raising the long end of the yield curve. And we know that cost-push inflation is inversely correlated with GDP growth; it is countercyclical. In this case, an upward sloping yield curve would certainly not be a prologue to healthy growth in the near future but, instead, an early warning for cost-push inflation and slower growth!

Hence, any instantaneous macro-predictions based solely on the shape of the yield curve, without accompanying analyses of the factors underlying the shape, need to be treated with a certain degree of caution.

9.5 THE AGONY OF A PARADIGM SHIFT: THE GREAT DEPRESSION

The year 1929 began on a glorious note. US real GDP exceeded potential GDP, and unemployment was a low 3.2 percent. The 1920s had witnessed years of economic strength that included tremendous booms in housing and in new technology. In fact, the period was optimistically labeled the "New Era".

Following the crash in October 1929, the stock market had lost more than one third of its value in two weeks. And this was only the beginning. By the time the stock market crash had deteriorated into the Great Depression by 1933, real GDP had fallen by 29% relative to its 1929 level. Prices had collapsed, with deflation at 24% compared to prices in 1928. Twenty-five percent of the work force was involuntarily unemployed with virtually no social security or unemployment benefits in place, and unemployment remained above 14% until 1940. Only the arming of the US, preparatory to its entry into WW2, finally shook off the vestiges of the lingering unemployment from the Depression.

The Great Depression was an inconceivable macroeconomic meltdown that remains permanently seared in the minds of those unlucky enough to have experienced it. And it was aggravated by four huge policy mistakes that, remarkably, turned a bad stock market correction into a singularly devastating macroeconomic calamity.

This book sidesteps the ongoing controversy between Keynesians and Monetarists regarding the primary causes of the Great Depression. Instead, the approach here focuses primarily on the effect of the four policy mistakes, compounded by a paradigm shift.

Mistake 1: Wage Floors

The operational model employed in 1929 was of course the Classical model with its vertical AS curve and with no role for discretionary fiscal and monetary policy. But this model was rendered defunct when President Hoover, in a well-meaning attempt to prevent workers' real purchasing power from falling, introduced wage floor legislation. These wage floors prevented nominal wages from <u>falling in the same proportion</u> as the collapsing prices in the months following the Crash. By legislating a system of minimum wages (wage floors) that did not adjust downwards with falling prices, Hoover inadvertently created Keynes' "sticky wages"! Nominal wages fell from 57 cents an hour in 1929 to 44 cents an hour in 1933, while prices fell by a significantly larger percentage. This wage floor—the first mistake— prevented W from falling in proportion with P, quickly demolished the fundamental assumption of full flexibility of W and P which was absolutely necessary for the vertical AS curve of the Classical Model. In fact, with "sticky wages", the AS curve quickly transformed into the familiar kinked Keynesian AS curve derived earlier in this chapter.

Unfortunately, this change in paradigm from Classical to Keynesian was not immediately obvious.[11] Policy makers were blind-sided—they continued to prescribe macropolicy based on the "wrong" (Classical) model, while in fact their world had changed to one where the AS had now taken on the positively sloped, kinked, Keynesian shape! They were unaware that the paradigm had shifted.

As confidence continued to plunge following the crash and the ensuing margin calls (at that time investors could borrow up to 90% of the value of the stock), the IS, and hence the AD, kept falling left along the Keynesian AS. As GDP thus fell to Y_{low}, and with national income falling, so did the tax base. Tax revenues fell, resulting in a small budget deficit.

Mistake 2: Tax Increases and decreases in G

At this point, policy makers made their second mistake. Continuing to operate in the now-defunct Classical AS model, they rapidly moved to increase tax rates to "do something" about the budget deficit. Tax rates were savagely increased. The Tax Revenue Act of 1932 nearly doubled income taxes (the highest tax bracket jumped from 25% to 63%), imposed excise taxes, and boosted corporate taxes from 12% to 13.75%.

As depicted in **Figure 10**, with a vertical AS, these increases would indeed generate a larger slice of tax revenues, given that national income was supposedly "fixed" at some natural rate. However, with the Keynesian AS, the sharp tax increases proved to be terribly contractionary. The recession only worsened as the IS pivoted clockwise with the AD matching this leftward movement over the sloping AS curve as depicted as (t) in Figure 10. GDP growth and inflation fell even further, and, with the sticky wages, unemployment began to increase rapidly. In addition government spending, although modest, was reduced in an attempt to respond to the deficits, further pushing the IS to the left! All along, as jobs were lost and unemployment soared and expenditures plunged, continuously collapsing consumer and
200

investor confidence formed a terrible backdrop to the crisis, further pulling the IS and AD to the left, denoted as (c) in Figure 10.

Things progressively got worse. The recession deteriorated inexorably. American social worker Frances Perkins wrote in 1934:

> But with the slow menace of a glacier, depression came on. No one had any measure of its progress; no one had any plan of stopping it. Everyone tried to get out of its way.

Mistake 3: Liquidity Crisis

Banks began to fail; almost 33% of all banks failed by 1933. Before the Crash in October 1929, bank loans had over expanded due to booming stock and property markets, but following the stock collapse, many borrowers could not make the interest payments on their loans or the repayment schedules. Panic spread as banks failed; there were "runs" on banks. Depositors rushed to pull their money—uninsured deposits in the era before FDIC—out before the banks went under.[12] There was a severe decline in the money stock, with M1, the most liquid measure of money, falling by 26.5% from 1929 to 1933, and M2, a less liquid measure, falling by 33.3% over the same period.[13]

Figure 10

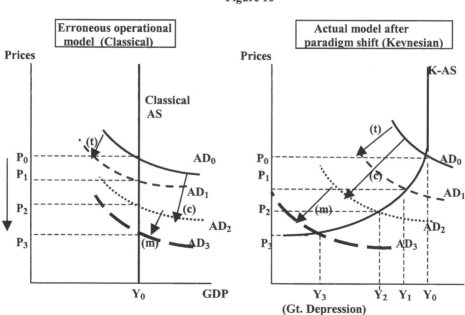

(t) = tax increase and decrease in G; (c) = ongoing collapse in confidence; (m) = effective monetary contraction

While the Federal Reserve did not deliberately enact a contractionary monetary policy, its reluctance to rush in, increase monetary growth, and inject liquidity to the liquidity-starved economy resulted in an <u>effective</u> reduction in M. Once again, policy makers believed that the only result of this effective decrease in M would be more deflation, since the model was still supposed to be Classical. Andrew Mellon, head of the Federal Reserve, was a deflationist. He believed that the increase in prices during the 1920s was the primary cause of the macroeconomic malaise, and he therefore wanted prices to fall to pre-World War I levels! He commented in 1930:

> Let the slump liquidate itself. Liquidate labor, liquidate stocks, liquidate the farmers, liquidate real estate….It will scourge the rottenness out of the system. High costs of living will come down. People will work harder, live a more moral life. Values will be adjusted, and enterprising people will pick up the wrecks from less competent people.

The tragic, erroneous implication of using the "wrong" model was that P would further fall as M fell, and Y would be unaffected since the AS was still supposed to be Classical (see Figure 10). So the Fed did nothing—it did not inject liquidity into the system by increasing M. Its silence was terrifying. The third giant mistake had been made.

In reality, the huge monetary contraction once again resulted in an AD shifting even further to the left over a sloping AS, depicted as (M) in Figure 10. The economy had now reached Great Depression status. Confidence was in total free-fall. Unemployment and GDP growth had reached their Great Depression levels with the economy contracting by 30%. Rampant deflation had set it, with prices collapsing to P_3 in Figure 10.

Milton Friedman and Anna Schwartz, in their <u>Monetary History of the United States</u>, have argued that the effective monetary contraction was, in fact, the proverbial straw that broke the economy's back. While we shy away from debates involving <u>the</u> principal factor responsible for the Great Depression, the result of this huge monetary contraction, coming on the heels of a major tax hike and a sharp drop in confidence, cannot be overstated.

Against this backdrop, President Hoover's 1931 comment epitomizes the sentiment of policy makers unknowingly trapped in the now-defunct Classical model. The laissez faire role for government intervention with a conspicuous absence of any role for G or M is clearly apparent:

> Economic depression cannot be cured by legislative action or executive pronouncement. Economic wounds must be healed by the action of the cells of the economic body, the producers and consumers themselves.

Mistake 4: Smoot-Hawley

As if these mistakes were not enough, a strong contender for the title of the principal factor was the Smoot-Hawley Act of 1930. This was a tariff (tax on imports), imposed on about one-third of US imports, resulting in a tariff increase from 45% in 1930 to 60% by 1933. Naturally, European exporters placed retaliatory tariffs on US exports, resulting in a global trade war that essentially shut down world trade. By 1933, the bottom had been reached. The inconceivable had happened—full-fledged depressions ravaged the US and its major trading partners worldwide.

Here we not only analyze the policies that caused the Great Depression, as most other texts do, but we place these policies against a backdrop of a paradigm shift. In this context the "mistakes" that led to the greatest macroeconomic cataclysm in US history may not seem completely preposterous. Policy makers were simply operating in the wrong model. By the time Keynes "looked out his window" and concluded that the "model had changed," it was too late. The Great Depression was in its darkest throes, laboring in the agony of a paradigm shift.

Could a Great Depression happen again?

First and foremost, it is clear that the Federal Reserve is extremely unlikely to ever again make Mistake 3. In times of great and grave national crises, the Fed has moved with amazing and impressive alacrity to inject liquidity into an economy in distress.

A striking example was the response following the terrorist attacks on the World Trade Center and the Pentagon on September 11, 2001. With thousands of flights loaded with uncleared checks stranded on the ground, and domestic and global financial institutions desperately in need of large infusions of funds, the Fed promptly injected liquidity into the system. Within three days of the attack, over $108 billion was lent to banks and investment dealers. Prior to September 11, 2001, injections of funds to the banking system had seldom exceeded $6 billion.

Another example of decisive Fed injections was the 14% increase in monetary growth in the days following the October 19, 1987 stock market correction—in fact, liquidity was being injected into the system on the very afternoon of the correction! Other examples are the infusions of liquidity following the 1995 Mexican Peso crisis and the 1997 Asian currency crisis.

Other positive factors that make a recurrence of the Great Depression unlikely are deposit insurance in the US (FDIC), that reduces bank panics and "runs" on banks, and unemployment insurance and benefits which would prevent sharp collapses in confidence and in spending at the first hint of unemployment. Furthermore, Mistake 4—despite the backlash against global trade—would be unlikely given the fundamental benefits of free trade in goods and services and in unrestricted global capital flows.

On the negative side, however, Mistake 2, unfortunately, keeps recurring. Policymakers find it difficult to understand that by increasing tax rates they may not be necessarily increasing tax revenues; the notion of output endogeneity is often lost in the analysis. This mistake was made in the US in 1990-91 even after the "No New Taxes" pledge of President Bush, and was (mistakenly) prescribed by the IMF to ravaged Asian economies in the wake of the 1997-98 currency crisis.

All in all, the chance of the concurrence of the 4 policy mistakes, discussed here, against a backdrop of a sharp collapse in stock prices and confidence, triggering another Great Depression seem highly unlikely.

During the post-World War II era, the world became Keynesian and exploited the Phillips curve relationship quite effectively. This was the era of "fine-tuning" and discretionary demand-side policy making. Economies were jump-started and soft-landed successfully and the "real world" cooperated with the model. But then, in the late 1970s, something went wrong. The Phillips curve relationship crumbled into a meaningless jumble of points. The output-inflation tradeoff had, apparently, ceased to exist. Suddenly, there was no clear unified model, and macroeconomic analysis and policy appeared to be irrevocably changed. A new and emerging group of macroeconomists insisted that the paradigm had changed yet again and that "Keynes was dead". Needless to say, the Keynesians strongly disagreed and continue to do so.

Before we come to yet another exciting phase in the evolution of macroeconomic policy, a discussion of some key questions and a review of "media articles" to allow us to fully understand the Keynesian model is in order.

9.6 DISCUSSION QUESTIONS

1. **It looks as if the vertical portion of the K-AS curve is identical to the vertical Classical AS curve. Are they essentially the same curves?**

They are "similar" in that they are both vertical segments, derived by the fact that W and P are fully flexible. But the similarity ends there. The Classical AS is vertical at some "natural" rate of output growth, Y_0, corresponding to some rate of employment n_0. The vertical segment of the K-AS curve, on the other hand, is at an overheated Y_{max}, corresponding to full employment and virtually no excess capacity in the economy.

2. **Is Stage 3 inflation (the rapid increase in inflation beyond the overheated stage) the same as hyperinflation?**

No. Hyperinflations are usually caused by non-sustainable deficits that necessitate monetization. Overheating and Stage 3 inflation are caused by excess demand that rapidly drive up wages and prices given the finite (maximum possible) aggregate supply.

3. **From a previous chapter, we know that foreign income, Y^*, can shift the global IS to the right, also driving the AD to the right. Why is this not listed under factors that can stimulate an economy?**

We only list changes in G, M, and tax rates, t, as factors that can jump-start or soft-land an economy because these are the three policy instruments available to us. Foreign income Y^* is an exogenous variable which is taken as given by the domestic economy. It certainly affects domestic IS and AD, but is not a policy variable that can be readily controlled by domestic policy makers to shift IS and hence AD.

4. **Wasn't it fairly obvious that the paradigm had shifted during and after the Great Depression? What would it have taken to convince the Classical economists that the model had changed?**

In hindsight and retrospect, yes, paradigm shifts seem obvious. But in reality, they are extremely difficult to detect during the contemporaneous time period. In Chapter 10 we will discuss a time-series problem known as the Identification Problem. This problem makes it extremely difficult to pinpoint the "correct" model, since several different models may "explain" the real-world data equally well. But in addition to this problem, there are the lags to consider—policy ineffectiveness may be misinterpreted simply as the lag before the policies actually show effects. In addition, data is often not very accurate and needs to be revised several times. And finally, there may be a sense of denial on the part of policy makers that the model that had worked so impeccably well in the past may now be defunct.

Please relate the underlined passages in the following articles to material covered in this chapter as well as in preceding ones. Use diagrams (ISLM-ADAS) liberally.

ARTICLE 9.1 **"WE HAVE OPTIONS," PM TELLS CABINET**

Tom Chamberlain, Belgravia Policy Review

As the latest economic data hit the stands, Dr. Norton Jones, Prime Minister of Belgravia, moved swiftly to assure the nation that plans were already afoot to counter the impending macro-economic problems.

"It is clear that our present

(a) slowdown is attributed to long recessions in our two biggest trading partners, the United States and Japan, but we have many tricks up our sleeve to counteract that," he told the powerful Belgravian Association of Model Train Builders at the National Hobby Convention in the tiny mountain principality of Luray.

The audience was not impressed. Zenobia Mistry, an expert in Swiss train sets, said, "I know something about finance; **(b)** when the yield curve points the other way, I know that a recession is coming." But Kevin Morgenstern, an American model train veteran specializing in early generation diesels conceded, "At least the guy (the PM) is trying. He has a plan that makes sense to me, and **(c)** let's just wait to see if he gets us through this. But now I have to get my Roanoke-built 611 off the main-line before that high speed TGV slams into it..." and with that he clambered hurriedly onto the tracks.

When questioned about his "plans" the PM stated, **(d)** "We have a budget surplus, and that allows us huge policy options. Given the fact that **(e)** we are still an emerging economy, fiscal expansion which includes a new expanded subway system, seven new power plants and dams, and, of course, the intercity high-speed train system will be the key."

He dismissed concerns from political opponent Bill Macla-shovsky regarding the financing of

206

the new infrastructure spending. The PM said, "Since we are running national budget surpluses, a **(f)** sustainable deficit is not a problem. In fact, it is part of the solution. I also expect a strengthening of our currency and capital inflows in the near future."

Dr. Jones has two other 'tricks' up his sleeve. The Belgravian central bank will cooperate by **(g)** lowering interest rates, and he is lobbying for an across-the board tax cut of 28% to stimulate consumption and capital investment. He also hopes that once investors see that these plans are in the works **(h)** the current trend of defeatism and gloom will be reversed.

"All in all, this is a **(i)** three-pronged Keynesian offensive," remarked Sophie DeSalle of France Polytechnique, a Loire Valley consulting house. "This is quite a standard package, actually. The important thing is that Dr. Jones has been quick to recognize the peril and quick to launch this stimulation package. We are quite sanguine about Belgravia in the near-term."

At the hobby conference, Al Silverman, a 77-year old model train buff, may have said it best. "While the 'locomotive' of the economy may need to be jump-started, and then later cooled down and all that—my trains need nothing! They run perfectly all the time!" More power to him (pun intended).

Mary Bonniebanks, <u>Houston World Business Weekly</u>

A recent visit to the kingdom of Bardoli is a study in contrasts. Just four weeks ago, this reporter spoke to Mr. Sudhir Gupta, owner of the Sea Breeze chain of hotels, who lamented that **(a)** <u>he had to "import" students from overseas during the busy summer months to staff the front desks of his hotels.</u> "It was my only option. Our labor market dried up months ago!"

The entire country had been desperate for workers until very recently. Employees for the service industries—hotels, amusement parks, general tourism, outdoor recreation—as well as sectors such as nursing, IT hardware and software specialists, engineers of all kinds, and high school teachers were virtually impossible to find.

"Personally, we have been riding this big high," says Bernice Fitzpatrick, a software engineer. "I know other engineers who changed jobs every two months for **(b)** <u>a salary increase of at least 25 percent with every change.</u> It was a crazy time," she says, shaking her head.

Professor Umbotu Ulundi of Bardoli Medical School added, "The **(c)** <u>over-inflated stock market and housing market added to the crazy salaries</u> that some sectors were getting. The **(d)** <u>central bank had to put an end to the madness.</u> It was really impossible to replace nurses as we couldn't afford the salaries demanded by new nurses. Sheer madness!"

The central bank certainly put an end to the "madness". **(e)** <u>Six interest rate hikes have cooled down the torrid labor market. The stock market is down by 19% relative to its high last year, and housing prices are also 24% lower.</u> And talk of a sharp cutback in defense spending is adding to expectations for further GDP slowdowns. The current GDP growth rate of 4.1% (down from the supercharged 7.8% last year) is expected to be down to 3.5% by this time next year, according to our survey of the nation's top economists. **(f)** <u>The price of gold has fallen by 32%, and other commodities futures have displayed similar drops in price.</u>

(g) <u>The rate of imports has also slowed, with the current account deficit posting its slowest increase</u> in six years. "This is all in line with macro theory," said Karen Chang, a recent MBA graduate from New Market University in Omaha, **(h)** <u>"I also expect long-term rates to fall over the next six months".</u>

Maximillan Porshe of the giant German real estate consortium, Haus, concurs. "I expect this to be a good time for mortgage purchases and refinancing. **(i)** <u>However, new home</u>

sales aren't just functions of interest rates. The question is how low will disposable incomes fall and how will the consumer feel as the central bank taps the brakes? Hopefully this will not be a hard landing."

ANSWERS AND HINTS

ARTICLE 9.1 "WE HAVE OPTIONS," PM TELLS CABINET

(a) Denote Y* as the foreign income (US and Japan) and show how recessions in these two countries affect the IS and hence the AD of the domestic economy. (You may need to refer to a previous chapter to review the effect of foreign recessions on the domestic economy.)

(b) Is Zenobia Mistry's conclusion incontrovertible? Explain why an inverted yield curve is thought to presage a slowdown and also explain why this may not necessarily be the only conclusion one could draw from an inverted yield curve.

(c) Kevin Morgenstern may be referring to the lags with which macroeconomic policies manifest themselves. Policies take time to make themselves felt.

(d) Yes, this allows Belgravia to increase G with impunity, and hopefully to reap multiplier effects. In other words, Belgravia has many fiscal "policy bullets" left in its arsenal of macroeconomic stimulus policies.

(e) Emerging economies are typically Keynesian, with the percentage change in prices usually far greater than the percentage change in nominal wages. This condition is necessary for a positively sloped Keynesian AS curve that will yield convenient multiplier effects stemming from the increase in G on infrastructure.

(f) Bond financing will inject the "idle" loanable funds back into the income expenditure stream and jump-start growth, as discussed in several earlier chapters beginning with the NSI in Chapter 2. Assume here that Belgravia is a safe haven country and, using the earlier NSI discussion, briefly discuss how and why Belgravia may experience a strengthening of its currency as well as a capital inflow.

(g) These are the other two policy buttons—cuts in tax rates and monetary expansion. Compare this exercise to the simpler case discussed in Chapter 5 (pre-ISLM) without the labor market and (i,Y) space and note the increase in sophistication post-ISLM.

(h) Consumer and investor confidence have apparently collapsed. However, a bold stimulus package may hopefully "turn around" the confidence parameters and further assist in shifting IS.

(i) Sophie DeSalle is referring to the three Keynesian macroeconomic policy instruments, namely changes in G, M, and tax rates.

ARTICLE 9.2 THE GOOD NEWS: ECONOMY IS SLOWING!

(a) Clearly, the labor market was tight—the service industry, and particularly the tourism industry, was in dire need of workers. The economy seemed to be close to overheating.

(b) Sounds like a SAP bubble existed in high skilled labor

(c) SAP bubbles in equity and real estate markets had created a dangerous wealth effect (discussed in earlier chapters) which, in turn, drove up demand for skilled workers.

(d) and (e) A soft landing and a deflation of SAP bubbles was engineered with contractionary monetary policy.

(f) Expectations of future inflation are now lower, given the monetary contraction and the "cooling down' of the economy. Hence, the attractiveness of gold and precious metals as inflation hedges has gone down, resulting in a drop in the price of gold.

(g) As national income (Y) falls during a soft landing, imports also fall as consumers now seek to purchase fewer foreign (and domestic) goods in a slowing economy. The current account (from Chapter 2) is defined as exports minus imports. If imports exceed exports, the nation incurs a current account deficit that increases at a slower rate when the growth in imports begin to slow.

(h) Include the Fisher effect and the inverted yield curve in this answer.

(i) Use the investment function to answer this. The effect of the slowing economy on investor confidence is the key.

---

[1] Cambridge is a highly recommended visit. This famous and exquisite university town, tracing its history to well before the Roman conquest, has a distinct "rural feel" which adds to its charm.

[2] The author remains grateful to Professor John Cathie of Cambridge University for pointing out "the window". This momentous event occurred soon after the Rutgers University Executive MBA students had just attended a private harpsichord recital by the renowned Dr. Gerald Gifford at King's College Chapel. The window is now a favorite "pilgrimage" destination during the annual Rutgers visit. While controversy swirls around the "authenticity" of the story pertaining to Keynes' office, the fact remains that Keynes is still considered to be one of our most globally influential and intriguing macroeconomists, and that he did indeed make history while at Cambridge.

[3] Here steps 3 and 4 of the survival guide are different from those of the Classical model. While prices may have changed, we do not bother going back to "adjust" the LM, even though technically the LM will shift with a change in P. The crucial effects here, namely the changes in P and in Y, are indeed captured and reflected by the

model in its diagrammatic analysis. Incorporating the final LM shift would make a diagrammatic representation somewhat intractable. While purists may disagree, the final twitch in LM does not add any additional value from a macroeconomic policy perspective, and is disregarded here in the interest of pedagogic convenience.

[4] In a later exercise in this chapter, we will examine why these policies have not been nearly as successful as the one in the example just discussed.

[5] The exact mechanism by which the major central banks change the money supply will be discussed in the Chapter 11.

[6] Recall that other instruments are cuts in taxes and, of course, increases in G, both of which take much longer to implement, given the necessary approval processes in government. On the other hand, monetary policy, especially in an economy characterized by an autonomous central bank, can be enacted very rapidly without being hindered by a lengthy and debate-ridden approval process.

[7] Here the overheating is being caused by relentless monetary stabilization. It needn't always be the case. The overheating could also be caused by excessive fiscal stimulus in the form of mammoth and ongoing increases in G and/or huge tax cuts, or some combination of all three "policy buttons". Finally, an "irrational exuberance" could also trigger overheating. Increases in the confidence parameters (perhaps in conjunction with any of the policies cited here) will also shift the IS remorselessly to the right, resulting in the AD being pushed towards the kink.

[8] The interest rates in ISLM space are short-term rates. Soon we will examine the effects of these policies on long-term rates when we revisit the role of expectations in the Fisher effect.

[9] A good example of this exercise is Japan in the 1990s and early 2000s. This scenario, which was briefly discussed earlier, is now being revisited in the context of a fully-articulated ISLM-ADAS model.

[10] This is reminiscent of the very low interest rates experienced by Japan in the early 2000s—virtually zero percent interest rates!

[11] In a following chapter, the Identification Problem will help explain why it is econometrically very difficult even today to "identify" the "real" model when dealing with time-series data.

[12] The Federal Deposit Insurance Corporation (FDIC) was a result of the Great Depression. Established in 1933, the FDIC insures bank deposits for up to $100,000 per deposit. This (it was hoped) would ensure that depositors no longer fear bank failures and thus recessions and depressions would not precipitate panics and provoke runs on banks.

[13] The monetary aggregates, M1-3 will be defined in Chapter 11. For now, M1 includes all cash and demand deposits, and M2 includes all of M1 plus interest bearing checking accounts.

10. THE SUPPLY-SIDE MODEL AND THE NEW ECONOMY

By the early 1980s, the macroeconomic landscape had changed significantly for the United States and several other Western European economies. Once-successful Keynesian discretionary demand-side stabilization policies appeared to be ineffective. The output-inflation tradeoff seemed to be no longer in evidence—expansionary fiscal and monetary stimuli only yielded additional inflation with no accompanying increase in GDP growth or employment. The Phillips curve, for all intents and purposes, appeared to be dead.

According to the rational expectationists, the emerging school of macroeconomics at that time, these changes were clearly indicative of the demise of the Keynesian model. They claimed that, once again, the paradigm had shifted and that the model that best described the economy, had changed from Keynesian to Rational Expectations.

Leading this revolution were economists such as Robert E. Lucas, Thomas Sargent, Robert Barro, JoAnna Grey, and E.S. Phelps, who ushered in the rational expectations paradigm with its attendant supply-side policy implications. These economists fundamentally believed in an optimizing, market-clearing approach to macroeconomics. A greater role of expectations, uncertainty, and asymmetric information, accompanied by more sophisticated time-series analyses, were the hallmarks of this school of thought.

This chapter begins with an examination of the causes underlying the so-called demise of Keynesian macroeconomics. We explore the transition from the Keynesian to the rational expectations paradigm by deriving the expectations-augmented aggregate supply curve (AE-AS). This will be followed by an analysis of the supply-side policy implications of the rational expectations model.[1] A case will then be made to link these supply-side polices to the advent of the New Economy in the United States (the slowdown during 2001-2 notwithstanding) and, to a lesser extent, in Western Europe.

The latter half of the chapter includes a discussion of the Keynesian response to the alleged paradigm shift propounded by the rational expectationists. This is followed by a Keynesian analysis and explanation of the "so-called" New Economy and the outlook pertaining to its longevity. Interestingly, the Keynesian explanation of the second paradigm shift, as well as the transition to the New Economy followed by the "hard soft landing" of 2000, may be as compelling as that provided by the supply-siders.

We then discuss the identification problem, which helps explain how and why both the Keynesian as well as supply-sider models can legitimately co-exist in the United States and other developed economies. Finally, this chapter explores whether the two paradigms can be reconciled—even in the short-run. Robert E. Lucas' well-known 'islands' model will be overviewed here in the context of the ability of policy makers to exploit perceived output-inflation tradeoffs in an economy characterized by imperfect information.

10.1   THE EXPECTATIONS-AUGMENTED AS CURVE: AN EXPLANATION OF THE PARADIGM SHIFT

In Figure 1, we derive the JoAnna Grey/Phelps expectations-augmented aggregate supply curve. This is a positively sloped AS curve that bears a resemblance to the positively sloped Keynesian AS curve of the previous chapters and has similar policy implications. Fiscal and monetary policies will indeed affect GDP and inflation, but the similarity ends there. The expectations-augmented AS, as the name implies, incorporates a significantly higher degree of sophistication pertaining to expectations formation over time. It is this feature that explains how this AS may have transitioned into the rational expectations AS curve by the early 1980s to usher in the shift from the Keynesian era to the supply-side model.

The four diagrams in **Figure 1** should be familiar from earlier AS derivations. The two plots on the left are the production function and the labor market, while the two on the right are the y-y reflector and (P,Y) space in which the expectations-augmented AS is to be derived.

The crucial assumption that "drives" this derivation is that information is asymmetric.[2] Here, demanders of labor (employers) are assumed to know the changes in contemporaneous prices as well as nominal wages. That is, they "see" changes in both P and W in the current time period. Suppliers of labor (workers), on the other hand, do not see/know changes in both P and W in the current period; they are only aware of the change in their nominal wages (W). In this sense, information in the labor market is asymmetric—workers know only one piece of information (changes in nominal wages, W), while employers know both pieces of information (changes in W and P) in the current time period.

Employers know both (all) pieces of information, not because they are necessarily any smarter than the "workers", but rather because employers have access to more information by interacting with wholesalers and sub-contractors, and have more knowledge about imported goods, inventories, transportation costs, etc.

We now turn to the derivation of the AS curve that will explain the paradigm shift and lead the way to the controversial New Economy. We will discuss its present version following the September 2001 terror attacks, and compare it to its heyday of the late 1990s. The New Economy has always generated a storm of controversy from the Keynesians who insist that the "old" paradigm is alive and well, and the whole business—the "so-called" paradigm shift in the 1980s to the "New Economy"—fits well into their original framework without necessitating a paradigm shift.

10.1.1 DIAGRAMMATIC DERIVATION: EXPECTATIONS-AUGMENTED AGGREGATE SUPPLY CURVE

Steps 1-7 are represented by corresponding numbers in Figure 1.

1. Initially, the economy is at Y_0 and prices are at P_0. We plot this point in (P,Y) space. For pedagogic simplicity, let $P_0 = 2$, and nominal wages, $W_0 = 12$. Equilibrium exists in the labor market at n_0. Let the initial Y_0 be some recessionary rate of growth that warrants stabilization.

Figure 1

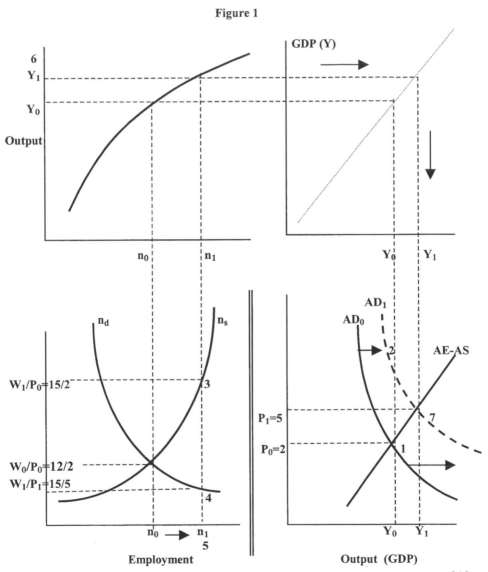

213

2. We are given that, following some demand-side stabilization, AD_0 shifts right to AD_1, causing Po to increase to P1, from 2 to 5, and nominal wages to increase from W_0 to W_1, from 12 to 15.

3. Given the assumption that information is asymmetric, employers know that prices have more than doubled but nominal wages have only gone from 12 to 15. However, workers "see" only the change in nominal wage from 12 to 15, and consequently think that they are "better off" as their salaries (W) have now increased. They are inadvertently "fooled" into believing that they are better off, and they supply more labor.[3]

4. This information asymmetry leads to an increase in demand for labor as well. Employers discern correctly that they are now paying only 3 in real wages (15/5), as opposed to 6 earlier (12/2), and they demand more labor (point 4, in Figure 1). In this stylized version of the Grey/Phelps model, point 3 in Figure 1 is where workers "think they are" in terms of real wage and labor supply, while point 4 is where producers "know" they are.

5. This increase in labor supply driven by asymmetric information on the part of suppliers of labor (workers), coupled with the increase in demand on the part of demanders of labor (producers), leads to employment increasing to n_1 in the labor market, in figure 1.

6. As employment increase to n_1, GDP growth increases to Y_1 as seen in the production function.

7. Reflecting this higher Y_1 into (P,Y) space and plotting, we obtain the second point, (P_1,Y_1). Joining this point to the initial given point (P_0,Y_0), we obtain the expectations-augmented AS curve.[4]

The expectations-augmented AS curve is indeed positively sloped like its Keynesian counterpart of an earlier chapter. The Keynesian AS was positively sloped by virtue of nominal wages being "sticky" and not changing in proportion to prices. The expectations-augmented AS, on the other hand, is positively sloped due to imperfect—asymmetric—information which leads workers to mistakenly interpret observed nominal wage increases for real wage increases and, hence, to supply more labor.[5]

The expectationists argue that this asymmetric information approach best explains the positively sloped AS curve which generated the successful output-inflation tradeoffs from the 1950s to the late 1970s in the US. After all, since nominal wage freezes were primarily in effect only during the Depression (1929-33), and given that an exploitable Phillips curve was indeed in effect during from the 1950s to the 1970s, the imperfect information theory would be the only viable explanation for the positively sloped AS.

In addition to explaining the output-inflation tradeoff, the heightened sophistication of the intertemporal expectations-formation structure also provides for a cogent explanation of Paradigm Shift II from the Keynesian to the supply-sider paradigm in the United States in early 1980s.[6]

10.1.2 PARADIGM SHIFT II: AN EXPECTATIONS-AUGMENTED EXPLANATION

How long can a tradeoff driven by imperfect information be exploited? Do workers misinterpret observed nominal wage changes for real wage changes only in the short and medium-term? Wouldn't suppliers of labor (workers) eventually realize that their real wages had actually deteriorated (from 6 to 3) over repeated episodes of demand-side stabilization policy?

Turning to **Figure 2**, we pick up where we left off in Figure 1. The positively-sloped, expectations-augmented AS curve facilitates output-inflation tradeoffs. But, over time, the relentless pursuit of expansionary fiscal and monetary policies with successive recessions result in workers eventually realizing that their observed increases in nominal wages (12 to 15) have not been in proportion to the actual increases in the price level (2 to 5).

In other words, workers now "catch on"; they update their information sets and revise their expectations. When another round of fiscal and monetary stabilization is anticipated, workers/unions now indulge in proactive long-term contracts to ensure that the real wage is not eroded by the next series of stabilization policies.

Thus, in our example here, workers/unions now contract for a nominal wage of $W_1=30$. This nominal wage W_1 ensures that real wages remains unchanged from $W_0/P_0 = 12/2 = 6$ initially, to $W_1/P_1 = 30/5 = 6$, once again.

At this point, information has become symmetric. Both suppliers as well as demanders of labor now accurately identify changes in all pieces of information, W and P. In Figure 2, this full (symmetric) knowledge on the part of both demanders and suppliers of labor translates to equilibrium employment n_0 once again corresponding to a real wage of 6. And, from the production function, GDP growth corresponding to employment n_0 is back to Y_0.

If we reflect this final Y_0 over to (P,Y) space and plot (P_1, Y_0) to join with the original point (P_0, Y_0), we obtain the rational expectations AS curve (RE-AS), which is the theoretical centerpiece of the new supply-side paradigm (figure 2). Since the RE-AS is a vertical line similar to the Classical model which predates the Keynesian paradigm, the RE-AS is also known as the new classical aggregate supply curve.

Economies that transition from the positively sloped expectations-augmented AS to the vertical RE-AS are typically those with (i) sophisticated labor forces with market power capable of influencing long-term nominal wage contracts, and (ii) fully-articulated and efficient bond markets that accurately "signal" expected inflation to workers as well as employers. Typically, developed economies are more likely to have these two criteria in place compared to emerging economies. The latter may be burdened with larger pools of excess labor incapable of affecting nominal wage contracts (as in parts of China, India, Eastern Europe, South America, Africa), and often lack well-developed government bond-markets.

Figure 2

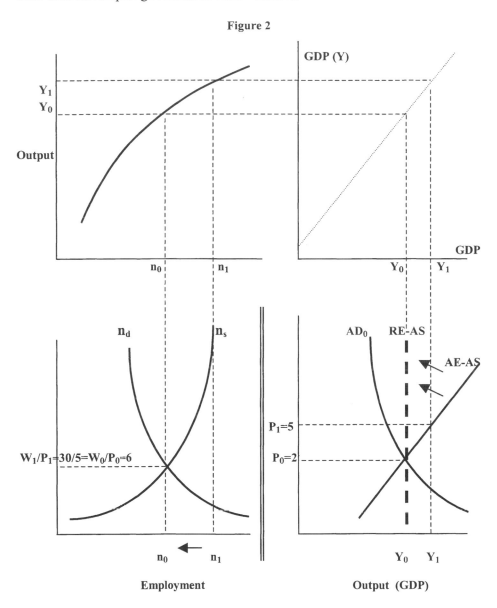

Remember that Keynesian discretionary fiscal and monetary policies have no effect on real GDP growth or employment in a classical-type model. In fact, demand-side stabilization, the mainstay of Keynesian policy, is neutral to real variables and affects only nominal variables such as inflation and nominal wages. This is now the case, as depicted in **Figure 3** where expansionary demand-side stabilization is attempted. Changes in G or M change only the rate of inflation—GDP growth remains at Y_0. The output-inflation tradeoff has vanished. The Phillips curve relationship, vital for jump-starting or soft-landing economies, is conspicuously absent. The paradigm has now "shifted" from K-AS to RE-AS.[7]

Figure 3

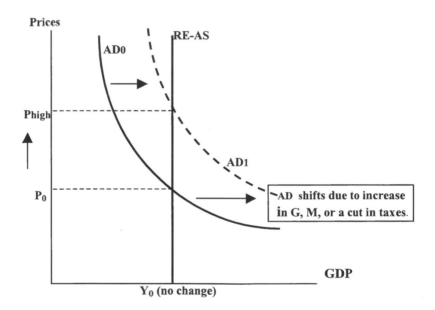

Against this new backdrop, if Y_0 is indeed some recessionary "low" rate of growth, how can GDP and employment be stimulated if expansionary fiscal and monetary policies have no effect? Since shifting the aggregate demand affects only inflation, leaving Y_0 unchanged, clearly the only viable policy option would be **to shift the aggregate supply** to the right to increase GDP growth. This radical emphasis on policies designed to shift the aggregate supply curve instead of the aggregate demand led to the aptly named "supply-side" model.

According to this theory, as once successful aggregate demand-side policies began to fail in developed economies possessing more sophisticated labor markets that are characterized by forward-looking information in efficient bond markets, policy makers began to focus their attention to shifting the aggregate supply.

10.2 SUPPLY-SIDE ECONOMICS

Three main elements of effective supply-side policy are:
(1) Significant income/personal tax cuts
(2) Sweeping corporate/business tax cuts
(3) Massive deregulation.

10.2.1 SIGNIFICANT INCOME TAX CUTS

The crucial assumption here is that in addition to stimulating after-tax consumption as discussed earlier, income tax cuts also impact the labor market. Tax changes now also result in shifts in labor supply and demand curves.

The Labor supply is now defined as:

Labor Supply = f(real wage, personal tax rates, macroeconomic outlook).
$$(+) \qquad\qquad (-) \qquad\qquad\qquad (+)$$
Here labor supply is positively related to the real wage and macroeconomic outlook, and negatively related to personal tax rates.

An intuitive explanation of a tax-cut-induced increase in labor supply is as follows. There is a sense on the part of suppliers of labor that these tax cuts are temporary, and hence currently employed workers may avail themselves of such tax cuts by working more hours. In addition, individuals not currently in the work force (not actively seeking employment, as discussed earlier), may now find it worthwhile to seek employment, thereby becoming a part of the civilian labor force, and increasing the participation rate. The pool of available workers increases as more and more disenfranchised individuals now "come back" into the active labor market, thereby shifting the labor supply to the right. These new entrants to the labor force now find it worth their while to re-enter the work force, given that, with the tax-cuts, the government is not siphoning away a disproportionate share of any additional income in the form of high taxes.

Conversely, personal tax increases result in shifts in labor supply to the left as individuals realize that, at the margin, it is not worthwhile to enter the labor force. For example, former homemakers turned workers might now choose to remain at home if higher income tax rates lead to very insignificant

218

(if any) real income gains after incorporating expenses such as child-care, housekeeping, and transportation.

An alternative explanation linking labor market shifts to tax changes is as follows. As presented in **Figure 4a**, initially at employment n_0 the real wage was $(W/P)_0$ and the initial labor supply curve is n_{so}. Let the government impose a tax of t. Income tax increases, in effect, decrease the after-tax real wage. In this situation, what increase in real wages would the workers have to be offered so that, once again, they supply n_0 labor? The answer is the after-tax real wage would have to be the same as it was before the tax increase. Thus, to induce employment of n_0 again, the real wages would have to rise by t to offset the tax increase. This translates to an upward shift in labor supply by t. This exercise holds true for any and all levels of employment, thus resulting in the labor supply curve shifting up ("left") from n_{so} to n_{st}.

The opposite holds for tax cuts; the labor supply shifts down (to the "right"), as presented in **Figure 4b**. Here, to maintain the original level of employment n_0 following the tax cut, the real wage would have to decrease by t to ensure that the after-tax real wage matches that before the tax cuts. Once again, this mechanism holds for all levels of employment thus shifting the labor supply down, or to the right.

While tax changes also affect disposable income and consumption as in the Keynesian model, one key difference between the two paradigms is that in the case of the rational expectations paradigm, taxes _also_ influence the labor market.

Figure 4a

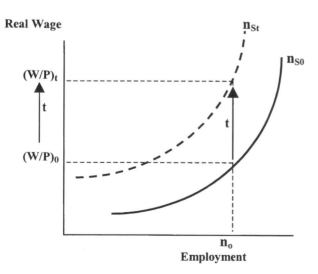

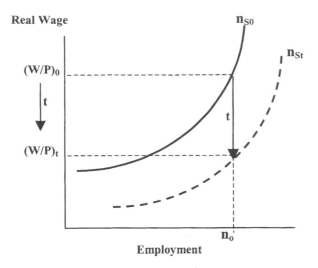

Figure 4b

The next main element of supply-side policy pertains to business tax cuts.

10.2.2   SWEEPING CORPORATE/BUSINESS TAX CUTS

Here, labor demand, depicted in **Figure 5**, is given by:
Labor Demand = f(real wage, business tax rates, macroeconomic outlook).
$$(-) \qquad\qquad (-) \qquad\qquad\qquad (+)$$
Labor demand is negatively correlated to real wages and business tax rates, and positively correlated to the macroeconomic outlook.

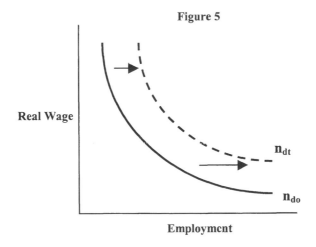

Figure 5

220

The assumption here is that with business tax cuts such as investment tax credits, and with accelerated depreciation, firms (demanders of labor) increase labor demand. Once again, the sense that the tax cuts are "temporary", coupled with an opportunity to increase shareholder wealth, leads employers to demand more labor.

Hence, cuts in corporate/business taxes shift labor demand to the right, from n_{d0} to n_{dt} as presented in Figure 5, while increases in these taxes do the opposite.

Changes in the third term, "macroeconomic outlook", also shift the labor demand and supply curves. As the outlook improves, both labor demand and supply curves shift right, and vice versa. This term, unlike tax rates, is not an exogenous policy instrument, but is, instead, determined by endogenously formed expectations. Discussions pertaining to stagflation and recessions, later in this chapter, will activate this term that lies dormant at this stage.

10.2.3 DEREGULATION

According to the supply-siders, government intervention is perceived to be intrusive and excessive and is believed to retard the productivity of the private sector, with "productivity" defined as output per worker per unit time. An economy unfettered by such excessive government regulation, therefore, is likely to experience an increase in productivity.

Figure 6 represents an economy with a sharp decrease in unproductive government regulation. With massive deregulation, at each and every unit of

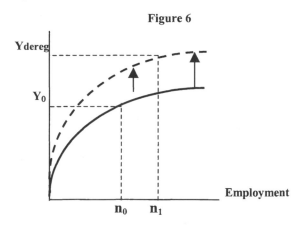

Figure 6

the labor force a higher output is now possible—n_0 labor now results in the higher Y_{dereg} as opposed to the initial output level Y_0 when the economy was highly regulated due to the increase in productivity.

For example, upon deregulation, industries such as airlines and trucking would now determine optimal routes, prices, and stops based on market forces, and not on required schedules and limits imposed by government. Similarly, financial institutions and utilities would determine their rates and fee-structures based on market-driven competition, and not on some government-imposed mandate. All these sectors would experience increases in productivity.

The United States embarked on an active deregulatory policy beginning in the later years of the Carter administration, followed aggressively by President Reagan and his successors to the present. Examples of deregulated industries in the US are airlines, trucking, financial services, telecommunications, and utilities. Western Europe, the United Kingdom, France and Germany have all seen deregulation adopted with varying degrees of intensity from the early 1990s to the present.

According to the supply-siders, an excessively regulated economy retards productivity in that private enterprise will not be "unleashed" to maximize the creative and risk taking instincts present in inherently dynamic economies. In this case, the reverse of Figure 6 occurs; the production function "bends down" with lower output produced at each and every level of employment.

Emerging economies have also embraced the concept of "less government," to some extent. However, these cases usually involve a two-stage process beginning first with privatization, eventually followed by gradual deregulation. Once again, with varying degrees of success, Mexico, Argentina, India, China, and Chile (to name a few) have, in fits and starts, attempted privatizations of industries once considered safely within the government domain. (Please refer to the discussion of State Owned Enterprises, SOEs, from Chapter 6).

10.2.4 SUPPLY-SIDE STABILIZATION

Integrating the three major supply-side policies, **Figure 7** displays the essence of shifting the AS curve to the right. Initially Y_0 is some low recessionary rate of growth corresponding to employment at n_{low}. The AS is a rational expectations AS curve in an economy characterized by symmetric information.

A combination of personal and business tax cuts set against a backdrop of government deregulation of key industries results in a final shift to the right in the RE-AS. Here, both labor supply and demand curves shift right due to the tax cuts, and the production function rises due to the surge in deregulation-driven productivity. This supply-side stimulus results in GDP growth increasing from $\dot{Y}_0$ to Y_1 and employment from n_0 to n_1 as depicted in Figure 7.

In this case, the increase in output growth is not matched by an increase in inflation, as was the case in the Keynesian paradigm. Here the rate of

222

inflation <u>actually falls</u> from P_0 to P_1. There is no output inflation tradeoff in this paradigm—the Phillips curve relationship is gone. Instead, increases in output and employment growth are accompanied by convenient <u>decreases</u> in the rate of inflation!

Figure 7

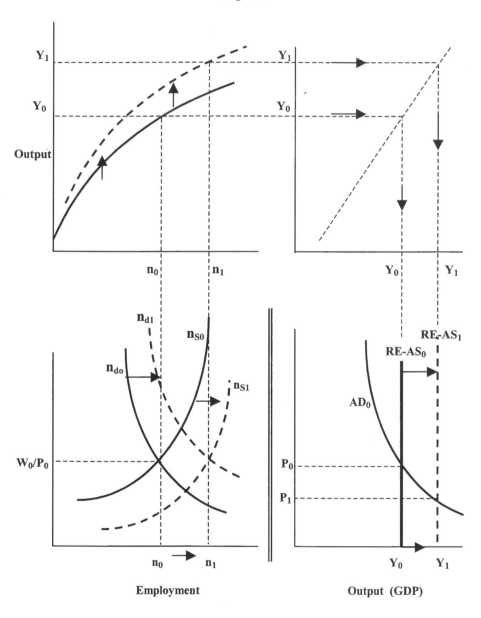

Ireland and Information Technology: A Supply-Side Story

Beginning in the late 1990s, Ireland embarked on a serious supply-side policy that may well have contributed to its re-engineered status as the Information Technology (IT) powerhouse of Europe into the early 2000s.

Corporate rates as low as 10%, coupled with a well-educated labor force, a five-year "tax holiday" for new foreign investment in IT, and a conspicuous absence of "meddlesome" government regulation, resulted in a huge global capital inflow primarily in the IT sector. More than 45 percent of American investment in Europe's electronic industry in the late 1990s was absorbed annually by Ireland. Consequently, by the late 1990s, Ireland was making one-third of all personal computers sold on the Continent, and GDP growth at times exceeded an annual rate of 10 percent.

The supply-side policies adopted by Ireland were not popular with continental Europe, where large government spending coupled with higher taxes dominated macroeconomic policy.

By 1998, the European Commission had labeled Ireland's policy of giving a preferential tax rate of only 10% to its financial services and manufacturing sectors as "unfair" to European Union (EU) members with higher tax rates (almost 32%). The Commission claimed that attracting global investment with low tax rates was tantamount to a hidden State subsidy to its champion sectors and, therefore, technically illegal.

Ireland responded to this pressure in the late 1990s by agreeing to eliminate the 10% rate for its few "championed" sectors. It then announced, however, that all its sectors would be taxed at a new uniform rate of 12.5%, one-third the average corporate tax rate in Europe! Ireland was determined to keep the continental penchant for taxation at bay, and to retain its hard-won title of "Celtic Tiger".

10.3   STAGFLATION

An economy in the throes of stagflation is characterized by a rising rate of inflation and an ominously falling rate of GDP growth and employment as described in **Figure 8**. Typically, "stagflation" brings to mind the severe episodes experienced by the US, Japan, and Western Europe in the 1970s which coincided with the oil crises.

Oil shocks slammed into the world economy following the October 1973 Yom Kippur War, when the Arab oil-producing nations sharply restricted oil exports. Another shock followed shortly thereafter in 1979, this time related to the Iranian revolution and the deposition of the Shah. Inflation rates soared to double digits coupled with similar rates of unemployment and shrinking national GDP rates.

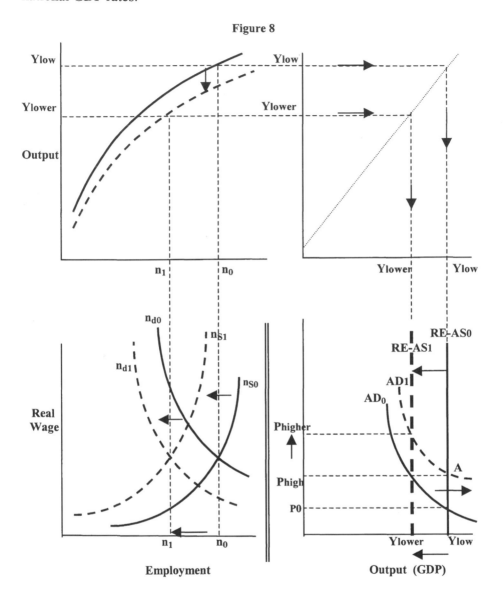

Figure 8

Further aggravating the situation may have been the paradigm shift from the Keynesian to supply-sider (rational expectations) model, in progress in many developed economies from the mid to late 1970s. According to the expectationists, policies designed to jump-start economies stuck at Y_{low} and mistakenly still considered Keynesian only served to worsen the rate of

225

inflation. Rightward shifts in the AD due to frequent and desperate attempts at fiscal and monetary stabilization only increased P_0 to P_{high}, labeled A in figure 8, without any accompanying relief in GDP or employment.

Superimposing the effects of the oil shocks and the accompanying reduction in productivity as production was forced to move to non-optimal, secondary sources of energy, resulted in a downward shift in the production function.[8] Additional leftward shifts in labor demand and supply caused by the deteriorating outlook, completed the dismal picture. The final toll of stagflation was an even higher rate of inflation at P_{higher} and a worsening recession at Y_{lower} as presented in figure 8.[9]

10.4   FROM THE SUPPLY-SIDE TO THE NEW ECONOMY

From a macroeconomic perspective, the 1990s could be characterized as the era of the New Economy in the US. Following the minor recession of 1990-91, and before the more sustainable phase that began in late 2000, the US economy displayed an amazing nine years of very strong GDP growth, productivity gains, and record low unemployment, set against a backdrop of virtually no inflationary pressure. The Europeans were quick to adopt such a performance as a policy goal, and in Singapore, Japan, and China policy makers became determined to put their own respective versions of the New Economy into operation.

According to the expectationists, the New Economy traces its roots to the supply-side policies put in place in the early 1980s. The massive deregulations, it is argued, paved the way for the eventual breakthroughs in technology. Firms and individuals were free to respond to market pressures, and to seek out market opportunities. The climate fostered risk-taking, massive private capital investment, and entrepreneurship. The unleashed creativity of US enterprise (according to this argument), in turn led to the inevitable internet-assisted economy, resulting in permanent structural increases in productivity (see the following box).

Technological growth, fostered in part by the early deregulations, shifted the production function up. Over time, labor demand and supply curves also shift right due to a stronger "macroeconomic outlook" fueled by expectations of yet more growth, thereby increasing equilibrium employment.

These combined labor-market and productivity effects resulted in a rightward shift in the RE-AS, resulting in the hallmark of the New Economy— growth in GDP without an accompanying increase in inflation. In fact, during the heyday of the New Economy in the US in the mid 1990s to 2000, quarterly GDP growth at times exceeded 5% with unemployment in the 3% range and with hardly any appreciable change in the rate of inflation.

The diagram depicting the New Economy is identical to figure 7, which presents the supply-sider paradigm. The only difference is that the production function in the New Economy is shifting up not to deregulation *per se*, but rather to a <u>result</u> of the deregulation—gains in productivity stemming from breakthroughs in technology. Additionally, in the labor market of the New Economy, the labor demand and supply curves do shift to the right but not due to large personal and business tax cuts. Instead, the curves shift right because of endogenous expectations of strong growth.

Labor demand also increases due to increased productivity, since this increased productivity implies an increase in the marginal product of labor. While this feature is not explicitly incorporated in our labor market for expositional convenience, we assume that the "outlook" term captures this shift in addition to expectations of future real growth. Indeed, the "outlook" term is positively correlated to productivity gains, and productivity has a strong procyclical component as discussed below.

The New Economy and the Productivity Puzzle

The New Economy lives and dies by its ability to influence overall productivity. Faster GDP growth with lower inflation, higher profits, and budget surpluses is vitally dependent on high and increasing productivity. While the US may be at the early stages of a more sustainable New Economy (Phase 2, if you will), the numbers from Phase 1 have been truly quite impressive. Labor productivity, defined as output per worker per hour, jumped from 1.4 percent during 1975-93, to over 3 percent during 1995-2000 in the US, by even the most conservative estimates. In the non-farm business sector, for example, growth of output per hour accelerated to a 2.8 percent annual rate during 1996-2000 as the New Economy blossomed, compared to just 1.6 percent for the previous 25 years.

The crucial question then is how much of this increase in productivity is structural (long-term/permanent), and how much is cyclical. After all, during boom times, employers do tend to work their employees harder to keep pace with additional demand, thereby contributing to increased productivity statistics. Conversely, as the economy slows, employers who are reluctant to shed employees at the first sign of a slowdown, keep them on the payroll but have them producing less output commensurate with the falling demand. This results in falling productivity numbers as the economy slows. This feature may account for a procyclical—moving "with" the business cycle—component of measured productivity.

Robert Gordon, long an outspoken skeptic of the New Economy, finds (from an ongoing series of empirical studies) that the productivity gains touted as "permanent" New Economy features exist only in the manufacture of computers (hardware) and a few other durable goods. The remaining productivity increases, he concludes, are cyclical. At the other end of the spectrum, however, New Economy proponents at the Federal Reserve find evidence that across-the-board labor productivity increases since the early 1990s have indeed been structural, implying a conservative rate of growth at just over 3%.

Superimposed on this vitally important debate is the enormous expenditure in the 1990s in the US on information technology (IT). Large capital spending on IT can influence labor productivity in two ways, by either (i) "capital deepening" which essentially increases the amount of capital available per worker, or (ii) affecting "total factor productivity" (TFP) which increases the efficiency with which units of labor and capital generate increases in output.

Very simply, total factor productivity is a residual defined as:

TFP = Percentage increase in real output per unit time – (percentage increase in labor + percentage increase in capital, per unit time)

Interestingly, by the early 2000s, several studies had found evidence to indicate that almost half of the acceleration in productivity growth between the first and second halves of the 1990s in the US was, in fact, due to capital deepening and not due to an increase in TFP. If capital deepening were indeed the case, a cut-back in IT spending would have serious ramifications for the New Economy by virtue of the rapid ensuing decrease in the supposedly large "capital deepened" component of productivity. Proponents of this theory point to the US experience in the early 2000s as evidence.

Accurate measures and determinants of productivity are absolutely vital in estimating the longevity and intensity of the New Economy. After all, with fiscal and monetary policy deemed ineffective, and given the advanced stage of deregulation in the US, macroeconomic growth (in this model) would now be dependent solely on productivity gains.

This crucial subject will be revisited when we summarize the outlook and nature of "Phase 2" of the New Economy towards the end of this chapter.

So how does the Keynesian paradigm reconcile itself to the observed "New Economy" behavior, namely the increases in productivity and growth without any accompanying increases in inflation during the late 1990s-early 2000s? How would the Keynesians explain the apparent demise of the Phillips curve and the "failure" of demand-side stabilization, as claimed by the supply-siders during this period?

To answer these questions and to discuss the Keynesian response, a brief overview of the identification problem in analyzing time-series data is in order.

10.5 THE IDENTIFICATION PROBLEM

Figures 9a and **9b** present two pairs of observed real world data points, (P_0,Y_0) and (P_1,Y_1), represented by $\boxed{A}$ and $\boxed{B}$. The rates of inflation, P_0 and P_1, and the rates of GDP growth, Y_0 and Y_1, are two sets of observed inflation and output growth rates, respectively. (P_0,Y_0) and (P_1,Y_1) can be interpreted as rates of inflation and GDP growth at two points in time, with (P_0,Y_0) being in Period Zero and (P_1Y_1) in some later time (Period One).

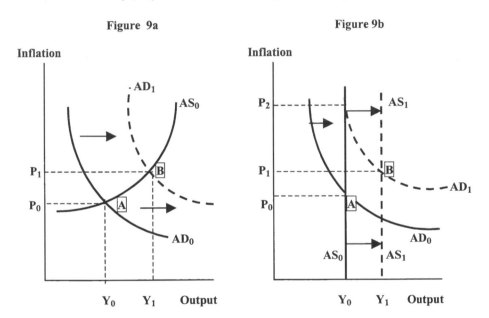

While the points A and B in 9a and 9b are directly observable, the <u>actual models</u> explaining how the economy progressed from (P_0,Y_0) to (P_1,Y_1) are not. In other words, while we "see" points A and B, we do not actually "see" the respective underlying AS and AD curves. It is up to macroeconomic theory to construct mathematically consistent models that can explain the movement of the economy from points A to point B, and in doing so, to form a "template" within which <u>all</u> future policies can be analyzed.

From Figures 9a and 9b we can see that two drastically different models can explain the observed path of the economy from A to B equally well. In Figure 9a, a Keynesian paradigm with expansionary demand-side policy (increasing G, M, or cuts in taxes) has jump-started this economy, taking it from point A at (P_0, Y_0) to point B at (P_1, Y_1). In this case, the output-inflation tradeoff has been realized.

However, in Figure 9b the <u>same points A and B</u> can now be linked within the context of a supply-side paradigm. Here the initial AS curve, AS_0, is shifted to the right, presumably by tax cuts, deregulation, a surge in productivity, and/or expectations of strong future growth. The AD is also shifted to the right by the same demand-side policies as in Figure 9a (increases in G or M or cuts in taxes). This combination of AD and AS shifts results in an economy transitioning from A to a new equilibrium at B in Figure 9b.[10]

Both paradigms, irrespective of their fundamentally different philosophies and policy prescriptions, provide us with perfectly reasonable explanations of an economy moving A to B. Herein lies a fundamental reason for the ongoing debate and confusion pertaining to "the" right model in developed economies—both paradigms legitimately co-exist because both fit the observed data equally well.[11] This is one very intuitive explanation of the **identification problem**, prevalent in the analysis of serially correlated time-series data, making it extremely difficult to identify the single "correct" model within which macroeconomic policy must be analyzed, prescribed, and conducted.

While the two paradigms diagrammatically "explain" the shifts from points A to B equally well, the policy implications remain fundamentally different. In 9a, for example, stimulative demand-side policy—increases in G or M or cuts in taxes—is solely responsible for the increase in national output from Y_0 to Y_1. Here, the shift in the AD "drives" real economic growth.

In 9b, on the contrary, the demand-side shift by itself, without an accompanying supply-side shift in the AS, would only result in an increase in inflation from P_0 to P_2, with output growth stuck at Y_0. It is <u>only</u> when the AS curve is shifted to the right due to some combination of deregulation, business tax cuts, and increases in productivity that output increases from Y_0 to Y_1. In sharp contrast to 9a, the boost to real economic growth in 9b is solely due to the AS shift.

10.6 A KEYNESIAN EXPLANATION OF THE "NEW" ECONOMY

Figure 10a presents the Keynesian response to what has been labeled the "new" economy. The Keynesians claim that there is nothing "new" about the economy, but that, once again, the confusion (according to this school of thought) may have been sown by the identification problem.

Keynesians do not deny the inescapable fact that productivity has increased in the US starting in the 1990s. While the exact nature and composition of this increase in productivity—structural versus cyclical, and "capital deepening" versus TFP—are vigorously debated in the academic and policy literature, the increase in productivity, powered by the internet economy, cannot be denied.

However, the Keynesians point out that <u>all</u> aggregate supply curves, be they vertical or kinked, will shift to the right as the production function bulges up with an increase in labor productivity. In Figure 10a, Keynesians demonstrate that even a Keynesian AS, shifted to the right by productivity gains, will replicate the exact same observed "New Economy" results of increasing Y and falling P.

Figure 10b reproduces the conventional expectationist view of the New Economy discussed earlier, with IT gains driving productivity increases and shifting a vertical AS to the right. Once again, thanks to the identification problem, both paradigms seem to fit the New Economy mantra of "growth without increasing inflation" equally well. Once again, the two sets of observed data, $\boxed{A}$ and $\boxed{B}$ in 10a and 10b, are identical, and the debate continues to rage.

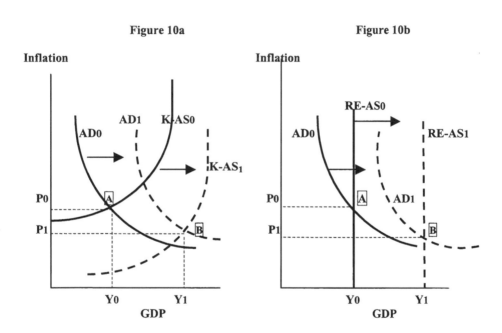

Figure 10a   Figure 10b

The major difference between the two explanations, however, is that the Keynesians believe that the "new" economy spawned in the 1990s was an episodic, one-off shift in the kinked K-AS curve. They argue that once this somewhat dramatic shift to the right of the K-AS slows down, and increases in technology and productivity eventually stabilize to some lower "more sustainable" level, the K-AS curve's rightward shift will be arrested.

They claim that, once again, demand-side stabilization, with its attendant Phillips curve and its symptoms of overheating and soft-landing will reassert itself with a vengeance. Once again, discretionary fiscal and monetary policies will stabilize output and employment. It is only in this transitional phase, they argue, that atypical results such as growth without accompanying increases in inflation are to be observed

The expectationists contend that while the identification problem technically leaves the door open for ongoing debate regarding the legitimacy of the New Economy, the episodes of stagflation were evidence enough that information had in fact become symmetric in developed economies. Fiscal and monetary stabilization would not have real long-term effects given the vertical nature of the rational expectations AS curve.

They insist that, in the long-run, any and all increases in real output and employment growth can only come about through shifts to the right in a vertical AS, driven by ongoing breakthroughs in technology-powered productivity gains. Shifting the AD, without any accompanying shift to the right in the vertical AS, would, according to their paradigm, only result in increases in inflation with no change in output or employment.

While the New Economy proponents attribute most of the increases in productivity to policies put in place in the formative days of supply-side economics in the early 1980s, Keynesians emphasize that the coincidental influence of a host of other contributing factors cannot be denied. For example, the strength of the US dollar from the early 1990s served to keep prices of imports down and to some extent may have mitigated incipient inflationary pressure. The Asian crises of 1997-8 followed by the rapid relative strengthening of the US dollar did much to lower prices of imports, and the drop in semiconductor prices through the 1990s was certainly a contributing factor. Furthermore, they point out that the worldwide glut in global commodities—not to mention fuel—also kept inflation in check. Keynesians stress that these factors, and not just supply-side initiatives, went a long way to contribute to the "growth without inflation" that has come to characterize the New Economy of the late 1990s and the early 2000s.

In the Keynesian view, GDP growth in the "new" economy was largely a result of a conventional text-book Keynesian stimulus—expansionary monetary policy. The significant monetary expansion in the US in the mid to late 1990s was the primary source of GDP growth, plain and simple. The AD was shifted to the right in a fairly standard Keynesian expansion, over a Keynesian AS due to an increase in M, thanks to a generally looser Fed monetary policy for much of the 1990s. This, coupled with a one-time shift to the right in the Keynesian AS (presented in 10a) due to the permanent increase in productivity stemming from the internet-powered economy, resulted in the so-called "growth without inflation" that was, in the Keynesian view, erroneously attributed to some permanent paradigm-shattering New Economy.

The new economists and their supply-side ancestors have argued that the Phillips curve was "dead". The Keynesian response is that the Phillips curve was simply lying dormant in the heyday of the New Economy. It was temporarily masked by the one-time rightward shift in the Keynesian AS due to the growth in productivity.

In fact, during the early 2000s, the not-so-soft landing by the Federal Reserve, followed by repeated attempts to jump-start growth by increasing monetary growth and decreasing interest rates, led many analysts to wonder if the Keynesian paradigm was indeed back on center-stage. These moves, followed by the fiscal and monetary stimulus package in the US following the September 11, 2001 terror attacks, smacked clearly of vintage Keynesianism.

10.7   CONTRASTING THE "NEW" ECONOMY WITH THE "OLD" ONE

The "old", or "traditional", economy is loosely interpreted to be the Keynesian model, while the New Economy is seen as the most recent iteration of the technology-driven version of the supply-side, rational expectations, vertical AS model. The differences between the two models go way beyond the obvious theoretical and diagrammatic ones. As discussed, the two paradigms clearly have very strong policy implications that are fundamentally polar extremes of each other.

The following **Table 1** will help recap and overview all the differences in the two paradigms.

Table 1

"New" Economy (Vertical AS)	"Old" Economy (Keynesian AS)
1. Changes in fiscal and monetary policies (increasing G or M, for example), result in no real effects. Only the rate of inflation is affected with no change in Y or employment. There is no role for activist fiscal or monetary policy in this economy, much like the earlier classical paradigm.	Expansionary fiscal and monetary policies generate multiplier effects. Rates of Y and employment increase, as do C and I. Conversely, contractionary policies can engineer soft landings. There is a distinct discretionary role for activist fiscal and monetary policy.
2. There is no output-inflation tradeoff. In fact, increases in output are matched by decreases in the rate of inflation.	There is a very evident output-inflation tradeoff. The Phillips curve relationship is evident. Increases in inflation are accompanied by

	increases in GDP growth and decreases in the unemployment rate.
3. Increases in GDP growth and employment are driven by technology-enhanced productivity growth that result in a supply-side stimulus. Furthermore, this productivity growth can be traced back to deregulation and the ensuing climate of risk-taking and entrepreneurship that it fosters.	Growth in GDP and employment are driven by demand-side policies that stimulate the aggregate demand (AD). Deregulation will also shift the K-AS to the right and may certainly increase productivity in some areas, but the rightward shift in the AS would be episodic—a one-time shift.
4. Large infusions of global capital are vital to fund the disparity between total demand for loanable funds and the total supply of loanable funds. Massive capital inflows finance high-technology startups fostered by the explosion in creativity and entrepreneurship. Please refer to discussion on the NSI (national savings identity) in Chapter 2.	Typically, as shown in the NSI discussion, large infusions of global capital are essential to fund bond-financed budget deficits. These deficits are caused by large increases in government spending necessary to generate Keynesian multiplier effects.
5. Changes in nominal wages and prices are (with short lags) fully flexible. Information is symmetric. Long-term government bonds operating in highly efficient bond markets signal future inflation effectively. Labor markets are relatively more deregulated, and workers have more market power. This allows them to negotiate long-term wage contracts and to maintain their real wages.	Nominal wages do not change fully in proportion to changes in prices. Some combination of excess supplies of labor (in emerging economies), imperfect information, or nominal wage rigidities, yield the positively sloped AS curve. Labor markets are relatively more regulated, and workers do not have the ability to negotiate real wage contracts—they have relatively less market power.
6. Inflation pressures are now harder to detect as increases in inflation are not positively correlated to GDP growth. Conventionally measured inflation may appear benign, but dangerous speculative asset price (SAP) bubbles in the stock market, the IT sector, and real estate may develop.	Overheating is easier to detect. Inflationary pressures are evident in conventionally measured indexes. Since inflation here is procyclical, an overheated economy "growing too fast" will exhibit dangerously rising inflation across the board. Long-bonds in this economy are good indicators of expected inflation.

7. In summary, this economy is driven by continuous increases in productivity in a highly deregulated economy, represented by ongoing rightward shifts in the vertical AS. There is no role for fiscal and monetary policy in influencing GDP growth or employment. There is no rapid-action "emergency package" to rescue a traumatized economy. For instance, there could be no supply-sider response on September 12, 2001, in the wake of the terrorist attacks and the ensuing drop in confidence.	In summary, these economies are primarily stabilized by active demand-side fiscal and monetary policies. Many Keynesian regimes would advocate privatization and eventual deregulation of large inefficient SOEs. Regarding productivity increases, constant (flat) productivity growth is usually viewed as the norm, with occasional, episodic, rightward shifts in the K-AS. This paradigm allows for an emergency stimulus package of rapid increases in M and planned increases in G when the economy is in crisis, as exemplified by the US \$100 billion stimulus package following the September 11, 2001, terrorist attack.

10.8   CAN THE TWO MODELS BE RECONCILED?

Purists from both camps would recoil at the suggestion. In the long-run, given the fundamental structural differences driving the two paradigms, any chance of a "compromise" model reconciling the two polar views would be extremely unlikely in developed economies. (Emerging economies are typically Keynesian, as discussed earlier.)

By the early 2000s, however, an increasing number of analysts along with mainstream policy-oriented economists, have proposed a model of a developed economy transitioning from a Keynesian-type AS curve in the short-run to a supply-side model in the long-run.[12] This quasi-paradigm, which could also be labeled the "synthesis view", is composed of "long-term" New Economy adherents who believe that, although the AS is eventually vertical, there is indeed room for short-term, demand-side stabilization. For example, in the very short term, the central bank may need to quickly "hit the brakes" to stem runaway growth or to re-ignite growth and confidence. This would provide the correct short-term impetus, but may not be a viable long-term policy.

Theorists point to the expectations-augmented AS curve discussed earlier as one explanation for the time-dependent change in the slope of the AS. As explained by the JoAnna Grey-Phelps model, in the short-term, in a world characterized by asymmetric information, when expectations of inflation do not actually match actual inflation, workers supply more labor. This additional labor, in turn, results in increases in output and employment that accompany increases in inflation, yielding the positively sloped expectations-augmented AS curve. [13]

However, over time, workers "catch on" and contract for higher nominal wages to keep their real wages constant. Information becomes symmetric and, as discussed, the AS becomes vertical, yielding the Rational Expectations AS curve. <u>Furthermore, according to Robert E. Lucas' seminal "islands" models (please see the following box), the rate at which the AS snaps back to its vertical position—the rate at which information becomes symmetric—is directly a function of the degree of attempted stabilization in an imperfect information environment.</u>

This "synthesis view", combining short-term Keynesian behavior with a long-term vertical AS curve, may explain why demand-side policies, such as changes in monetary growth that attempt to jump-start and soft-land economies, may be successful only for short periods in developed economies. Typically, these policies may be successful only at inflection points in the business cycle when growth is just about to lose momentum or the economy is on the verge of a recovery. Eventually, however, only structural changes in taxes, deregulation, and technology-induced productivity would be remedies for long-term macroeconomic growth. (Keep in mind, this "synthesis" view is espoused by long-term expectationists/supply-siders).

Lending credence to this synthesis view are the actions of the Federal Reserve and the European Central Bank (ECB). After all, the attempt by the Federal Reserve to engineer a US soft-landing in 2000 by contracting monetary growth and increasing interest rates was a "text-book" Keynesian policy prescription. So were the almost frantic attempts to jump-start growth with a sequence of significant interest rate cuts, beginning in 2001.

The European Central Bank, too, in spite of strident claims of <u>only</u> inflation control as its policy objective, has at times indulged in decidedly Keynesian behavior. It has lowered interest rates on several key occasions to invigorate growth in the larger German and French economies, despite strong signals of impending increases in inflation in the Eurozone. Since the ECB's well publicized policy objective is to ensure that inflation in the Eurozone is at most 2 percent, these actions have led a growing body of central bank watchers to wonder if the major central banks, such as the ECB and the Fed, are indeed subscribing to a "synthesis" model that combines a Keynesian AS in the short-run and a vertical AS in the long-run.

Keynes famously said, "in the long-run we are all dead". In the context of this section, however, the more appropriate version may be, "in the long-run we may be either die-hard Keynesians or supply-siders, but in the short-run we are all Keynesians". [14]

236

Explaining the Synthesis: Robert E. Lucas and his 'Islands' economy*

In, "Some International Evidence on Output-Inflation Tradeoffs," (AER, 1973), Robert E. Lucas cleverly introduced the notion of imperfect information by constructing a radically new model—the "islands" economy—that soon spawned a whole new body of macroeconomic modeling. Here, producers scattered randomly over individual "islands" are independently able to observe price changes. They cannot, however, distinguish relative changes in prices from economy-wide nominal changes in prices. For example, when producer X sees an increase in price, he/she does not know if this change results from a real increase in excess demand for the product on the producer's island, or if the price increase is simply due to an increase in inflation that affects all islands.

In the Lucas model, the producers cannot communicate with any other islands. Hence, given this imperfect information, they must hedge. If the price increase is indicative of excess demand for the product, then increases in output are warranted. In this case, the observed price increase would be accompanied by an increase in output, resulting in a positively sloped AS curve.

If, on the other hand, the price increase is perceived as simply due to an "ocean-wide" inflation that affects all islands, producer X would have no incentive or motivation to respond to this observed increase in price with an increase in supply. In this case, islanders promptly attribute any observed price increases to inflation caused by central bank monetization. Consequently, they do not increase output, resulting in a vertical AS curve.

Borrowing the concept of signal extraction from electrical engineering, Lucas found that economies with very disciplined monetary policies were indeed represented by AS curves that were positively sloped. (Monetary discipline was characterized by a central bank that had a history of not indiscriminately and constantly attempting to tweak the money supply or resort to vast debt monetization.)

On the other hand, in economies where monetary discipline was low, Lucas found that islanders attributed most (if not all) of the observed price increase simply to inflation, and the AS was indeed found to be steeper depending on the degree of monetary variance. In other words, in the Lucasian economy the slope of the AS was found to be inversely proportional to the degree of monetary discipline.

Perhaps most interestingly, Lucas' model also demonstrated how expectations adjusted rapidly and efficiently. Positively sloped AS curves in economies known for their high monetary discipline would mercilessly adapt and get steeper at the first sign of a deterioration in monetary discipline. The AS curve would snap back to vertical, with the rate of adjustment directly proportional to the rate of deterioration in monetary discipline!

In terms of policy these findings have huge implications. Some economies may indeed be characterized by positively sloped AS curves by virtue of asymmetric information. However, the output-inflation tradeoffs <u>are only perceived tradeoffs—they are not exploitable</u>. <u>Any attempts to exploit these tradeoffs would quickly result in the AS becoming vertical</u>. The perceived tradeoff would rapidly disappear.

Many years later, this model was experimentally reconstructed with live "producers" in a simulated islands economy by the author (<u>Journal of Economic Behavior and Organization</u>, 1994). The "producers" (MBA and EMBA students) were located on "islands" characterized by imperfect information and subjected to prices from both disciplined as well undisciplined monetary policies. The Lucas results were faithfully replicated. As in the Lucasian economy, the greater the monetary discipline, the flatter the AS and the greater the perceived output-inflation tradeoff. As monetary discipline progressively deteriorated, the slope of the AS curves predictably increased. Eventually, producers simply began to ignore posted price increases, and the AS curves became vertical.

In conclusion, according to the synthesis view, there may be tradeoffs in the short run driven by asymmetric information. The AS curve in the short run may look like a conventional Keynesian AS curve, but the similarity ends there. Unlike its Keynesian counterpart, there is no long-run exploitable Phillips curve relationship. Instead, only a shimmering mirage of a Phillips curve is perceived here. The faster we attempt to approach this mirage, the more quickly it disappears. Therein lies the theoretical elegance of the Lucas islands model.

* Robert E. Lucas Jr., of the University of Chicago, was the recipient of the Nobel Prize for Economic Sciences in 1995.

10.9   THE OUTLOOK FOR THE NEW ECONOMY

Is the New Economy a one-time episodic event as claimed by the Keynesians, or is this a paradigm that is here to stay? At the epicenter of this discussion lies the issue of the longevity of the productivity gains. These, after all, "drive" the New Economy.

How long will the productivity gains last? Have we entered a "phase 2" of the New Economy since 2001, with lower yet more sustainable productivity gains? Economic research has provided several insights into the matter.

1.   The first issue, discussed earlier in this chapter, pertains to the nature of the productivity gains. Are they structural or cyclical? While the evidence is mixed and controversial, the general consensus is that until the economy has completed one real business cycle—boom followed by a real recession—it will be extremely difficult to sift out cyclical changes in productivity from structural ones.

2. A huge contributing factor to the New Economy was the massive drop in semiconductor prices in the early-mid 1990s. To some extent, this may have prevented inflation from increasing in proportion to the explosion in growth. Annual multifactor productivity growth (defined earlier) in the semiconductor sector was 30.7% from 1974-90, and 22.3% from 1990-95, and then it exploded to 44.0% from 1996-99 (Oliner and Sichel, 2000). Industry experts (Jorgensen, 2001) expect price declines to continue well into the second decade of the new millennium.

3. The IT revolution, the centerpiece of the New Economy, may be just another breakthrough in a long series of technological revolutions. By the end of the 19th century, the widespread adoption of electricity was followed by the internal combustion engine. These inventions revolutionized travel (land and air), and manufacturing. In the 20th century, these breakthroughs were followed by others in medicine (vaccines, antibiotics) and communications (radio, television). If the IT revolution was then just another in a series of technological developments, expectations of a trend increase in the rate of growth may be unjustified. Rather, the IT economy could be interpreted as simply ensuring the sustainability of recent growth rates.

4. Finally, even if the IT economy is indeed different from preceding technological revolutions, it is not clear if the economy's long-term growth rate will be higher, or if just the level of national income will be ratcheted up, followed by the same long-term post World War II trend rate of growth (3-4%). Evidence from "phase 2" of the New Economy since 2001 seems to indicate a return to the long-term post World War II real rate of growth of the US economy. Once again, data from a full business cycle would be necessary to obtain any meaningful empirical estimates.

10.10   WHICH MODEL FOR DEVELOPED ECONOMIES?

The fact of the matter is that, in the United States, productivity numbers reminiscent of the 1960s were evidenced again in the late 1990s (the heyday of what has been labeled the "New Economy"). The causes and prospects of the New Economy have generated considerable interest from research as well as policy perspectives. Due to the identification problem, both paradigms, Keynesian as well as supply-sider, offer equally plausible explanations for the phenomenon labeled as the "New Economy". In addition, both models can also be found to fit a range of other macroeconomic outcomes in developed economies.

Against this macroeconomic backdrop, it remains to the reader to decide not just which model best explains the "New Economy", but also which model <u>consistently</u> explains <u>all</u> macroeconomic behavior in the developed economy that is being analyzed.   In my macroeconomics classes, both paradigms are discussed in detail, and finally the students have to decide for themselves.   While analyzing developed economies, they can choose to be either long-term Keynesians or long-term supply-siders; they can all be Keynesians in the short-run.   (The choice is clear for emerging economies where the Keynesian paradigm applies in the short-term and the long-term.)

In some cases, the long-term choices for developed economies are based on the plausibility of the theoretical and technical assumptions underlying the derivation of the model, or the logical and intuitive elegance of one paradigm relative to the other.   The richness of the labor market and the clear policy implications of the Keynesian model are admired by many.   Others are impressed by the elegant simplicity and the bold, uncluttered, policy strokes of the supply-side paradigm.

In other cases, individuals choose their model based on their own real-world experiences and instincts, or on moral and/or philosophical grounds. For example, the absence of a role for government intervention in macroeconomic stabilization may be seen by some to be highly desirable. The fundamental belief that market forces and not government intervention should determine business decisions, and that private enterprise must be allowed to compete freely and to succeed or perish in such an environment, resonates with the expectationists.

Others, however, may strongly believe that it "ought" to be government's responsibility to be involved in activist macroeconomic policy, especially to cure unemployment.   And there "should" be a minimum level of regulation to ensure that environmental, moral, and non-commercial concerns are not swept aside by unregulated businesses interests.

Both paradigms would agree that privatization and deregulation can indeed increase productivity.   Both emerging and developed economies have pursued privatizations.   While the intensity and determination with which privatizations are undertaken may be higher in supply-sider regimes, in enlightened emerging economies (China, India, Mexico, Brazil, to name a few), there is a growing conviction that state-owned enterprises (SOEs) eventually have to be allowed to "sink or swim" in the sea of global competition; a rightward shift in a Keynesian AS has undeniable merits.

After all the discussion throughout this book, and armed with the two diametrically different paradigms and their implications, the reader is finally equipped with all the tools for choosing the long-term paradigm for analyzing developed economies.

We now turn to questions that clarify and discuss some key concepts, followed by simulated media articles. The next chapter discusses the mechanisms by which central banks change interest rates, along with the objectives (and challenges) of prudent central bank policy in the global economy.

10.11   DISCUSSION QUESTIONS

1. Does the "synthesis" view imply that one need not adopt a polar model—Keynesian or Supply-sider—but could, instead, comfortably adopt the compromise version just described?

The synthesis version is purely a short-run compromise driven by observed real-world macropolicy—especially monetary policy. As long as short-run imperfections and asymmetries in information exist, or as long as wage-contracts remain "sticky" (rigid) in the short-term, such tradeoffs will be successful. According to the expectationists, however, as the asymmetries disappear, the vertical AS will re-emerge along with its attendant supply-side oriented polices. As discussed earlier, Robert E. Lucas constructed his "islands economy" in 1973 to demonstrate that the greater the attempts to try and exploit information imperfections in the short-run, the faster the convergence of the economy to a vertical AS curve, and the quicker the demise of any perceived short-term tradeoff.

Of course, die-hard Keynesians would have no problem with the "synthesis" view in the short-run. In the long-run, however, they would advocate simply a continuance of the Keynesian policies. After all, for them the AS is positively sloped in both the short-run as well as the long-run.

2. If there are two diametrically different paradigms for developed economies, why do the bond market and often the stock market behave in a predominantly "Keynesian" fashion? For example, monetary policy announcements are immediately assumed to be fully capable of attaining the desired objectives regarding GDP, employment and inflation.

Bond markets in the US and in Europe certainly tend to display "Keynesian" tendencies. An announcement by the central bank that the short term rate will be lowered by, say, 50 basis points, is often seen as an indicator of greater GDP growth, greater employment, and an accompanying increase in the inflation rate. These indicators, after all, are hallmarks of Keynesian output-inflation tradeoffs. Typically, the yield curve might get steeper soon after the central bank's announcement, as long bonds incorporate higher expected inflation resulting from the rate cut. Anticipation of renewed economic

241

growth often results in a stock buying frenzy as investors re-enter the equity market, which may result in a spike in stock prices following a central bank announcement of looser monetary policy.

Conversely, immediately following an announced rise in interest rates, yield curves often get flatter as bond markets recognize the attempt by the central bank to cool down the economy by means of a monetary contraction. Expected inflation falls as a soft landing is expected, driving down long-term rates. Investors may take profits and sell out of a market on the verge of being slowed down, thereby causing a drop in stock prices, in this instance.[15]

One can indeed make a case that stock and bond markets in most developed economies either are "mostly Keynesian", or that these markets subscribe to the "synthesis" view and are Keynesian in the near-term.

3. How would you explain a recession in the supply-side (New Economy) paradigm?

The labor market is the key to explaining a recession in the New Economy paradigm, presented in **Figure 11**. In the version done in this chapter, both labor supply and demand were functions of the real wages, tax rates, and a term labeled "macroeconomic outlook". We discussed how cuts in taxes (personal and/or business) either shifted labor supply or labor demand to the right, and vice versa. To explain recessions, we now need to activate the "outlook" term.

Simply, the "macroeconomic outlook" is composed of forward-looking consumer and investor confidence. If the future looks bleak, the "outlook" term will decrease and labor demand will shift to the left as presented in Figure 11. The effect on labor supply is uncertain. Discouraged workers may simply opt out of the labor market, thereby removing themselves from the civilian labor force, or they may work more hours in anticipation of leaner financial times ahead. Hence, we leave labor supply curve unchanged. Equilibrium employment in the labor market will fall as labor demand shifts left.

From the production function diagram, as employment falls, output falls too, and this causes the vertical AS to shift to the left. Furthermore, the production function itself drops as the economy worsens. Typically employers tend to hold on to most of their workers until a recession is well under way. In doing so, each worker's output per hour (productivity) drops since the demand for the product has fallen in the slowing economy. Worsening macroeconomic conditions will also affect conventional consumer and investor confidence terms, $\underline{C}$ and $\underline{I}$, which account for the drop in AD, as shown in Figure 11.

The final effect on inflation is ambiguous and depends on the relative magnitude of the AD and AS shifts.

Figure 11

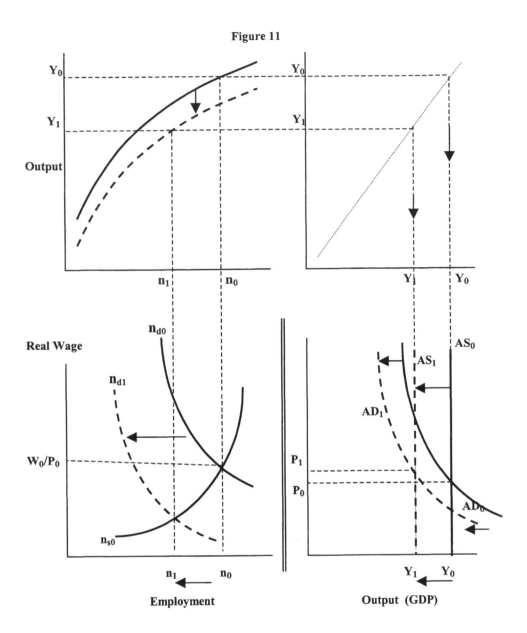

In the following articles, please comment on the underlined passages using material presented in this and preceding chapters. Use diagrams liberally.

Article 10.1   SHIKOKU NEEDS LESS STIMULUS

James McVie, Aberdeen World News

Last weekend, Mr. Keichi Nagumo, Minister of Finance of the Republic of Shikoku, unveiled the country's most recent "economic stimulus" package. The event followed the graduation ceremony of the prestigious National Engineering Institute at the Koda Hotel. Even though the event was studded with the usual luminaries, there was something missing—a real expectation of success was conspicuously absent from the proceedings.

In spite of the eighth stimulus package in six years, Shikoku, one of the most formidable economies of the recent past, remains mired in recession with no end in sight. A total of 400 trillion units of domestic currency have already been **(a)** spent on gigantic infrastructure projects ranging from the Kaga desalination complex to one of the most modern airports in the world, not to mention the super high tech magnetic levitation (maglev) train system currently under development. But all these huge expensive projects have only managed to **(b)** nudge the economy from its severe bouts of deflation, up to about 2 percent inflation for short periods, before sinking back down again..

We interview Mr. Mitsubishi, who is enjoying a walk in the Fujimoro lotus gardens with his 5-year-old grandson. "We spend and spend, and I know that my hard earned savings are **(c)** being borrowed by our government to build expensive toys. But these are toys that we can't use, and this is not what we need now. I have not worked in 18 months, and all my close friends are now out of work; all six of us once designed the best ships in the world. What will become of us?" he says keeping one watchful eye on his grandson who is feeding the ducks by the water's edge.

Dr. Midori Konda, well-known author of Shikoku's Agony stresses that "Its not just fiscal profligacy." She points out, "They have **(d)** constantly hit the 'money button' to revive their economy, with the result that **(e)** interest rates are virtually at zero percent! But nothing is happening! The central bank and the government are praying for a Keynesian recovery **(f)** but they're praying in the wrong temple. It's the wrong model, and the sooner they accept this the better!"

On Monday, at the Eastern Heaven Ice Cream Bar, we ran into owner, George Haromi, "Listen guys, I don't need a PhD to figure this. The (central) bank **(g)** brought down the stock market with those crazy interest rate hikes four years ago, remember? And the country **(h)** went into chronic depression when the stock market collapsed. People's entire retirements evaporated overnight—can you imagine? The elderly are wiped out—my wife's mother had to move in with us. Why would you take a loan at a time like this—I'm an experienced businessman and **(i)** I'm not borrowing anything for a LONG time!" He then excused himself to scoop out Mango Mayhem icecream for two school-girls.

Now, Shikoku has yet another stimulus package, but there are no expectations of success. Despondency is epidemic. The bond market's reaction did nothing to help; **(j)** rates sprang to 12 percent, as the government deficit/GDP ratio crossed over 10 percent. The **(k)** currency continues to plunge, hitting its 20-year low last Tuesday. So what can be done?

"Throw away the old model," says Dr. Konda. "Politically this will be tough, but we have to let all the sick companies and institutions die. We can't and shouldn't keep spending trillions to bale them out. Unemployment will get worse before it can get better. **(l)** Get government out of decisions on manufacturing, trade, and specialization. No more government subsidies, directives, or 5-year national plans. Order the **(m)** central bank to stop printing money at once. Shikoku needs less stimulus. Let the free market rule. **(n)** Unshackle the labor market by scrapping all the employment regulation—this is vital. And most important, slash all business taxes significantly."

Dr. Konda then flies off to Scotland for a conference in Aberdeen. This reporter and his camera crew decide to walk by the Eastern Heaven. There are no customers. It is a nice evening. A cool breeze blows in from the bay. George Haromi sees us and waves us in. "Here, have some free Mango Mayhem," he beams, as he hands us small ice cream cones.

Maybe things are looking up after all.

Article 10.2 IMPLICATIONS OF THE "NEW" ECONOMY

Alcina Varghese, Kansas City Financial Examiner

"The implications go way beyond academic discussion," intones Dom Panelli, at the National Policy Bureau's Conference on the New Economy in Minneapolis. "What we have here is a fundamental sea change in policies prescribed by respective governments and in the way we do business."

With the elections never too far away in the US, this opinion has profound implications. Panelli's comment is countered by an article published by <u>Policy Today</u> that insists that it was **(a)** <u>low interest rates, cheaper imports, and a "one time boost in productivity"</u> that resulted in the New Economy. This kind of thinking is immediately chall-enged by last month's <u>Engineering Outlook</u> which presents rigorously measured productivity numbers in virtually all major sectors. Most areas show a huge jump since the late 1990s, and all **(b)** <u>indicate no slowdown</u> in their growth rates. In view of this backdrop of conflicting data, believers on both sides remain adamant.

As the experts debated the issues, this newspaper took the matter to the practitioners. Art Vandalay, Dircctor of JKV, an Oklahoma-based wireless bio-metric equipment manufacturer, says, "This whole industry basically grew overnight, and we haven't even scratched the surface. Technology has a long way to go, and we are coming up with more potentially path-breaking innovations literally on a daily basis." He vehemently adds, "I have been an engineer for 34 years, and I know that we are in a new phase since the IT explosion of the 1990s. My only problcm is getting enough skilled labor to keep pace with the new ideas."

Jerry Kitsmiller, controller at Cyber Lock, an encryption company in Richmond, adds an ominous note. "This new world of e-commerce fueled by the internet is real. No doubt about that. But it can come crashing down if these folks in Washington enact **(c)** <u>even more legislation to regulate our industry.</u> It worries me a lot….stagflation would be terrible."

But at StatsOnLine, the global statistical analysis giant, Perin Guzder admits, **(d)** "<u>We can't say for sure</u> if it was monetary policy against a backdrop of favorable world events that 'caused' the New Economy, or some big tech-nological revolution set in a new paradigm".

This was not good enough for Isabella Soprano, researcher at the Carson Mountain Radio Telescope in Colorado. "We can detect an object as small as a VW at the edge of the universe, and those **(e)** <u>folks can't write a program</u> to find out which 'model' works! Come on! Get serious!"

In Ireland, a similar debate has long been under way. **(f)** <u>Did huge transfers from the rich European Union countries "cause" Ireland's remarkable growth</u>, or was it textbook supply-side economics leading to the New Economy? "I admit that the transfer did help enormously. And the tax cuts could also be called

246

'old economy,' but **(g)** I really think that huge pro-business initiatives and the fact that our government has stopped meddling in the economy may have given us our miracle," says Mike Kelly, bartender at the Celtic Rebel pub in Dublin, as we waited for the head on our glasses of Guiness to stop rising.

The mood has spread globally. In China, Jiao Xianquan, President of the Shanghai Consortium of Business told us, "We really must **(h)** privatize our key sectors, force them to compete globally, allow our bright young men and women to take risks and unleash their minds and energies."

All are not convinced. Dr. Mica Fischer, Chairman of the Dresden Group in Dresden, Germany, scoffed at the debate in a television debate last night. **(i)** "There is nothing to debate. We raise interest rates, things slow down, and unemployment goes up. We lower rates, the opposite happens. End of story. Nothing 'new' about this New Economy!"

ANSWERS AND HINTS

Article 10.1   Shikoku Needs Less Stimulus

(a) This illustrates the basic Keynesian fiscal multiplier driven by large infrastructure spending.

(b) As AD is shifted right, inflation is pushed up as the economy barely enters Stage 2 of demand-pull inflation….but then the AD drops back down….why is this happening? (Please be sure to read through the whole article before answering.)

(c) This is typical bond-financed government deficit spending. What may be some factors causing manufacturing and heavy industry to bear the brunt of the slowing economy?

(d) and (e) Monetary stimulus has also been relentlessly applied. As money supply has increased, interest rates have progressively fallen, until apparently they are now close to zero. Both G and M were increased to attempt a rightward shift in AD. Use diagrams to explain how these policies were supposed to have revived Shikoku's economy.

(f) Could Shikoku be in the throes of a paradigm shift? Use diagrams to explain.

(g) Sounds like the central bank contracted monetary policy to deflate a potential SAP bubble in the stock market—and succeeded. Apparently the contraction in M was severe. Use diagrams here.

(h) It is hardly surprising that the collapse in perceived wealth following the central bank's bursting of the SAP bubble has led to plunges in $\underline{C}$ and $\underline{I}$.

(i) This relates to low $\underline{I}$. A healthy demand for loanable funds is crucially dependent on investor confidence and not just on interest rates, as discussed in earlier chapters. Even though interest rates are close to zero in this economy, expectations of future growth are dismal. Investor confidence is at rock bottom, and businesspersons like George are not even contemplating any borrowing.

(j) Central bank policy directly influences very short-term interest rates. However, long-term rates, as discussed in earlier chapters, are endogenous. Use this fact, coupled with Shikoku's deficit/GDP ratio, to explain the rise in "rates" to 12 percent.

(k) An exodus of capital into safer and healthier economies results in investors selling domestic currency to purchase assets denominated in foreign (hard) currency. This causes the domestic currency to plunge.

(l) A smaller role for government is advocated here; deregulation is the mantra. This is clearly a supply-side proposal.

(m) Further emphasis on the supply-side. Basically, demand-side fiscal and monetary stabilization is not effective any more. The paradigm has shifted. The emphasis ought to be on attempting to shift the aggregate supply curve instead of the aggregate demand curve. Illustrate, using diagrams.

(n) These are textbook supply-side policies. Deregulation is vital—especially in the labor market. And tax cuts are absolutely necessary to a supply-side stimulus. Illustrate, using diagrams.

Article 10.2 Implications of the "New" Economy

(a) Dom Panelli is referring to the Keynesian explanation for the New Economy. Use diagrams to explain.

(b) This is the supply-side perspective. Productivity growth is real, ongoing, and here to stay. The New Economy is not an episodic one-time event.

(c) Use the set of four diagrams (production function, labor market, reflector and (P,Y) space) to show how, in this supply-sider perspective, an increase in government regulation could result in stagflationary effects.

(d) Why can't statistician Perin Guzder "say for sure"? Use diagrams.

(e) It is not technical deficiency, but the nature of the time-series data that results in the problem.

(f) Was it just an increase in donor-funded government spending in Ireland that produced a nice Keynesian recovery in that country?

(g) Or was it a genuine supply-side stimulus? Refer to the chapter.

(h) Here is an example of attempts to generate a shift in the AS even though the economy may almost certainly be Keynesian.

(i) In the short-run we can all be Keynesians. But in some economies, we cannot perpetually exploit short-run tradeoffs based on imperfections or rigidities. If the AS eventually becomes vertical (according to long-term supply-siders), the output-inflation tradeoff ceases to exist. Furthermore, according to Robert E. Lucas, in this case the more we try to exploit short-term tradeoffs, the faster will they converge to vertical AS world.

---

[1] In this chapter and the remainder of this book, rational expectationists and supply-siders will be used interchangeably. Technically, in the context of this chapter, rational expectationists were the theoretical macroeconomists who constructed fundamental mathematical models that validated the paradigm shift. Their supply-sider colleagues then prescribed real-world macroeconomic policies consistent with this new rational expectations model.

[2] The model presented here is a synthesis of the JoAnna Grey/Phelps class of asymmetric information models that were key in the early development of the paradigm shift. Once again, in keeping with the policy-driven focus of this book, the theoretical aspects are de-emphasized to make way for expositional convenience and intuition.

[3] The numbers used for P_1 and W_1 are purely for discussion. The point is that increases in nominal wages do not match increases in prices, and this disparity leads to an erosion of the real wage.

[4] This AS is also called the adaptive expectations AS curve.

[5] The asymmetric information theory for a positively sloped AS is only one of several theories. Another explanation is the rigidity in long-term nominal wage adjustments caused by long-term wage contracts. According to this theory, unexpected increases in inflation in a labor market characterized by fairly rigid long-term contracts will have the same effect as in our model. Once again, nominal wage increases will not match increases in inflation, resulting in a positively sloped AS.

[6] This is the view propounded by the expectationists. Later, in this chapter, the Keynesian explanation of the "so-called" paradigm shift will be discussed.

[7] Paradigms, in the context of this chapter, are basically differentiated by their AS curves. ISLM space and the AD curve are identical for both Keynesian as well as RE-AS models. It is only the AS curves derived from crucial assumptions in their respective labor markets that separate the two major paradigms.

[8] Both oil shocks have been combined into one "composite" shock as shown in the diagram.

[9] US macroeconomic statistics during the stagflationary bouts in the 1970s were indeed bleak, and included double-digit inflation and unemployment. Relate stagflation to the earlier discussion on cost-push inflation, where similar countercyclical movements in prices and GDP were discussed.

[10] The AD shifts are independent of the AS curve, and hence are identical in 9a and 9b.

[11] The problem exists primarily in developed economies because these economies are almost certainly Keynesian. Developing economies are characterized by excess labor supply and the inability of this excess labor supply to enforce and influence nominal wage contracts. Information is imperfect and asymmetric, and there is an absence of

efficient bond-markets that signal expected inflation. All these characteristics point to Keynesian models as "default" paradigms for emerging and even for newly industrialized economies.

[12] Mainstream macroeconomics texts by authors such as Michael Parkin and Richard Froyen also propose short-term and long-term AS and Phillips curves.

[13] In the example where prices went from 2 to 5 while wages only went from 12 to 15. Here workers did not "see" the increase in price—they only "saw" their nominal wage increases from 12 to 15 in the short run, and responded by supplying more labor. Thus, output increased with increases in price, resulting in a positively sloped AS.

[14] In this section, we deliberately shy away from specific definitions of short- and long-run. The point is that information asymmetry can exist only for so long. Eventually, workers will know all pieces of information. And besides, this process may be of different duration in different economies. An economy with a more sophisticated labor market will go from short to long-run far more quickly than one with a less developed economy possessing a less sophisticated labor market.

[15] This assumes that all other macroeconomic factors—tax rates, government spending, confidence, foreign GDP—remain constant and dormant. This is a purely linear, simplified causality from interest rate announcements to typical long-bond and stock market behavior, immediately following the Fed's announcement.

11. CENTRAL BANKS AND MONETARY POLICY

After analyzing monetary policy in both Keynesian and rational expectations paradigms, and across emerging and developed economies, the time has finally come to explore the exact mechanism by which central banks enact monetary growth.

We begin by reviewing the institutional structure of major central banks that include the US Federal Reserve (the Fed) and the European Central Bank (ECB). This will be followed by a discussion of the three major methods by which monetary growth, and hence, short-term interest rates are changed. The discussion pertaining to the instruments of monetary policy includes the conventionally accepted ("textbook") version of changing monetary growth followed by the <u>empirically observed reality</u> of current monetary policy.

We then explore and evaluate the objectives of monetary policy in both emerging and developed countries. How <u>should</u> monetary policy be conducted? Section 11.3 begins with a discussion of Keynesian stabilization, followed by the Friedmanian x-percent rule, and ends with the Taylor rule. The European Central Bank's attempts to maintain an inflation target (discussed earlier) will also be revisited in this context.

Issues such as the implication and attainment of monetary discipline, and the policy of pegging one's currency to the hard currency of another country to enable monetary discipline, will be covered towards the end of this chapter. The "impossible trinity", the undoing of the East Asian economies during the currency crises of 1997-98, as well as Argentina's 2001-2 crisis, are also discussed in some detail.

11.1   INSTITUTIONAL FRAMEWORK: THE FEDERAL RESERVE

The Federal Reserve (the Fed), the central bank of the United States, was founded in 1913 by an act of Congress. It should be noted that in the early years of the 20th century, there was strong resistance to the idea of one central bank in the US. However, a series of banking panics culminated in a particularly vicious run on banks in 1907, and this finally led to a consensus for a central bank. The objective (at that time) was to manage the nation's money supply more effectively and allow it to be more flexible in times of monetary crises.[1]

The key bodies within the Federal Reserve are the **Board of Governors** and the **Federal Open Market Committee (FOMC)**. The Board of Governors is based in Washington, D.C., and is composed of seven governors who have non-renewable 14-year terms, staggered by two years. The governors are appointed by the President and confirmed by the Senate. The Chairperson and the Vice Chairperson have renewable 4-year terms, and are both designated by the President and confirmed by the Senate.

The fairly long terms serve to insulate the Board of Governors from political pressure and to ensure that the Federal Reserve (and therefore monetary policy) is indeed independent of government pressure to either monetize a runaway deficit or to indulge in excessive and possibly detrimental changes in money growth and interest rates. The 2-year staggering is to limit the number of Presidential appointments to the board to a maximum of four members—presumably this would reduce the possibility of a certain president "stacking" the board of governors with individuals that subscribed only to his/her macroeconomic paradigm.[2]

Some economists believe that this provision also reduces the possibility of "political business cycles" (PBCs) wherein a "government-friendly" Federal Reserve attempts short-term stimulation by lowering rates shortly before an election, allows the incumbent to get re-elected as growth temporarily picks up, and then, months after the election, lets society incur the costs of the ensuing inflation and the original lower rate of growth.

As a result of the relatively long terms and the staggering by two years, the Board of Governors is basically a quasi-independent body. The Federal Reserve is, of course, a creation of Congress, and the chairperson is required to report to Congress on a regular basis and to be subjected to long afternoons of demanding grilling. Nonetheless, the Federal Reserve remains independent in that it takes monetary action first and later explains and reports its actions to Congress.

The **Federal Open Market Committee (FOMC)** is primarily responsible for the course and conduct of monetary policy in the US. By law, the FOMC is required to meet at least four times a year in Washington, D.C., but since 1980 they have met at least eight times a year. The committee comprises the 7-member Board of Governors plus five of the presidents of the 12 regional Federal Reserve banks. The President of the New York Federal Reserve is always included since the New York Federal Reserve is always an integral part of the money supply process. The other four presidents are rotated into the FOMC every January 1. All 12 Federal Reserve presidents are invited to participate in the deliberations, but the final voting on the course of monetary policy is done only by the 12 members (7 Governors + 5 Presidents).

The presidents of the regional Federal Reserve banks are selected by the directors of their respective banks. Each Federal Reserve bank has nine directors, six of whom are elected from the member banks in the district while the three others are appointed by the Board of Governors in Washington, D.C.

Ever since the system of the Board of Governors and the FOMC was instated in 1935, there has been an ongoing debate regarding the independence of the central bank and the influence of the Federal Reserve presidents on the course of monetary policy. However, advocates of central bank autonomy have prevailed, with the result that the Fed, along with the

German Bundesbank (and possibly the European Central bank in the years to come), is among major central banks that have acquired strong reputations for monetary discipline over the last few decades.

The **Federal Advisory Board** is another component of the Federal Reserve. It is composed of 12 prominent bankers who represent the interests of the financial services in their respective districts, and, as the name implies, their role is purely advisory.

In addition to prescribing and implementing the course of monetary policy, the Federal Reserve also regulates and supervises all the financial institutions that transact money. These institutions range from around 8,000 commercial banks to small savings and loans. In addition, the Fed is also a major lender of last resort (as discussed later in this chapter), and it also provides financial services such as clearing interbank payments, managing wire transfers, and managing exchange rates and reserves.

We now turn to a discussion of how money policy is implemented by central banks. In the previous 10 chapters we deftly increased or decreased M and shifted the LM back and forth to analyze the effects of monetary policy. Now we examine the mechanism by which M is actually changed.

11.2 THE MONEY CREATION PROCESS: HOW THE FEDERAL RESERVE CHANGES THE MONEY SUPPLY

Central banks use three methods to change a nation's money supply:

(i)   Open Market Operations (OMOs)
(ii) Discount Rate Policy
(iii) Changing the Reserve Requirement (RR)

Prior to discussing these, a description of one aspect of the implementation mechanism of major central banks—reserve requirements (reserve ratios)—is in order. In the following two sections, we discuss the widely accepted "textbook" version of the theoretical working of the money multiplier and Open Market Operations. This is followed by the reality of the state of Open Market Operations in 11.2.2.1.

11.2.1 RESERVE REQUIREMENTS AND THE MONEY MULTIPLIER: THE THEORY

Under this system, all depository institutions are required by law to hold a minimum fixed percentage of deposits as reserves. The Reserve Ratio (RR) is defined as the ratio of reserves to deposits.

Required Reserve Ratio = Reserves/Deposits

Although in the US the Federal Reserve determines the required ratio for each type of deposit, we assume a flat reserve ratio of 10 percent in this chapter, for convenience.[3] Hence, a deposit of $1,000 made to the First Bank of New York by Person 1 would result in the First Bank putting $100 in reserves and being able to loan out $900, in this simplified example in which we have multiple banks. This loan is made to Person 2 in Florida who then buys computer hardware from a store in Orlando for $900. The store owner deposits this check into the Bank of Orlando, which then has to hold $90 in reserve and be able to lend out only $810 to Person 3 who need to remodel her home office, and so on.[4]

We can write the string of total deposits generated by the initial $1,000 of deposits, given the 10 percent reserve ratio, as:

$$\$1,000 + \$900 + \$810 + \$729 + \ldots\ldots \tag{1}$$

Since each successive bank obtains only 0.9 of the deposits of the previous bank, the above string of numbers can be re-written as:

$$\$1,000\ (1 + 0.9 + 0.9^2 + 0.9^3 + \ldots\ldots\ldots) \tag{2}$$

Since the sum of the infinite series $1 + x + x^2 + x^3 + x^4 + \ldots = 1/(1-x)$, the series in our example works out to be:

$$(1 + 0.9 + 0.9^2 + 0.9^3 + \ldots\ldots\ldots) = 1/(1 - 0.9) = 1/(0.10) = 10 \tag{3}$$

In other words, the infinite sum is equal to $1/[1 - (1-R)]$ where R is the reserve ratio. This simplifies to simply $1/(R)$, which is $1/(0.10) = 10$

Substituting the result from (3) into (2), we obtain the total increase in checking account balances throughout all the banks to be:

($1,000)(10) = $10,000 = (Initial Deposit)(1/Reserve Ratio)

In general:
The total increase in deposits = (Initial Deposit)(1/Reserve Ratio)   (4)

Economists refer to the term 1/Reserve Ratio as the money multiplier, and in some ways it is identical to the fiscal multiplier of the earlier Keynesian chapters.

11.2.2 OPEN MARKET OPERATIONS (OMOs)

With the review of reserve ratios and the money multiplier, we now explore Federal Open Market Operations, the most frequently used method by which the Federal Reserve and other major central banks change money supply.

The FOMC meets in Washington. The setting is splendid; white and gold wallpaper dating back to the art deco era graces the walls. The committee sits on plush brown-colored swivel chairs around an immense oval 27-foot Honduran mahogany table. A green light is switched on whenever the proceedings are being taped. Large numbers of staffers, statisticians, econometricians, and technical assistants are also present prior to the main deliberations. Until the mid-1990s, the announcements of FOMC meetings had been typically relegated to inside columns of inner pages of business newspapers. But things changed in the mid-1990s—since then, FOMC meetings have often attracted as much media attention as royal weddings.

We begin with the case where the FOMC meets and decides that the economy needs a looser monetary policy (lower interest rates), and decides to increase M by $1,000, in this simplified example.

The committee then instructs the Trading Desk at the New York Federal Reserve to buy $1,000 worth of government securities (US Treasury bills and notes) from a Government Securities Dealer (GSD). "GSD" is a prestigious designation reserved for only a few highly regarded financial institutions. The Federal Reserve then pays the GSD with a check for $1,000 drawn on itself. The GSD then deposits this check in its account at its commercial bank (New Jersey National Bank, for example). The New Jersey bank then sends this check to the Federal Reserve for credit. The Federal Reserve "pays" New Jersey National Bank by crediting this bank's account at the New York Federal Reserve by $1,000. In other words, the Federal Reserve increases the reserves of the New Jersey bank by $1,000.

Assuming a reserve ratio of 10 percent, the New Jersey Savings bank must place $100 in reserve and can now lend out $900, and the effect of the initial injection of $1,000 now ripples through the economy as discussed. As the money "changes hands", a string of successively smaller deposits and loans are made in the process described in the preceding section.

As banks now have a greater supply of loanable funds, competition between them to lend these newly-available funds rapidly translates to a lowering of interest rates.[5] Throughout the book we deftly shifted the LM to the right to signify an increase in the money supply M, resulting in a lower interest rate as presented in **Figure 1**. Now, finally, the mechanism has been described.[6]

The rate lowered by the Federal Reserve in our example is the short-term rate—the **federal fund rate**. This is the overnight rate that banks and other depository institutions charge each other while trading their non-interest bearing reserves. Banks, whose reserves may have fallen below the ratio required by the Fed, borrow at this overnight lending rate from other banks that happen to have excess reserves. In our example, as the FOMC authorizes an open market purchase of government bonds, and as reserves generally increase, the federal funds rate, perhaps the best indicator of current Federal Reserve policy, tends to fall.

Figure 1

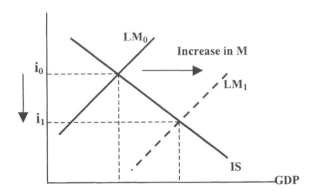

While the money multiplier implies that the total loans generated (money "put into circulation"), should be ($1000)(10) = $10,000, the actual money multiplier for the US is not 10 but lies between 2 and 3. This difference is due to the fact that our formula assumes that there is no "leakage" in the money creation process and that all the loans make their way directly into other checking accounts which are then promptly deposited into banks 2, 3, 4, and so on. However, this process ignores the fact that individuals tend to hold a portion of their loans in cash. This tendency to hold cash constitutes the "leakage" in our example as deposits held as cash are not available for other banks to lend out. As cash holdings increase, the money multiplier decreases as successive shrinking bank deposits in turn rapidly decrease future loanable funds.

From this discussion, it becomes clear that an efficient market with large volumes of tradeable government bonds is a necessary condition for effective open market operations. Economies not possessing such bond markets and, more importantly, such relatively risk-free and easily traded government debt would certainly be unable to readily change the growth of the money supply and short-term interest rates using OMOs.

To decrease money growth and to increase short-term rates, the reverse process takes place. The FOMC instructs the Trading Desk at the New York Federal Reserve to sell bonds to a GSD, resulting finally in a removal of reserves from the GSD's commercial bank (New Jersey Bank). The ensuing decrease in the supply of loanable funds in New Jersey Bank and its competition results in a rapid increase in the interest rates. In previous chapters, this was evidenced when we contracted M and shifted the LM to the left, thereby increasing interest rates.

In summary, open market purchases of government securities from the private sector result in an increase in bank's reserves and the resultant increase in national money supply, accompanied by a drop in short-term rates. An open market sale of government securities does the opposite: banks' lending abilities decrease as their reserves fall. The money supply shrinks, resulting in higher interest rates in the short-term.[7]

Typically, the media announce the FOMC's decision in terms of the final intended change in the federal funds rate.[8] In reality, though, the FOMC sets the target range for the intended federal funds rate, and then indulges in open market operations to attain it.

We now turn to the empirical reality of open market operations and the money multiplier. Unfortunately, the money growth process is, in reality, not nearly as clinical and convenient as that presented in the pedagogic-academic literature, and in this and the preceding section.

11.2.2.1 RESERVE RATIOS AND THE MONEY MULTIPLIER: THE EMPIRICAL REALITY

The author is most grateful to Prof. Giles Mellon of Rutgers Business School, with whom he co-authored and presented "Effective Monetary Policy in a World of Non-Binding Reserve Requirement," at the National Business and Economics Conference, 2002. This section incorporates portions of the working paper.

Monetary legislation in the 1990s has caused fundamental changes in the way that money/credit creation results from open market operations. In 1990, the Fed abolished completely all reserve requirements on time deposits for US banks. (Similar regulations also went into effect in Japan, the UK, Canada, Australia, and in several Western European economies.) Since time deposits for US banks made up some 80% of total deposits, the result of this legislation was to free-up the bulk of US bank net deposits from reserve requirement obligations.

Reserve requirement on demand deposits were retained, though the ratio was lowered to 10% in the US in 1992. But even this moderate system of reduced legal reserve obligations soon ceased to be a binding constraint on bank expansion of deposit and credit for two reasons; (i) The rapid expansion of ATM systems containing huge amounts of cash, and (ii) the institution of "sweep accounts" where the banks moved large amounts of demand balances into time accounts with legal reserve requirements.

As a result of these developments, the great majority of US banks now hold no reserves at all at the Fed to meet reserve requirements, and, indeed, can satisfy their reserve requirements with only a portion of the cash balances in their ATM systems which count as legal reserves. Most banks in the US now hold significant excess reserves on a permanent basis, well in excess of the legally binding minimum amount—legal reserve requirements have ceased to exert any binding limit on monetary expansion.

It should not, however, be thought that under this new system, open market operations are useless, or, alternatively, any injection of new reserves through open market operations would allow the banks to expand deposits and credit without limit.

The cash holdings of banks in ATM machines, though they far exceed legal required reserves, are not "excess" in the operational senses. The reserves are "excess" only in the sense of the legal reserve ratio. In reality, they may be optimal reserves at "desired" levels necessary for the banks to do business. In other words, "effective" although not legally established reserve ratios are now found to exist—an injection of reserves via open market operations will still increase the rate of monetary growth, and vice versa.

The key issue is, however, the computation of the size of the so-called money multiplier, now that the clean conventionally-accepted mechanism of the multiplier presented in 11.2.1 has been muddied by the recent events and legislation pertaining to reserves. The existence of "effective" and non-binding reserve ratios does indeed complicate the conventional money multiplier and significantly increases the difficulty in accurately determining its magnitude. However, this sub-section does not invalidate this chapter's discussion on open market operation and the general money creation process. Instead, this discussion places OMOs in a real-world context and emphasizes the formidable challenges faced by modern central banks in exercising at least some discretionary control on the rate of monetary growth.

Before we transition to the second method of changing monetary growth, we briefly discuss the very important distinction between Open Market Operations and the monetization of outstanding government debt discussed earlier in Chapter 3 and 6.

OMOs, the Federal Reserve and the Treasury

The operations are considered to be "open market" because transactions involving government securities are conducted by the Federal Reserve in an open market with commercial banks and the general public, but not with the government. The exclusion is to ensure that there is no possibility of monetization of national budget deficits incurred by the government. A central bank that buys new bonds directly from the US Treasury effectively

---

"prints money", and this could be the dangerous first step on the road to eventual hyperinflation.

The Fed's open market purchases and sales of government securities should not be confused by the Treasury's sales of government debt to individuals and institutions. The Treasury issues <u>new</u> debt to finance large increases in government spending and to finance the ensuing budget deficits. As discussed in detail in the national savings identity (NSI) in Chapter 3, these sustainable bond-financed budget deficits are linked to current account deficits and to large accompanying capital inflows.

In sharp contrast, the government securities that are bought and sold in open market operations by the Federal Reserve to change the money supply, are not new securities, but instead are <u>outstanding</u> (preexisting) government securities.

Another difference between Treasury issues of new debt and Federal Reserve open market operations lies in the nature of the transaction. Domestic and foreign investors voluntarily purchase the Treasury's new issues of government bonds at national bond auctions.

11.2.3   CHANGING THE DISCOUNT RATE

The rate at which the Federal Reserve lends reserves to banks is called the **discount rate**. In this section we begin with the conventional discussion of how discount-rate policy is, theoretically, designed to be a tool of monetary policy—that is, how discount rate policy is supposed to work. This will be followed by a discussion of the actual effectiveness of discount rate policy in the US.

How is discount rate policy supposed to change money growth?

If a major customer in the private sector requires a loan from, say, Citibank, and if Citibank does not have the amount on hand, it is reluctant to turn away the major customer. Generally, Citibank would first try to borrow from other banks through the federal funds market, at the federal funds rate, discussed earlier. If this rate is too high, or the reserves are simply not available from other banks, then Citibank can borrow directly from the Federal Reserve at the discount rate.

By changing this discount rate, the Federal Reserve affects the amount borrowed by banks and signals a change in monetary policy. Announced raises in discount rate indicate a tighter money-growth policy, while drops in the discount rate imply and "easier" (looser) money-growth policy.

While federal funds rate policy is conducted by the 12-person FOMC, the discount rate is administered only by the 7-member Board of Governors.

Discount rate changes are highly visible signals of the Fed's intent regarding near-term changes in monetary growth. Even though discount rate changes are not made as frequently as changes in the federal funds rate, they are usually synchronized with appropriate open market operations. A fall in the discount rate, for instance, is usually accompanied by an open market purchase of government securities, and vice versa.

Perhaps one of the largest infusions of liquidity using the discount rate window was on the day following the September 11 attacks on the World Trade Center and the Pentagon. On Wednesday, September 12, the Federal Reserve lent a staggering $45 billion from its discount window to banks that needed to finance uncleared checks that were stuck in grounded aircraft all over the country. In sharp contrast, lending for the whole week prior to the attack was just under $200 million.

How is observed (actual) discount rate policy different?

Aside from significant discount window activity in such times of crisis, the discount rate in recent times has not been a proactive tool of monetary policy. Borrowed reserves have constituted an extremely small percentage of total member bank reserves from the late 1990s to the present. In fact, on average, since the mid-1990s, borrowed reserves have only constituted less than 1/200th of total bank reserves!

In addition, there is strong empirical evidence that the discount rate actually follows the 3-month Treasury Bill (T-Bill) rate, which is the interest rate paid by the government when it borrows from the public for a period of three months. Typically, the Fed is almost never proactive in its discount rate policy, with the discount rate closely mimicking or, at times, lagging, the short-term T-Bill rate.

The reason for adopting the T-Bill rate as a benchmark is that if the discount rate were to fall below the T-Bill rate, a clear arbitrage opportunity would present itself. Banks could now borrow reserves from the Federal Reserve at this low discount rate, and then lend these out risklessly to the government at the 3-month T-Bill rate for a guaranteed profit. Conversely, if the discount rate were to exceed the T-Bill rate, borrowing from the Fed would rapidly shrink. Barring national crises such as the attacks in September 2001, only banks in dire financial straits would be forced to borrow reserves from the Fed under these circumstances.

As a consequence, instead of using discount rate policy as a proactive monetary policy instrument as the conventional wisdom indicates, the Fed has been found to adopt a discount rate policy that very closely mimics the 3-month T-Bill rate.

11.2.4   CHANGING THE REQUIRED RESERVE RATIO

This is the least frequently used method of changing the money supply. By changing the required reserve ratio, the Federal Reserve changes the quantity of deposits that can be supported by a given level of reserves. For instance, increasing the reserve ratio from 10 percent to 12 percent would increase the reserves to be held "at the Fed" by local banks, thus lowering their lending ability, and vice versa.

In our earlier example, the theoretical final money multiplier would now drop to $1/(0.12) = 8.33$, thus lowering the eventual amount of deposit creation that would eventually ripple through the economy.

Changes in the RR are disruptive as banks have to undergo a sudden, finite change, whereas they can now lend out more/less of their deposits, and hence the RR is changed very infrequently. Increases in the RR, in particular, are uncommon and are highly unpopular with banks since reserves are non-interest-bearing.

Following this discussion of the institutional structure of the Federal Reserve and the three methods by which the money supply can be changed by central banks, the next logical question explores the objectives of effective monetary policy.

11.3   THE ROLE OF THE CENTRAL BANK: HOW SHOULD MONETARY POLICY BE CONDUCTED?

In addition to making discretionary changes in the money supply, the Fed has several functions. These include clearing interbank payments, supervising and regulating the banking system by reviewing the quality of loans and ensuring that the banks are maintaining the reserve ratio, managing exchange rates and the nation's foreign exchange reserves, and acting as the **lender of last resort** for the banking system.

This last role is perhaps the most dramatic. The Federal Reserve must quickly inject liquidity into an economy during times of great national crisis. Following the attack on the World Trade Center and the Pentagon on September 11, 2001, the Fed moved with impressive speed and determination to rapidly pump funds into a system that was suddenly in a grave liquidity crisis.

Within two days of the attack, the Federal Reserve had injected over $108 billion to meet demands from banks to cover uncleared checks that were in planes stranded on the ground in airports all over the country. Such rapid injections of liquidity are typically done by overnight (short term) repurchase agreements (known as RPs or repos). Here the Fed buys securities from banks and provides liquidity to them, with the agreement that on a specified date (usually the next day) the banks will repurchase the securities back from the Fed at a fixed price. In other words, this arrangement enables the Fed to make a short-term loan to financial institutions in need of short-term liquidity. While repos are usually for one-day (overnight) lending, such an agreement could span a 2-week period.

A similar injection (though on a much smaller scale), followed the stock market correction in October 1987, when a liquidity crisis prompted a money growth increase of 14% during the week following the correction. Other examples are monetary infusions following the 1995 Mexican peso crisis and the 1997 Asian currency meltdown.

While the Federal Reserve has to perform the functions described above, its single most important responsibility remains the control of the growth of the money supply in the United States. How should this be done? What policy should the Federal Reserve adopt for changing M? And what about central banks of emerging economies? How is their policy prescription different?

To answer these questions, we begin with Milton Friedman's role for monetary policy, followed by the Taylor rule and the Humphrey Hawkins legislation, the bane of the US Federal Reserve. An overview of the European Central Bank is followed by a discussion of challenges for monetary policy within the Eurozone.

11.3.1   MILTON FRIEDMAN AND THE ROLE OF MONETARY POLICY

Long before the advent of a formally recognized "New Classical" AS curve, decades before the arrival of the rational expectations paradigm, Milton Friedman outlined a role for monetary policy consistent with a vertical aggregate supply curve **(Figure 2)** for developed economies.

In Friedmanian doctrine, monetary policy would be <u>unable</u> to <u>consistently</u> attain the following objectives on a long-term basis:
1. Full employment
2. High GDP growth.

In Figure 2, we establish interest rates, output, and employment "targets" for monetary policy.[9] Note the vertical AS curve implicit in Friedmanian monetary doctrine. An increase in money growth (an open market purchase) leads to a rightward shift in LM_0 to LM_1, resulting in attainment of the interest rate target, i_{low}, and output target, Y_{high}, depicted as (A) in Figure 2. (The employment target is also attained, but the labor market diagram from Chapter 9 is not reproduced here).

However, these would be just the immediate short-term impact effects of monetary policy. Milton Friedman pointed out that, in developed economies, prices would increase from P_0 to P_1, thus resulting in the LM "snapping back" to LM_0, presented as (B) in Figure 2. As discussed earlier in Chapter 8, in a classical AS curve model, nominal wages would adjust with prices, rendering the real wage unchanged. The labor market would be finally at the original rate of employment, and GDP growth corresponding to the original rate of employment would still be the same. Thus, with the shift (snap-back) in LM, GDP growth would again fall back to Y_0 in the long-run.

The <u>only</u> lasting effects of the monetary expansion in this case would be an increase in inflation from P_0 to P_1 (accompanied by an increase in nominal wages as discussed earlier), and <u>no long-term increase</u> in output growth or in employment. Interest rates would also "snap back" to i_0. In fact, by the Fisher effect (Chapter 6), long-term rates would rise right away due to expectations of future impending inflation.

Clearly, according to Friedman, monetary policy cannot and should not be used to try and attain long-term output, interest rate, and employment targets. The results would only be progressively increasing cycles of higher inflation and long-term rates.

So how should monetary policy be conducted?

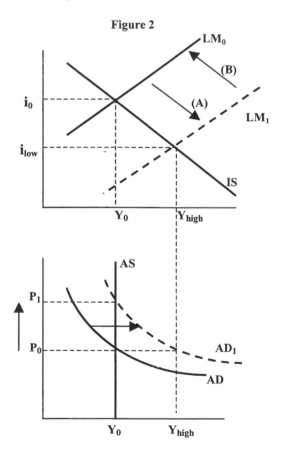

Figure 2

Milton Friedman advocated an **"x percent money-growth rule"** for developed economies. Here, the central bank resolutely maintains a publicly announced and rigidly adhered-to fixed money growth rule that would not be sacrificed to attempt any futile demand-side stabilization. In this case, the central bank makes it very clear that drops (changes) in GDP growth and employment will not, and cannot, be cured by expansionary monetary policy. While the magnitude of the announced growth rate in money could be tied to the real trend growth rate of the economy, the exact percentage growth is not nearly as important as the unwavering nature of the x-percent rule, and the implied determination of the central bank to adopt a noninterventionist monetary policy with regard to output and employment.

In the US, such a policy was adopted by Fed chairman Paul Volcker, who finally succeeded in eradicating the ravaging inflationary legacy of the 1970s. Inflation consequently fell from 10.5% in 1980 to under 3 percent by the mid-1980s, thanks to a resolutely-fixed 2% money growth rule, single-mindedly aimed at attaining the well-announced money growth rate. While Keynesian critics may argue that the recession of 1980-81 may have been exacerbated by such determined Fed policy, inflation ceased to be an ongoing macroeconomic concern.

The Volcker monetary policy is, however, an exceptional episode and an unpopular one, given the attendant accompanying recession of 1980-81. In reality, central banks that adopt x-percent money-growth rules often come under intense pressure from the public (and governments) to lower interest rates and to "do something" to spur employment and growth. For central banks, a Friedmanian x-percent money rule can be, understandably, a lonely and unpopular policy objective.

Therefore central banks settle instead for a more practical or "second-best" version of the x-percent rule, wherein monetary policy's only objective is inflation control instead of an unwavering money-growth rule. Here, monetary policy attempts to target the only major endogenous variable that it can actually influence over the long-term—inflation. The central bank's sole objective is to hit the inflation target, P_{target}. The objective of monetary policy is to continuously make appropriate changes in monetary growth to offset any shifts in the AD from domestic or global exogenous shocks or changes in fiscal policy, and to thereby ensure that the inflation rate P_{target} in constantly attained.

The European Central Bank, perhaps, epitomizes this policy of inflation targeting. In fact, it comes closest to adopting a true Friedmanian monetary policy by adopting two targets—an inflation target as well as an x-percent money growth target (please see following box).

However, the fact remains that even while both the hard-core x-percent rule as well as the slightly gentler "inflation-only" policy may be academically sound in a vertical AS paradigm, they are likely to be politically

264

difficult and, at times, distinctly unpopular. This may be true even when the central bank enjoys a high degree of autonomy, as experienced by the European Central Bank (ECB) in the late 1990s and in the early 2000s.

The European Central Bank: Early Trials and Tribulations

While membership in the Eurozone with its one common monetary policy and common currency is subject to the Maasticht criteria discussed in Chapter 6, the policy objective of the ECB itself is fraught with controversy.[10] The European Central Bank's only policy objective is to manage the money growth of the member countries to attain and ensure an inflation target. The ECB has unambiguously and adamantly announced that a target of less than (or equal to) 2% inflation is the only macroeconomic goal that it will attempt to attain.[11]

During the formative years of the ECB, potential member countries' governments were "right-of-center," but by the time the ECB came "on line" in 1999, most of the countries in the Eurozone (and in the European Union) were labor governments and socialist regimes that were decidedly "left-of-center". These governments, almost uniformly Keynesian, believed in the power of monetary policy to alleviate unemployment as well as sluggish growth via lower interest rates.

The ECB, on the other hand, with its publicly-declared "inflation-only" target set in a vertical AS curve paradigm, found itself in a clash of paradigms with Keynesian governments and the public when it repeatedly refused to "do something" to increase jobs and growth by lowering interest rates. The notion that monetary policy in certain economies may be ineffective in stabilizing output growth and employment is not intuitive, not fully-understood, and understandably unpopular in high-unemployment economies.

Compounding the matter further is the German Stability and Growth Pact, adopted by the Eurozone countries. Basically, this pact prohibits the use of government spending to jump-start economies. Upper limits on government spending and deficits are specifically prescribed by the Pact, and any violation of these upper bounds may result in severe fines that may equal 0.05% of GDP!

The Stability Pact, as it is usually referred to, is based on a vertical AS paradigm, and hence it ascribes no benefit to GDP and employment resulting from increases in government spending, since fiscal multiplier effects are claimed to be non-existent in this paradigm. Hence, the Eurozone economies can rely on tax changes only if they are to attempt demand-side stabilization—changes in M and G are not possible. The ECB's inflation-only target prevents monetary fine-tuning, while the Stability Pact precludes changing (increasing) government spending to manage growth and employment.

As the Eurozone economies slowed along with the US economy by late 2001, policy makers, under increasing pressure from an exasperated public, increasingly wondered if, perhaps, the Stability Pact could be relaxed somewhat to allow at least some increase in government spending to explore if multiplier effects were truly non-existent. As unemployment increased by 2001, it was becoming increasing untenable to "do nothing" to attempt to stabilize the economy aside from the usual supply-side prescriptions of tax cuts and deregulation, that would, eventually, result in endogenous increases in productivity.

Another challenge faced by the ECB is more fundamental than a "clash of paradigms"; it pertains to the institutional design of the ECB and to the administration of its open market operations. The 6-member Executive Board of the ECB is equivalent to the Board of Governors of the Federal Reserve. The Executive Board members based in Euro Towers in Frankfurt have 8-year non-renewable appointments, and consist of the President, Vice-President, and four other members. Monetary policy is formulated and implemented by the Governing Council (similar to the Federal Open Market Committee), comprising 18 members; 6 Board members plus the 12 governors of the central banks of the member countries.[12]

Unlike the Federal Open Market Committee (FOMC), where only 5 out of 12 Fed Presidents vote, all 12 central bank governors of the respective member countries are involved in the voting process in the ECB's Executive Board. This has caused some concerns among academic circles. By virtue of allowing all 12 governors to vote, the "center," composed of the Executive Board in Frankfurt, can be outvoted—in fact, blocks of countries could collude to determine the course of monetary policy for the Eurozone independent of "Frankfurt".

This was the case in the US before the Great Depression. All 12 Fed Presidents were included in the FOMC, with the result that the Board of Governors was often paralyzed when it came to enacting policy that might adversely affect one sector of the nation or the other; the 12 Fed Presidents would outvote the Governors, thereby neutralizing any central control of national monetary policy.

With more countries soon to enter the Eurozone, analysts fear that the ability of the ECB's Executive Board to direct and enact monetary policy may be further jeopardized.

Central banks of emerging economies are, of course, not constrained by inflation-only targets. In the Keynesian paradigm, monetary stabilization is indeed an effective tool for macroeconomic stabilization. Monetary policy is effective in attaining higher GDP growth and higher employment, or in engineering soft landings. China and the East Asian economies (possible excepting Japan), Central Europe, India, Africa, and Latin and South America are examples where central banks may be successful in demand-side stabilization. However, these economies run the risk of relying excessively on monetary policy. Without accompanying fiscal reform and discipline, the specter of surging inflation and permanently high long-term rates that accompany excessive demand-side stabilization lurks in the background.

11.3.2 IS MONETARY DISCIPLINE WORTH THE PAIN?

Proponents of an inflation-only rule, conducted by a central bank that resolutely adopts a New Classical paradigm (vertical AS curve), would list the benefits as follows:
1. Lower inflation rates. This is the one variable that the central bank can consistently control in the long run using monetary policy.
2. Lower long-term interest rates. Since expectations of inflation will be curtailed given the policy of adopting some low to moderate inflation target, long-term nominal rates will be consequently lower, by the Fisher effect. Low long-term rates are vital in the formation of long-term capital growth (housing, new plant and equipment, for example.)
3. With lower inflationary expectations, unions may be more agreeable to lower increases in nominal wages, thereby breaking any wage-price spiral.
4. Stable exchange rates. This is particularly important for small economies with large exposure to the trade sector (Singapore, Taiwan, Hong Kong. A fixed money growth rule will yield less volatility in nominal exchange rates and hence in the prices of tradeable goods (imports as well as exports).
5. Monetary discipline breeds fiscal discipline. Empirically, countries with highly disciplined (tight) monetary policies have been positively correlated with low and highly sustainable budget deficits. With no possibility of monetizing away any fiscal profligacy thanks to a tight money-growth rule, policy makers are forced to incur only the deficits that they can bond-finance.
6. Monetary and fiscal discipline is the necessary condition for the "safe haven" status that attracts global capital inflows. An economy incurring a bond-financed deficit and/or a current account deficit must also be a safe haven economy to attempt NSI-type financing as discussed in Chapter 3.

Now that we have discussed how monetary policy ought to be conducted and having listed the benefits of monetary discipline, it quickly becomes evident that the Federal Reserve (as well as the ECB, to some extent) may really not be adopting inflation-only targets. There is clear evidence of attempts to engineer a soft landing in the US 2000, to deflate the tech sector's SAP bubble, and then to jump-start the US economy in 2001 with seven interest rate cuts before the terrorist attacks in September 2001, followed by four more thereafter.

Instead of an inflation-only rule, the Fed seems to have displayed decidedly Keynesian behavior. Why? The answer lies in a discussion of the bane of the Federal Reserve—the 1978 Humphrey Hawkins Act.

11.3.3   THE "CURSE" OF HUMPHREY-HAWKINS

In the **1946 Employment Act**, Congress declared that it was the "...responsibility of the Federal Government to...promote maximum employment, production, and purchasing power". Congress then went one step further in 1978 with the Full Employment and Balanced Growth Act, commonly referred to as the **Humphrey-Hawkins Act (H-H)**, which specified unemployment targets for the Federal Government. Every year, around the 20th of every February and July, the Fed Chairperson has to testify before the Senate Banking Committee regarding the degree to which the H-H targets were achieved and to forecast the course of monetary policy over the next 18 months.

At first glance, Humphrey-Hawkins seems like a perfectly reasonable set of policy objectives. Closer examination yields just the opposite— Humphrey-Hawkins is macroeconomically inconsistent and fundamentally unsound. From both a theoretical and a monetary policy perspective, simultaneously attaining the H-H targets of low unemployment and low inflation is an exercise in futility.

In Chapter 10, we discussed how both Keynesian and supply-sider models could legitimately co-exist in the US due to the identification problem. We now analyze the implications of H-H for each of the two paradigms in turn.

We begin by assuming that the US is operating in a Keynesian paradigm. This model is characterized by the output-inflation tradeoff and the Phillips curve. Demand-side stabilization resulting from an expansionary monetary policy would increase GDP growth, decrease unemployment, but also increase the rate of inflation! Clearly, in a Keynesian model, Humphrey-Hawkins targets of low unemployment and low inflation would be impossible.

We now assume that the US is operating in a supply-sider paradigm with the vertical rational expectations aggregate supply curve. In this paradigm, increases in output growth (due to a rightward shift in the AS) and decreases in unemployment are accompanied by falling rates of inflation. In this case it may appear that the Humphrey Hawkins targets of low inflation and unemployment have been attained.

However, on closer examination, it becomes clear that these results are not the results of monetary (demand-side) policy. They are, instead, the products of shifts in the aggregate supply curve due to increases in productivity, deregulation, and so on. A monetary stimulus by itself (a shift in AD), without any accompanying supply-side stimulus (shift in AS), would only result in a higher rate of inflation at the same rate of GDP growth, as discussed in the previous chapter.

Therefore, from a monetary policy perspective, Humphrey-Hawkins is a macroeconomic impossibility. No matter what the paradigm, the targets are fundamentally impossible to hit using monetary policy. It is no wonder that several policy makers have undertaken the abolishment of H-H as a personal agenda. In fact, European Central Bank officials consider themselves lucky to have just one policy objective—keeping inflation below 2 percent—instead of the impossible challenge of Humphrey-Hawkins.

Is the Humphrey-Hawkins Act really a liability?

Cynics point out that despite its fundamental macroeconomic inconsistency, Humphrey-Hawkins may actually benefit the Fed by giving it some "wiggle room". Instead of single-mindedly having to direct monetary policy towards attaining a highly visible monetary aggregate target or an inflation target, H-H actually allows the Fed some discretion by prescribing both an unemployment/output target as well as an inflation target.

If the economy were to slip into recession and actual unemployment were to rise above the full employment target, H-H would legitimize monetary loosening by the Fed and the subsequent lowering of interest rates. On the other hand, if the economy were to signal imminent overheating, the Fed could legitimately contract money growth to engineer a soft landing.

Hence a case could be made that, conveniently, Humphrey-Hawkins allows the Federal Reserve to indulge in short-term discretionary policy. Unlike its European counterpart, the ECB, the Federal Reserve isn't constrained by an official, rigid and transparent inflation-only policy.

Cynics further contend that, unlike the ECB that agonizes every time it deviates from its policy objective to lower interest rates under pressure from slowing economies in the Eurozone, the Federal Reserve has no such compunction, thanks to the (inadvertent) flexibility provided by the "impossible" Humphrey-Hawkins.

Hence, given the discussion presented on H-H, it is hardly surprising that the ultimate significance of Humphrey-Hawkins, whether curse or convenience, remains open to debate.

11.3.4   THE TAYLOR RULE

What is the Federal Reserve's policy response given the dual unemployment and inflation objectives? The answer lies in the **Taylor Principle** and the **Taylor Rule**.

Named after John Taylor of Stanford University, the Taylor Principle (1993) states that changes in the central bank's policy interest rate must be disproportionally larger than changes in the inflation rate.

An increase in the inflation rate of one percent, for example, should result in a monetary policy response whereby interest rates increase by greater than one percent. According to the Taylor Principle, this action would increase the real interest rate, defined as the nominal rate minus inflation in Chapter 6. The rise in the real rate, in turn, reduces spending, slows down the economy, and with the implicit leftward shift in aggregate demand, results in the inflation rate dropping back down to its target.[13]

The Taylor Principle is not without its hazards. Using the expression for the Fisher effect from Chapter 6, $r = i - \pi$, we can see that if the increase in the policy interest rate (i) is not disproportionally larger than the increase in inflation (π), real rates will actually fall, thereby stimulating the economy and hence pushing the inflation higher. Hence, the exact amount by which the policy interest rates need to be changed, is crucial to the final outcome.

In response to these policy hazards, John Taylor formulated the **Taylor Rule.** This rule enables policymakers to determine exactly how much the Fed should change the policy interest rate (the Federal Funds rate) in response to deviations of actual inflation and output/employment from their specified H-H targets.

While several versions and extended forms of the Taylor Rule exist, we begin by discussing an early and simplified version, expressed as:

Federal Funds Rate $= i_t = 2 + (\pi_t) + 0.5(\pi_t - \pi_t^*) + 0.5(Y_t - Y_t^*)$

Where:

i_t = the Federal funds rate, the policy interest rate controlled by the FOMC, in the current period t

π_t = Prior 4-quarter inflation rate

π_t^* = FOMC's inflation target

Y_t = Current rate of real GDP growth

Y_t^* = Trend rate of growth of real potential GDP (long-term target)

According to this simple Taylor rule, the FOMC contracts monetary growth and increases short-term interest rates (Federal Funds rates) if actual inflation

π_t exceeds the target $\pi_{t,}^*$, or if real GDP growth Y_t exceeds the long-term trend rate Y_t^*. The $(Y_t - Y_t^*)$ term is also referred to as the "output gap".

The constant term, 2, is the assumed long-term average of the real interest rate defined as the long-term average difference between the nominal interest rate i and the rate of inflation, and the coefficients of magnitude 0.5 are the degrees to which the FOMC responds to the deviations of inflation and output from their "targets". Taylor contends that since 1999, the FOMC has responded more vigorously to deviations in inflation from the target rate of inflation, thereby implying that the coefficient is probably higher than 0.5 at the present.

Taylor assumed that the equilibrium long-term real rate was 2 percent, and that the long-term output gap is zero, on average. By substituting the expression $i = r + \pi_t$, with r =2 into the Taylor Rule, we obtain a long-run target inflation rate equal to 2 percent. That is, $\pi_t^* = 2$.

Extended Taylor rules are more sophisticated versions of the rule discussed here, with targets that include the S&P 500 stock price index (as well as exchange rates and long-term interest rates). In the case of a stock price index, if a dangerous SAP bubble were to develop, with average stock prices exceeding some implicit target, the Taylor Rule would advocate an open market sale of government bonds, leading to an increase in short-term (Federal Fund) interest rates along the lines of the Fed's deflation of the perceived SAP bubble in technology stocks in 1999.

11.3.5   EXCHANGE RATE PEGGING AND CURRENCY CRISES

As introduced in the pre-ISLM Chapter 6, in economies where the central bank has no significant institutional autonomy, and where legislation pertaining to monetary discipline is absent, exchange rate pegging has often been the only option left to central bankers hoping for some modicum of monetary independence from the government. Here, the country seeking monetary discipline (Country A), locks—pegs—the exchange rate between its currency and that of another country with a longstanding reputation for monetary discipline (Country B). In this case it announces that monetary policy in A would be directed <u>only</u> towards ensuring that the exchange rate remained fixed (pegged) at 10 units of A's currency to 1 unit of B's currency.[14]

Such a well-announced peg would allow the central bank, presumably striving for some form of independence from fiscal pressure in the conduct of monetary policy, to reject pressure to increase M to "do something". Perhaps more importantly, under a self-enforced system of pegged exchange rates, the central bank now has a mechanism by which it can resist pressure from the government to monetize non-sustainable deficit spending.

With a peg of 10A = 1B, if the central bank were to buckle under pressure from a fiscally irresponsible government and increase monetary growth to finance large deficits, the domestic currency would immediately weaken and the peg would be instantly threatened. Instead of 10A =1B, it would tend to drop to 12A = 1B (in this simplified example), and this would immediately signal, to domestic and foreign investors, a breakdown in A's monetary discipline. With interest in A lower than in B due to the increase of monetary growth in A, and coupled with the loss in confidence in A's ability to maintain monetary discipline, capital would rapidly flow out of A to B as soon as it becomes evident that the 10A = 1B peg is about to "break".

If, however, the peg is viable and if A does indeed successfully pursue a disciplined monetary policy aimed only at managing the 10:1 currency ratio, domestic and foreign investors will increasingly see A as a safer haven. Global capital flows into A, and foreign investment increases as it becomes evident that A's monetary policy basically mimics that of a high-monetary-discipline country, B. Good examples include the incredible capital inflows experienced by Mexico in the early 1990s and later that decade by the East Asian economies. Expectations of growth combined with signals of macroeconomic discipline resulted in massive inflows into these economies that were pegged to the US dollar.

In a sense, from a central bank perspective the adoption of a hard peg would be a "pre-emptive strike" against any attempts at fiscal profligacy. Hopefully, the scenario describing a breaking peg (from 10A = 1B to 12A = 1B) would be only a hypothetical warning of the dire consequences of losing macroeconomic discipline. Central bankers would make clear to those advocating unrestricted monetization that the peg would indeed be broken if the central bank were pressured to increase money growth to pay for excessive and non-sustainable government spending. Country A would experience a traumatic hot capital outflow, resulting in a sharp spike in domestic interest rates.[15] Capital investment would, subsequently, fall due to the rise in domestic interest rates, threatening the country with recession.

Perhaps most damaging, any monetary credibility attained by Country A after adopting the peg and after enduring the subsequent macroeconomic straightjacket over a significant period of time would be, unfortunately, wiped-out "in an afternoon." The long end of the yield curve for Country A would, in all probability, begin to rise as nervous (and disappointed) lenders now began to add additional risk premiums to long-term debt issued by that country.

However, the policy of pegging is fraught with questions. Given the benefits of pegging and despite the dire macroeconomic consequences of forsaking the peg, are there any drawbacks to designing monetary policy solely towards managing the exchange rate? Why do pegs often "blow apart" with severe consequences for the country attempting to "import" monetary discipline from a type-B country? Why did the Mexican and East Asian attempts at pegging their currencies to the US dollar come to naught?

In our initial example, monetary policy in A was solely directed to ensuring that 10 units of country A's currency were pegged to one unit of B's currency. In a world economy characterized by global capital mobility, a hard peg implies that A's central bank must ensure that domestic interest rate changes match those in County B. In other words, if B's bonds were to yield higher interest rates, A would experience a capital outflow as domestic and foreign investors quickly switched to B's higher-yielding bonds. As investors sold A's currency to invest in B, this would put downward pressure on A's currency and threaten the peg of 10A = 1B. To prevent such a result, A's central bank would have to quickly increase its own interest rates to match the increase in the interest rates in B.

As long as both A and B are in similar phases of their respective business cycles, interest rate changes in A can indeed mimic those in B. If both A and B are in recessions, then lower rates in B will certainly be welcomed by matching lower rates in A and the peg will remain intact. Likewise, if both A and B were to overheat, interest rate hikes in B would be gladly matched by similar hikes in A and both economies would soft-land with the peg intact. But if their two economies were to be in different phases of their business cycles, the peg would come under severe pressure. For example, an overheated B would prescribe higher interest rates, but if A were in a recession, then A would find it impossible to increase rates to match B's rates.

Country A's central bank would have to make a hard choice—to increase rates to match the rise of rates in country B and to maintain the integrity of the peg, or to lower rates at home and provide domestic relief to an economy in the throes of recession. Usually the second option dominates. As Country A lowers domestic interest rates with interest rates rising in County B, the peg snaps. The domestic currency typically loses significant value as mobile capital rushes out. Vital imports into Country A become significantly more expensive and its domestic interest rates spike as the supply of loanable funds drops, and macroeconomic credibility, attained at such great cost, collapses.

Pegging, therefore, is a temporary measure of attaining monetary independence and discipline. It works only as long as the economies of both A and B are in similar phases of their respective business cycles. As real GDP growth slowed in Mexico and East Asia, while the US economy supercharged its way into the New Economy in the mid-late 1990s, their respective pegs were eventually doomed.

Currency Crisis: Europe 1992

The precursor to the Euro, the European Currency Unit (ECU), was based on a system of pegged exchange rates within 12 European economies. Basically,

273

the European currencies were quasi-locked in managed pegs to the German currency, the Deutsche Mark (DM). Economies were bound to the DM by a narrow band and allowed +/- 2.25% fluctuation with respect to the DM. British, Italian and Spanish currencies, on the other hand, needed more monetary flexibility and adopted a "wide band" with fluctuations of +/- 6%.

This system, known as the Exchange Rate Mechanism (ERM), worked very well from its inception in 1979 till the early 1990s. The managed pegs to the German currency resulted in Teutonic monetary discipline in the other European economies. Inflation plummeted and wage growth was contained. Monetary discipline, in turn, bred fiscal discipline as governments now realized that monetization of runaway spending was not possible any more. The central banks' only policy objective was to transact domestic and foreign currencies to manage the exchange rate within the prescribed bands with respect to the DM.

And then The Wall came down. Massive infrastructure expenses in the former East Germany resulted in a German budget deficit that looked dangerously non-sustainable. Adding to their woes, monetary growth increased by a staggering 19% in the year following German unification as East German currency was swapped at a 1:1 rate with the DM in a burst of political euphoria. Faced with rapid monetization and non-sustainable deficits, the Bundesbank drove up interest rates to send a clear signal to the German fiscal authority that monetization would not be forthcoming.

As German rates shot up, to ensure the integrity of the peg the other member nation of the ERM would also have had to contract monetary growth and drive up their respective interest rates. But this move would have been problematic. Several member economies were actually dangerously close to recession. They needed the exact opposite interest rate prescription— monetary loosening and lower interest rates! As the peg was tugged by the German economy at one end and by the slowing British, Austrian, Spanish, and Italian economies at the other, the Exchange Rate Mechanism blew apart in Fall 1992. The Bank of England actually lowered rates, and the British pound subsequently fell by as much as 20%.

Once again, the peg (ERM) had worked well as long as all 12 economies moved together, in the same phase of their respective business cycles. However, after 13 years, when the interest rate requirements inevitably differed, domestic considerations (such as the alleviating of domestic recessions), clearly dominated any attempts to preserve the peg.

Not all pegs are designed and implemented to "import" monetary discipline from some country B. Countries like Singapore, for example, adopt managed pegs to reduce fluctuations in the Singapore dollar. Since global trade is the primary engine of Singapore's growth, stable export and import prices are imperative. To prevent this relatively small country's currency

274

from being constantly buffeted by global exogenous factors and market forces, a peg to the more shock-resistant US currency has been adopted since the early 1980s.

11.3.5.1 THE IMPOSSIBLE TRINITY

The concept of the "impossible trinity" is linked to the effects on domestic discretionary monetary policy in a economy where capital is globally mobile and where the central bank has had to adopt a system of pegged exchange rates.

The "impossible trinity" lists three macroeconomic features that <u>cannot simultaneously</u> exist from a theoretical perspective.

An economy cannot:
(1) Exist in a regime characterized by perfectly mobile capital,
(2) Have its exchange rates pegged to that of an economy with monetary discipline, and
(3) Have the ability to influence its own interest rates using monetary policy.

Any combination of two of the three macroeconomic features listed above may be possible—<u>but not all three</u>, and hence the "impossible trinity".

For example, as discussed in the previous section, in a world of perfectly mobile capital an economy (Country A) pegged to, say, the US dollar would find that any attempts on its part to unilaterally change—decrease, for example—its domestic interest rates, would result in an outflow of capital, causing an accompanying incipient depreciation of the domestic currency, thereby breaking the peg.

In other words, Country A would be unable to change domestic interest rates with perfectly mobile capital flows <u>and</u> with its peg intact. Features (1) and (3) hold, while (2) is not possible; all three together are impossible.

We now turn to discussion questions followed by the articles that highlight key topics covered in this chapter.

11.4   DISCUSSION QUESTIONS

1.   In the past, currencies were "backed by gold". What backs the world's major currencies now?

All that "backs" the strength and value of a nation's currency today is the credibility of that country's macroeconomic policies. An economy perceived as a safe haven for its longstanding fiscal and monetary discipline and political stability is considered an economy with a "hard currency".

2. **Since the New York Federal Reserve bank is always directly involved in open market operations, isn't it unfair to always allow the New York district area to be the first beneficiary of newly created money?**

While the New York Fed is indeed a vital cog in the money creation process, there are around 64 government securities dealers (GSDs) spread over the US. Hence, the injection of new funds is spread over the country, and market forces cause the interest effects of the monetary change to be spread very rapidly through the economy.

3. **While H-H has been criticized as macroeconomically "impossible", weren't the two targets of low unemployment and low inflation attained for most of the 1990s, during the era of the New Economy?**

While the two targets were indeed hit, they were not achieved <u>by monetary policy only</u> as H-H directed, but instead by combinations of monetary <u>and</u> fiscal policy. In the New economy explanation, the increase in GDP growth was due to the explosion in productivity stemming from the internet-assisted economy, which was, in turn, unleashed by earlier deregulation. In essence, a shift in AS, not a shift in AD, was the principal driver of the "growth without inflation" result.

4. **The People's Bank of China (PBOC) and the Monetary Authority of Singapore are not endowed with high degrees of institutional autonomy. Yet, over several decades, they have conducted monetary policy that ranges from good to exemplary. How can this record be reconciled with no/little independence?**

These central banks have been blessed at critical times with central bankers (Zhu Rongji, Dr. Richard Hu) who had a firm grasp on the essentials of effective monetary policy. The system, however, cannot depend on a perpetual stream of accomplished individuals, and must insure against the possibly of errant macropolicy. Hence, the safeguard of central bank autonomy becomes important.

5. **In attempts to change monetary growth, why do most emerging economies eschew OMOs in favor of policies that resemble changes in reserve ratios or discount rate policies?**

The essential ingredients for open market operations are risk-free national government bonds and an efficient forward-looking bond market. Many emerging economies are in the process of building globally recognized national bond markets and bringing national deficits to sustainable proportions over a significant time period. But the existence of efficient bond markets also implies relatively high degrees of capital mobility, more importantly pertaining to capital outflows, and attaining this mobility remains one of the greater challenges for emerging economies.

The following simulated articles that highlight some key concepts. Please relate the underlined passages to material covered in this and in preceding chapters.

Article 11.1   THE ROLE OF EFFECTIVE MONETARY POLICY

Justin Chen, <u>Michigan Business Quarterly</u>

At the recent symposium on monetary policy conducted by the Economic Research Group in Portland, Oregon, the role and effectiveness of monetary policy was discussed passionately. Opinions ranged from the effectiveness of Federal Reserve policy to claims of monetary policy impotence. Participants included mid to high-level executives, academics, entrepreneurs, financial analysts and, of course, economists. In addition, there was a strong showing from attendees of the National MBA Conference, also being held at the same complex.

This paper interviewed several participants at the coffee break. Christina Hansen, senior purchasing executive of the Far Hills department store in Knoxville, Tennessee, said, "Honestly, that last seminar was an eye-opener—if the **(a)** discount rate policy is really a lagged effect of market-determined rates, then why this fuss over Fed announcements regarding the discount rate!"

At this comment, Jeff Caruso, a hospital executive chimed in, "and we now realize that **(b)** even long-term rates are really not controlled by the Fed—hey, I was in shock..." But, at this, Melinda van Eyksson, pharmaceutical marketing VP for Europharma in Morristown, New Jersey, muttered, "Folks, it's the **(c)** Fed Funds rates that we must watch— over long periods", and she shot us a meaningful look, "right? That will tell us what the Fed is trying to do to the monetary base over a sustained period of time."

"Yes, yes," added Dr. Fred Waterstone, of the Carmella Graduate school in Dayton, Ohio, as he got emotionally worked-up and threatened to spill his coffee,

"Watch the short rates and you will see the Fed's hand on the steering wheel—and keep in mind who **(d)** came to your rescue after the terrorist attacks on September 11!"

With this, the pendulum again swung in favor of the Fed, till we ran into Michael Smithkline, CFO of the Jamaica Coffeebean Company. "With all these countries pegged to the US, I wonder **(e)** how this affects our (US) monetary policy." He then grimaced as he sipped the coffee, "awful coffee—they should try the coffee we make in Jamaica. Now that's coffee!"

"Well, it is clear to me that the Humphrey Hawkins legislation is a 'necessary evil' for monetary policy. **(f)** It is 'impossible' as the speaker indicated, but **(g)** it allows the Fed some wiggle room. But this was not clear to me before this conference! I always thought that one clear monetary policy goal was best!" remarked Arijit Bose, President and owner of the Bose Trading company in San Francisco, "now please excuse me, I need to see how I can import that Jamaican coffee...."

"All in all, even though China does not have the huge quantity of government debt outstanding as the US does, we have done pretty good in terms of monetary policy," remarked Xiao-Min Wang, of Beijing Techsat, a technology research institute focusing on medical/laser systems, **(h)** "But the point about institutional autonomy is well taken."

Conversation was lively. Participants clearly felt that the seminars were most enlightening. But Michael was right. The coffee could have been better.....

Article 11.2   HOSINTAHL IN TROUBLE. END IN SIGHT?

Armelle Vernet, Macroeconomic Times

The Republic of Hosintahl has its back to the wall. Its currency, the Hosin, is pegged to the US dollar, and it is beginning to hurt.

Last week, the Prime Minister, Larbuz Xindal, announced that, "Lord Keynes taught us that **(a)** multipliers occur due to large government spending. But Ms. Wadine Gystro (Central Bank President) insists that she will not increase money growth to pay for this! This is unpatriotic!"

This sentiment has found strong support. Walso Komtree, **(b)** president of the textile workers union, urged the government to spend more and to force the central bank to "print a little money to fund the new highway project so our poor can get employed." He even accused Ms. Gystro of "caring more for her equations than for her people and not really relating to the working class."

In a related interview with the news agency, All-World, Ms. Gystro responded to these charges against her. She said, **(c)** "they can obviously fire me if they want to, but as long as I am the head of the central bank we will maintain the integrity of the peg at the announced rate of 250 Hosins to 1 US dollar."

General Nuypal, head of the air force remarked, "we should **(d)** increase money growth and re-peg at say, 300 Hosins to the dollar. This will give us a realistic peg, and create jobs!"

Upon hearing this, Gystro exploded in a TV interview, "What! No way! That would be the **(e)** 4th time we 're-adjust' the peg since we adopted it two and a half years ago. We started at 150 (Hosins) to 1 US$ and now look where we are." She added that the **(f)** whole experiment with pegging was to bring back the global investment that had fled after the hyperinflation and the coup by General Nuypal several years ago.

"With the **(g)** deficit/GDP ratio already at 9.9 percent, I cannot sanction this. Fire me if you like—the peg stays as long as I'm in charge. **(h)** We will create more jobs with foreign capital investment, and that will only happen if we are serious about both monetary and fiscal discipline," she told the Prime Minister in a televised statement last Tuesday.

She also added that her father was a sheet-metal worker, and she could relate to the "working class" better than her critics.

In the meantime, as the debates and public accusations continue, **(i)** more foreign invest-ors are selling Hosins and pulling out capital. This is straining the peg even further. Unemployment inches up, angry demonstrations by laid-off workers are now a daily feature, resentment mounts, and, most ominously, **(j)** long-term rates continue to increase—the last four weeks have already seen a 5% gain in long-term rates! And no compromise seems likely between the Prime Minister and his Generals and the Central Bank President.

Alas, the perils of macro-economic discipline. **(k)** Is it worth all this pain?

ANSWERS AND HINTS

Article 11.1   THE ROLE OF EFFECTIVE MONETARY POLICY

(a) Explain why this is so. Describe the clear arbitrage opportunities that would arise if the Fed allowed its discount rate to be significantly out of line with the 3-month T-bill rate.

(b) Long-term rates are endogenously determined. They embody market driven expectations of future risk and inflation a la the Fisher Effect.

(c) The federal funds rates are exogenously determined by Fed policy, and long-term sustained trends in fed funds rates would indeed indicate the intent of US monetary policy.

(d) Perhaps the most crucial role of the Fed is to be the "lender of last resort", and to inject huge amounts of liquidity in times of great crisis, as following the terror attacks on September 11, 2001.

(e) Having a number of countries wouldn't affect US monetary policy, per se, aide from the fact that the FOMC would have to, at the least, consider the ramifications of its proposed policy on other economies pegged to the dollar.

(f) This discusses the fundamental infeasibilty of Humphrey-Hawkins.

(g) Here Mr. Bose is referring to the options available to the Fed. It can indeed adopt the Taylor rule and attempt to tweak output and inflation in the short run, unlike the ECB that has one unequivocal policy objective.

(h) Ms. Wang is referring to the discussion pertaining to the dependence on enlightened policy makers in regimes where the central bank has very little institutional independence.

Article 11.2   HOSINTAHL IN TROUBLE. END IN SIGHT?

(a) Ms. Gystro does not want to monetize government spending. It seems that bond-financed increases in government spending are not an option. Clearly Ms. Gystro and PM Xindal are operating in two different paradigms.

(b) There is huge pressure to increase government spending and alleviate the suffering of unemployed workers. Ideal macroeconomic policy that may benefit the whole economy is often overshadowed by more pressing local interests.

(c) This is exactly what the peg is designed to do in an economy where the central bank obviously has no institutional autonomy—the peg allows the central bank to resist pressure to increase monetary growth. In this case, apparently not for much longer, given the pressure on Ms. Gystro.....

(d) This form of "managed" peg allows the central bank to loosen monetary growth, and re-peg at a new rate, with the domestic economy now worth considerably less in terms of foreign currency. However......

(e) .....repeated "adjustments" of the peg—four times in a little over two years, in this case—defeat the purpose of pegging! When domestic and global investors realize that the peg is indeed very "soft" and subject to buckling under government pressure, it will be a peg "without teeth" and will not be treated seriously.

(g) This answers the question posed in the answer (a) above—the deficits cannot be bond-financed any more. They are non-sustainable. Lenders are not forthcoming for obvious reasons, and hence the severe pressure on Ms. Wadine Gystro.

(h) A clear signal to global investors that Hosintahl is swallowing some bitter medicine to adopt fiscal and monetary discipline would make it a "safer haven" and perhaps induce capital investment back into its textile and mining sectors.

(i) The outflow has begun. Perhaps this is the beginning of a hot capital outflow as investors realize that it is just a matter of time before Ms. Gystro is fired and the peg is broken. As investors sell Hosins to divest themselves of their Hosintahl assets, the downward pressure on that currency increases.

(j) Bonds know best, after all. Even the fledgling Hosin bond market is signaling risk and inflation warnings in the near future. Monetization is very likely at this stage, and the bond market is flashing red.

(k) The benefits of monetary discipline have been listed in this chapter.

---

[1] The "compromise" solution was to have 12 Federal Banks representing different regions of the US, instead of just one central bank in the capital, as in most other countries.

[2] If governors cannot finish their terms, and if more than four slots become available, the President has to leave those unfilled. The President can appoint only a maximum of four members to the board of governors over a 2-term Presidency.

[3] This is actually very close to the reserve ratio in the US. Please note that "reserve requirements" and "reserve ratios" will be used interchangeably in this chapter.

[4] Note that the reserves earn no interest. In this simplified Federal Reserve example, we also assume that no funds are simply held by the banks and individuals as cash. Such holdings would affect the magnitude of the final result as explained in the next section.

[5] Remember that the Federal Reserve has most influence on very short-term (overnight) interest rates, by monetary policy. Short-term rates are exogenously determined. Long-term rates, on the other hand, are endogenously determined by expectations of future risk and inflation formed by processing information efficiently in forward-looking bond markets that "know best" (Chapter 6).

[6] In the US recession of 1990-91, despite several interest rates cuts the confidence levels were so low that the only "borrowing" was from homeowners who already held mortgages but were attempting to refinance them at the prevailing lower rates.

[7] These processes assume that all other factors, including the demand for loanable funds, remain unchanged.

[8] The federal funds rate changes are usually expressed in terms of basis points, with each point being 1/100th of a percent. Thus, 25 basis points will be a change of

0.25%. Note that the "prime rate" is simply the rate that commercial banks charge their biggest and best (prime) customers.

[9] The employment target is not specifically displayed in Figure 2, as the labor market is not displayed here. We assume that employment is positively correlated to output growth.

[10] As discussed earlier, the Maastricht convergence criteria include upper limits on the deficit/GDP ratio (3%), debt/GDP ratio (60%), long-term interest rates, and inflation. Prior to 2001, new member countries joining the European Union (EU) had an option—if they qualified, they could choose to also participate in the monetary union (the Eurozone). The UK, Sweden and Denmark are members in the EU, but they chose to "opt out" of the monetary union in the early 2000s. However, after 2001, if a new country (Poland, Hungary, Czech Republic) joins the EU, and its macro-statistics satisfy the Maastricht convergence criteria, then it has no choice—it <u>has</u> to be part of the monetary union (Eurozone) along with the European Union. Before a new country can be formally inducted into the Eurozone, it must lock its currency to the Euro for two years and demonstrate that it can indeed sustain the fiscal and monetary discipline entailed in joining the Eurozone.

[11] In addition to the inflation target, the ECB also has a concurrent monetary aggregate target. The inflation target, however, is the binding constraint and apparently grabs all the attention of both the public as well as policy makers. Nevertheless, both targets add to monetary policy being clearly prescribed for an economy with a vertical aggregate supply curve.

[12] Note that the Eurosystem is composed of the ECB plus the various national central banks. The latter, not the ECB, are responsible for supervising their national financial institutions.

[13] Clearly, the Taylor principle attempts to exploit short-term output inflation tradeoffs. Please see Carl E. Walsh, "The Science and Art of Monetary Policy", FRBSF, Economic Letter, May 2001, for an excellent overview.

[14] We adopt 10A = 1B as the peg here, purely as an example for discussion. Such a "fixed" peg is known as a "hard" peg. Thailand's peg to the US dollar in the mid-late 1990s, before the 1997-98 East Asian currency crisis, is a good example. Most pegs, however, are "managed". The ratio of A's currency relative to B's is managed within certain target ranges by A's central bank by continuously buying and selling the currencies of A and B on global foreign exchange markets.

[15] As discussed in the section on Hot Capital outflow in Chapter 3, the supply of loanable funds curve shifts left as capital rushes out of country A.

REFERENCES

Aghion, P., and Peter Howitt. 1998. *Endogenous Growth Theory.* Cambridge, Mass. MIT Press.

Bank of Canada. 1996. *The Transmission of Monetary Policy in Canada.*

Bank of Japan. May 1995. "Reserve Requirements System and Their Recent Reforms in Major Industrialized Countries: A Comparative Perspective", *Quarterly Bulletin*, pp. 54 – 75.

Barro, R.J. 1976. "Rational Expectations and the Role of Monetary Policy," *Journal of Monetary Economics*, 11: 1-32.

Bartolini, L.B., and Alessandro Prati,. September 2000. "Day to Day Monetary Policy and The Volatility of the Federal Funds Interest Rate," *Staff Report No. 110,* Federal Reserve Bank of New York.

Burdekin, Richard C.K., and Marc D. Weidenmier. December 2001. "Inflation is Always and Everywhere a Monetary Phenomenon: Richmond vs. Houston in 1864," *American Economic Review.*

Burdekin Richard C.K., and Leroy Laney. 1988. "Fiscal Policymaking and the Central Bank Institutional Constraint," *Kyklos*, 41: 647-62.

Burdekin, Richard C.K., and Farrokh K. Langdana. 1992. *Budget Deficits and Economic Performance*, Routledge, London.

Burdekin, Richard C.K., and Farrokh K. Langdana. 1993. "War Finance in the Southern Confederacy, 1861-65," *Explorations in Economic History*, 30: 352-76.

Burdekin, Richard C.K., and Farrokh K. Langdana. 1995. *Confidence Credibility and Macroeconomic Policy: Past, Present, Future*, Routledge, London.

Case, Karl E., and Ray C. Fair. 1999. *Principles of Macroeconomics*, Prentice Hall.

Clarida, R., Jordi Gali, and Mark Gertler. 1999. "The Science of Monetary Policy: A New Keynesian Perspective," *Journal of Economic Literature*, 37, pp. 1661-1707.

Cox, W. Michael and Richard Alm. 1999. *Myths of Rich and Poor: Why We're Better Off Than We Think*, Basic Books.

Cox, W. Michael and Richard Alm, "Information Age Economics: Good News on Inflation," May 11, 2000. IntellectualCapital.com.

European Central Bank. 2001. *The Monetary Policy of the ECB*, Frankfurt.

Federal Reserve Bank of New York, April, 1993, *Reduced Reserve Requirements: Alternative for The Conduct of Monetary Policy and Reserve Management.*

Feinman, Joshua N. June 1993. "Reserve Requirements: History, Current Practices, and Potential Reforms", *Federal Reserve Bulletin*, pp. 569-589.

Friedman, Milton and Anna J. Schwartz. 1963. *A Monetary History of the*

United States, Princeton University Press.

Friedman, Milton. March 1968. "The Role of Monetary Policy", *American Economic Review*, 58: 16.

Froyen, Richard T. 1998. *Macroeconomics: Theory and Practice*, Prentice Hall.

Fuhrer, J.C. 1993. "What Role does Consumer Sentiment play in the US Macroeconomy?" *New England Economic Review*, Jan/Feb. 32-44.

Gavin, William T. and Rachel J. Mandel, "Economic News and Monetary Policy." *National Economic Trends*, Federal Reserve Bank of Saint Louis, July 2001.

Goodhart, Charles. June, 2000, "Can Central Banks Survive The IT Revolution?" *Institutional Finance*, pp. 189 – 200.

Gordon, Robert J. 1999a. "US Economic Growth since 1870: What We Know and still Need to Know." *American Economic Review* 89, 123-8.

Gordon, Robert J. 1999b. "Does the New Economy measure up to the Great Inventions of the Past." *Journal of Economic Perspectives*, 14, pp. 49-74.

Grey, Joanna. 1976. "Wage Indexation: A Macroeconomic Approach," *Journal of Monetary Economics*, 2: 221-35.

Henke, Stephen. 4/28/1999. "Yugoslavia Destroyed its own Economy," *Wall Street Journal.*

Hertzel, Robert L. Spring 2000. "The Taylor Rule: Is it a Useful Guide to Understanding Monetary Policy?" *Economic Quarterly*, Federal Reserve Bank of Richmond, Spring 2000.

Jackman, Michael. 1984. *The Macmillan Book of Business and Economic Quotations*, Macmillan.

Jorgensen, Dale W., and Kevin J. Stiroh. 1999. "Information Technology and Growth." *American Economic Review,* 89, 109-15.

Keynes, John Maynard. 1936 (reprinted 1964*). The General Theory of Employment, Interest and Money*, Harcourt, Brace and Jovanovich, London.

King, Meryvn. August, 1994. "Monetary Policy Instruments: The U.K. Experience", Bank of England *Quarterly Review,* pp. 268 – 276.

Katona, G., and E. Mueller. 1953. *Consumer Attitudes and Demand, 1950-52.* University of Michigan Press.

Langdana, F.K. 1990. *Sustaining Budget Deficits in Open Economies,* Routledge, London.

Langdana, F.K. 1994. "An Experimental Verification of the Lucas 'Islands' Approach to Business Cycles," *Journal of Economic Behavior and Organization*, 25: 271-80.

Langdana, F.K., and Giles Mellon. October 1995. "Fiscal and Monetary
284

Stabilization in a Confidence-Driven Rational Expectations Economy," *International Journal of Finance.*

Lucas, R.E. 1972. "Expectations and the Neutrality of Money," *Journal of Economic Theory*, 4: 1-3-24.

Lucas, R.E. 1973. "Some International Evidence on Output-Inflation Tradeoffs," *American Economic Review* 63: 326-34.

Lucas, R.E. 1977. "Understanding Business Cycles," *Carnegie-Rochester Series on Public Policy* 5: 7-29.

Lucas, R.E. 1981. *Studies in Business Cycle Theory*, Cambridge, MIT Press.

Meyer, Laurence H., "The Future of Money and of Monetary Policy", Address Delivered at Swarthmore College, December 5, 2001: Federal Reserve System, Release of same date.

Oliner, Stephen D., and David E. Sichel. 2000. "The Resurgence of Growth in the late 1990s," *Journal of Economic Perspectives*, 14, 4, pp. 3-22.

O'Sullivan, Arthur, and Steven M. Sheffrin. 2001. *Macroeconomics: Principles and Tools*, Prentice Hall.

Pakko, Michael. May 2000. "Capital Deepening," *National Economic Trends*, The Federal Reserve Bank of St. Louis.

Pakko, Michael. May 2001. "Accounting for Computers," *National Economic Trends*, The Federal Reserve Bank of St. Louis.

Parkin, Michael. 1996. *Economics*, Addison Wesley.

Phelps, E.S., and John Taylor. 1977. "Stabilizing Powers of Monetary Policy Under Rational Expectations," *Journal of Political Economy*, 85: 163-90.

Pugh, Peter, and Chris Garratt. 1994. *Introducing Keynes*, Totem Books, Cambridge, England.

Santomero, Anthony. 2001, Second Quarter. *Review*, Federal Reserve Bank of Philadelphia.

Sargent, T.J. 1979. *Macroeconomic Theory*, New York: Academic Press.

Sargent, T.J., and Neil Wallace. 1981. "Some Unpleasant Monetarist Arithmetic," *Quarterly Review,* Federal Reserve Bank of Minneapolis 5: 1-17.

Sellon, Gordon H., Jr. and Weiner, Stuart E. 1996. "Monetary Policy Without Reserve Requirements: Analytical Issues", *Economic Review*, Federal Reserve Bank of Kansas City, pp. 5 – 24.

Sellon, Gordon H. and Weiner, Stuart. 1997. "Monetary Policy Without Reserve Requirements: Case Studies and Options for the United States", *Economic Review*, Federal Reserve Bank of Kansas City, pp. 5 – 29.

Stevens, R. J. 1993. "Required Clearing Balances", Federal Reserve Bank of Cleveland *Economic Review,* pp. 2 – 14.

Stiroh, Kevin, "What Drives Productivity Growth?" March 2001. *Economic Policy Review*, Federal Reserve Bank of New York.

Taylor, John B. "Discretion versus Policy Rules in Practice." December 1993. *Carnegie Rochester Conference Series on Public Policy*, pp. 195-214.

Taylor, John, B. "The Robustness and Efficiency of Monetary Policy Rules as Guidelines for the Interest Rate Setting by the European Central Bank." 1999. *Journal of Monetary Economics*, 43, 655-79.

Walsh, Carl E. May 4, 2001. "The Science and Art of Monetary Policy." *Economic Letters*, Federal Reserve Bank of San Francisco.

INDEX

288